Dickens and the dream of cinema

MANCHESTER
UNIVERSITY PRESS

VILLA JULIE COLLEGE LIBRARY
STEVENSON MD 21153

Dickens and the
dream of cinema

GRAHAME SMITH

distributed exclusively in the USA by Palgrave

MANCHESTER UNIVERSITY PRESS Manchester and New York

Copyright © Grahame Smith 2003

The right of Grahame Smith to be identified as the author of this work has
been asserted by him in accordance with the Copyright, Designs and
Patents Act 1988.

Published by Manchester University Press
Oxford Road, Manchester M13 9NR, UK
and Room 400, 175 Fifth Avenue, New York, NY 10010, USA
www.manchesteruniversitypress.co.uk

Distributed exclusively in the USA by
Palgrave, 175 Fifth Avenue, New York,
NY 10010, USA

Distributed exclusively in Canada by
UBC Press, University of British Columbia, 2029 West Mall,
Vancouver, BC, Canada V6T 1Z2

British Library Cataloguing-in-Publication Data
A catalogue record for this book is available from the British Library

Library of Congress Cataloging-in-Publication Data applied for

ISBN 0 7190 5562 8 *hardback*
ISBN 0 7190 5563 6 *paperback*

First published 2003

11 10 09 08 07 06 05 04 03   10 9 8 7 6 5 4 3 2 1

Typeset in Photina and Frutiger display
by Koinonia, Manchester
Printed in Great Britain
by Bookcraft (Bath) Ltd, Midsomer Norton

This book is dedicated to my computer:

'The biggest electric train set any boy ever had!'

(Orson Welles on seeing a film studio, in Brady, Frank, *Citizen Welles: a biography of Orson Welles*, London: Hodder and Stoughton, 1990, p. 208.)

Contents

Illustrations

Figures 1, 2, 6 and 11 reproduced by permission of BBC Television.

Figures 3, 9, 10, 12 and 13 reproduced by permission of The Bill Douglas Centre, University of Exeter.

Figures 4, 5, 7, 8 and 14 reproduced by permission of The Dickens House Museum, London.

Acknowledgements

I am pleased to acknowledge the assistance provided in the research for this project by an Emeritus Fellowship awarded by The Leverhulme Trust. Ideas contained in the book have been presented in the form of papers to colleagues at the Universities of Stirling, Keele and Essex, and Williams College, Massachusetts. I am grateful for their stringent as well as enthusiastic responses.

Visual material is reproduced by courtesy of The Dickens House Museum, London; BBC Television; and the Bill Douglas Centre for the History of Cinema and Popular Culture, University of Exeter.

Aspects of this book have appeared in various forms in other publications and I am grateful to their publishers for their permission to reprint. Material on Paris as panorama appeared in *Dickens Quarterly*, September 1999, vol. 16, no. 3 and is reprinted by permission of The Dickens Society of America. 'Novel into Film: the case of *Little Dorrit*' appeared in the *Yearbook of English Studies*, 1990, vol. 20. A version of the material on Dickens, theatre and spectacle appeared as 'Dickens and Adaptation: imagery in words and pictures' in *Novel Images: literature in performance*, edited by Peter Reynolds in 1993, Routledge.

A number of individuals have made significant contributions to this book. Manchester University Press's reader offered a challengingly positive critique of the manuscript, while Matthew Frost was a cheerfully encouraging editor. John Bowen provided a vigorous response to Chapter 1. The lively interest in film of Emily Nance and Matthew Smith in Melbourne was a source of inspiration. Dan Smith's insight into film was translated into constantly valuable comments while his computer production skills were indispensable. Helena Smith is a brilliant editor, not merely in terms of detail, and her love of Dickens made her unfailingly supportive. Angela Smith read the whole manuscript several times; her analysis of weaknesses was unsparing, and so hugely beneficial. Teaching film with John Izod in the early, heady days of the University of Stirling was a joyful way of acquiring knowledge. My intellectual life as a whole has benefited immeasurably from discussion over many years with Ieuan Williams.

Exploratory 1

We are such stuff as dreams are made on[1]

This book, rooted in dreams and dreaming, takes its inspiration from a specific dream in which, according to Walter Benjamin, 'every epoch sees in images the epoch which is to succeed it'.[2] My inflection of this suggestive claim focuses on the nineteenth-century dream of cinema, and specifically the ways in which Dickens anticipates in images the medium that would only come into being after his death. This book is, then, a contribution to cultural history and a critical study of a great writer, but the history and criticism both concentrate on my attempt to explain the genesis of cinema. Substantiating such claims may itself seem dreamlike, but not inappropriately, given how often cinema is understood as being akin to dreaming. For Orson Welles film is 'a ribbon of dreams',[3] an insight given extended form in Gore Vidal's novel *Hollywood*. One of its major characters, Caroline Sanford, whose screen name is Emma Traxler, finds herself 'day dreaming about the movies' in relation to the character she plays in a film:

They were insidious. They were like waking dreams that then, in sleep, usurped proper dreams. There was a power here but she was not sure what it was ... The audience knew, of course, that the story was made up ... but the fact that an entire story could so surround them as a moving picture did and so, literally, inhabit their dreams, both waking and sleeping, made for another reality parallel to the one they lived in. For two hours in actual time Caroline was three different people as a light shone through a moving strip of film.[4]

Dreams, daydreams and fantasy intermingle here, and all play a part in Abel Gance's delirious claim that 'Shakespeare, Rembrandt,

Beethoven will make films',[5] a moment when common sense bristles until it is chastised by the memory of Gance's *Napoleon* (1927), a film of such panoramic grandeur, grandiosity even, that it has the effect of having been made by its own hero.

Despite the apparent fancifulness of Gance's claim there is a sense in which Shakespeare *has* made films or, at least, permitted their existence through the longing of artists of the calibre of Kurosawa, Kosintsev and Welles to make what Welles has called 'a violently sketched charcoal drawing of a great play'.[6] And the epigraph of this chapter extends the dream scenario a stage further. The line is Prospero's, from *The Tempest*, and the character has been read in many ways, as magician, tyrant, God even, all roles played by Shakespeare as the creator of his own play. With the advantage of hindsight, these roles might be collapsed into their twentieth-century equivalent, the film director as author. Shakespeare's *The Tempest* is full of magic as well as dreams, and so is cinema; indeed, these qualities are shared by the humblest of films. The effect of the passage of light through a strip of celluloid at a fixed speed never loses its power to fascinate, and even mere mortals, to say nothing of directors and editors, can feel Godlike if they are lucky enough to be able to play with an old-fashioned editing machine. Actually to control the movement of that magical substance, to slow it down and speed it up, is to exist, however briefly, in a realm of seemingly supernatural power.[7] This is how the point is made by Simon Callow in relation to Orson Welles's discovery of 'a new passion, one that lasted to his dying day ... editing':

He had discovered the Frankenstein element of film-making. Sitting at the Steenbeck, it is really possible to assemble your own creature, and give life to it. The sense of power is intoxicating: a slow scene can be made fast, a funny one sad, a bad performance can be made good, and actors can be expunged from the film as if they had never been. To shoot is human; to edit, divine.[8]

If dreaming, then, is to be a central focus of my enterprise, one could hardly find a more congenial companion than Dickens since, in the words of Fred Kaplan, the 'dream state was his domain, permeating his fiction and non-fiction...a metaphor for his exploration of what he considered the most meaningful aspects of human consciousness and the human predicament'.[9] And his letters reveal how central the metaphor was to his conception of his own life, and the lives of others. In consoling a younger friend, Edmund Yates, on the death of his mother, an actress, he remarks 'I think of your mother, as of a beautiful part of my own youth, and this dream that we are all dreaming seems to darken'.[10]

Darkness is even more evident in his letter to one of his closest friends, the great actor Macready: 'What a Dream it is, this work and strife, and how little we do in the Dream after all! Only last night, in my sleep, I was bent upon getting over a perspective of barriers, with my hands and feet bound. Pretty much what we are all about, waking, I think?'[11]

If Walter Benjamin is a dreamer, like Dickens, dreaming takes a somewhat different direction; for Benjamin it is a way of grasping the past, however tenuously, a facet of the antagonism he sees between the anecdote and conventional history: 'Uprising of the anecdotes ... The constructions of history are comparable to instructions that commandeer the true life and confine it to barracks. On the other hand: the street insurgence of the anecdote. The anecdote brings things near to us spatially, lets them enter our life. It represents the strict antithesis to the sort of history ... which makes everything abstract'.[12] In making his distinction between the fruitful dreaming of the anecdote and the abstractions of conventional history, Benjamin has recourse to urban metaphors that contain hints of revolution and the Paris Commune; and the city as metropolis, with London and Paris its prime nineteenth-century exemplars, are central to this book. It is within the city that Dickens lives, moves and has his being, not merely in terms of his novels' subject matter, but in the pulse of their language and form. And, initially, film was inspired to reflect and embody the city as well as to find its audience there, although it also soon began to explore its capacity to reflect the wide open spaces of, say, the Western. Whatever its subject matter, however, the mechanisms of film-making and projection align it with the practices of the urban Industrial Revolution.

Dickens and the cinema do, then, belong to a related phase of nineteenth-century history, but if a space is to be found for Dickens in the history of a form – film – which came into being only after his death, this will have to be a special kind of history, a history which allows for dream or, alternatively, prophecy, as in the words of Wallace Stevens: 'Little of what we have believed has been true. Only the prophecies are true'.[13] This is how the point is made by André Breton: 'The work of art is valuable only in so far as it is vibrated by the reflexes of the future'.[14] The extremity of these statements is their justification, not their objective truth: Stevens leaves a space, however tiny, for some beliefs to be true, while for Breton art is valuable for only one reason. The usefulness of these unreasonable statements is their power to extend and disturb the mind, as in Benjamin's larger claim that 'the traditional art forms in certain phases of their development strenuously work towards effects which later are effortlessly attained by the new ones. Before the rise of the movie the Dadaists' performances tried to create an audience reaction which Chaplin later evoked in a more natural way ... unspectacular social changes often promote a change in receptivity which will benefit the new art form'.[15] I do not myself believe that one 'of the foremost tasks of art has always been the creation of a demand which could be fully satisfied only later'.[16] Take out the 'foremost' and the 'always', cries common sense, and I will keep quiet. But, as so often, common sense is pusillanimous. To leave them in and take from the statement what one can is, in the end, more enlightening. Put another way, this book is not Benjaminian; only Benjamin can be that. In other words, if Benjamin exaggerates, obfuscates, repeats himself, is sometimes downright tiresome and boring, that is his problem. It's not my job to make something internally consistent out of a body of work which may lack logical coherence. It is enough for me that Benjamin is frequently brilliant, profound even, and that his insights are offered with a rare kind of intellectual generosity for others to make of them what they will. What I want to make of these insights is a narrative about Dickens's dream of cinema, and it is time to explore this in a bit more detail.

I will begin, then, with Dickens and film. Yes, and why not Dickens and circus, ice-skating or any other form of entertainment? For the fact is that Dickens must be one of the most highly adapted figures in the whole of literature, a process that began before his first smash hit was even finished. *Pickwick Papers* was nowhere near completion when piracies, rip-offs and every possible form of commercial exploitation exploded with an energy that continued unabated throughout his lifetime and seems not to have run its course even at the beginning of the twenty-first century. The fact that there is in Stirling, close to where I write, a branch of Oliver's Hot Bread and Coffee Shop is a small, but not entirely unimportant, testament to that. This appropriation of his work evoked every possible response in Dickens, from comic outrage – on one theatrical outing he lay down on the floor of his box in anguished protest and remained there for the whole performance – to genuine anger and disgust. But his most consistent reaction was probably his resentment at not being paid for these piratical incursions! For if Dickens was exploited, it remains true that he himself was one of the most determined exploiters of his own work, producing what some materialist critics have called commodity fictions and 'working ... the copyrights' on them, as he himself described it, with determined energy.[17] Indeed, one factor in attempting to account for Dickens's quite extraordinary fame in his own lifetime is that his work was circulating in a large number of forms throughout his career. His second novel, *Oliver Twist*, was serialised in a monthly magazine called *Bentley's Miscellany*, but published in volume form before the serialisation was completed. Thereafter, it continued to appear in a whole number of guises, from cheap formats to de luxe editions. Dickens's novels were frequently re-issued in serial parts years after their first serialisation, and when we remember that Victorian reviews of fiction consisted mainly of large chunks taken verbatim from the novels being considered, we can see that Dickens's work was circulating throughout his society almost like oxygen in its blood. I exaggerate, of course, since many other oxygens flowed through the blood of the nineteenth century, but one of my major themes is the importance of Dickens's contribution to society's system of circulation. It is hardly surprising, then, that his work was so widely adapted and exploited when he might be said to be its own most inveterate adaptor and exploiter.

There is, perhaps, a second major reason why Dickens's novels were adapted into other media in his own day: the flexibility of the format in which they first made their appearance before the public. Dickens stumbled by chance into this mode of publication through *Pickwick Papers*, and the overwhelming success of that venture ensured that he never departed from the format for the rest of his career, apart from those occasions when he published weekly, rather than monthly, serialisations of his fiction in his own magazines.[18] In the Preface to a later edition of *Pickwick Papers*, Dickens recounts with glee how his friends tried to talk him out of this undignified mode of publication which, they assured him, would destroy his chances of being recognised as a great writer. There is an undoubted note of triumphalism in Dickens's rejoinder: 'How right my friends were, the world has now some cause to know'. The ideological assumptions underlying his friends' worries become clear, I think, when we contrast a monthly part with the classic form of Victorian novel publishing, the so-called three-decker – three volumes at a guinea a volume – the very appearance of which asserted their status as serious and weighty, in every sense of the word, literature.

What of the ideological assumptions underlying a monthly serial part, or number as it was called? What did avid Victorian readers find in their hands when they held, say, a monthly part of one of the novels? They saw a pale green cover with a densely illustrated title page which remained the same throughout the series. Like the overture to an opera, this engraving contained hints of the delights to come and possible clues to the complex narrative that would be revealed over its nineteen-month publication period. Turning the cover took the reader into the world of Victorian commerce with as many as seven pages of advertisements, most of them illustrated, for everything from 'Laming's Effervescing Cheltenham Salts' to an invitation to 'Reform Your Tailors' Bills!'. Commerce gave way to two vivid illustrations, most characteristically by the brilliant 'Phiz' (Hablot K. Browne), and only then did the reader finally get to the text itself, with another few pages of advertisements to round the whole thing off. What this suggests is an element of continuity, rather than an absolute break, between the novel and the social world from which it emerged. In this way, the novels can be seen as commodity fictions presented in a manner not dissimilar to the 'classic' television series, a text sandwiched between commercial breaks. The experience of handling these little pamphlets is inviting rather than intimidating, fleeting rather than timeless, and democratic, I would suggest, in not even pretending to be set apart from the commercial factors which are necessary for the circulation of all art in a capitalist society. Above all, given the aims of this book, they offer themselves as a mixed media experience in which the visual aspect, while not on a par with the astonishing richness of Dickens's language, is certainly part of the package. (When we remember that these illustrations were suffused with the genius of George Cruikshank in *Sketches by Boz* and *Oliver Twist*, and the vividness of Phiz in the novels up to and including *Little Dorrit* we can see that the Victorian public was getting value for money.)[19]

We are, of course, on the edge of a morass of cliché here, nonsense of the 'if Dickens were alive today' variety. If Dickens were alive today he would be a television scriptwriter, for example. André Bazin dismisses this kind of thing in his own inimitable style: 'There is no sense in asking ourselves what the author of *Phèdre* would have written in 1740 because he whom we call Racine was not a man answering that identity, but "the-poet-who-had-written-*Phèdre*". Without *Phèdre* Racine is an anonymity, a concept of the mind'.[20] Reading any paragraph by Dickens should be enough to convince anyone that he was deeply and profoundly a *writer* in the same sense that we can say this of Shakespeare, someone utterly committed to words in their fullest, most complex expressiveness. Nonetheless, comparisons between then and now may be instructive, especially when we remember the crucially distinctive fact of Dickens's career as a novelist, that he did not merely publish serially, but he also wrote serially. A monthly part – embedded in a commercial context and with the visual attractions of its unchanging cover and varied illustrations – is obviously inhabiting a similar cultural context to the television series, and seriality may well be a factor in any attempt to account for the phenomenon of adaptation. The pleasures of serialisation have rarely been expressed better than in this anonymous tribute to Dickens in the *Illustrated London News* shortly after his death:

> The obvious effect was to inspire all his constant readers – say, a million or two – with a sense of habitual dependence on their contemporary, the man Charles Dickens, for a continued supply of the entertainment which he alone could furnish. He was personally indispensible to them ... If each of his stories had appeared complete in three octavo volumes, with the lapse of a couple of years between one work and another, the feeling of continued dependence on the living author would have been less prevalent among us.[21]

The monthly or weekly reading of a novel, the weekly visit to the pictures (in the 1940s and 1950s), the human needs satisfied by repetition with variation on television are surely all part of a common world of experience which helps to make exchanges between media seem unsurprising, although the full meaning of this phenomenon will become clearer as the argument proceeds.

It must have seemed 'natural', at least to early film-makers, to have taken Dickens's novels into the new form of cinema because they had already been adapted, and not only for the stage. Like Shakespeare's plays, Dickens's novels were performed on horseback (horseback!) in places such as Astley's Circus[22] and, to anticipate material that will be discussed in detail later, they were also reproduced as slides for magic lantern shows, appeared in panoramas and dioramas, were illustrated in engravings, exploited in advertisements, adapted for clothing, and the list goes on. This saturation in a variety of media, coupled with the widespread nature of his fame, made Dickens seem an obvious subject for those desperate to exploit their new medium.

It is at this point that I want to shift the focus gradually towards my interest in Dickens's dream of cinema, and not just Dickens and film. There is a seemingly uncanny phenomenon at work here: if we look at Dickens's work in the light of the form that followed – and of which he of course knew nothing – then it is possible to trace what might be called proto-filmic elements in his writing. I'll begin this topic, which is one of this book's major themes, with two passages from Dickens's work. The first is a striking example of the economy of writing which is a marked feature of the novels serialised in weekly parts, rather than the more ample monthly numbers. It is from *A Tale of Two Cities* and illustrates Dickens's ability to effect a transition from one venue to another with maximum speed:

> 'Have you finished your repast, friend?' he asked, in due season.
> 'Yes, thank you'.
> 'Come, then! You shall see the apartment that I told you you could occupy. It will suit you to a marvel'.
> Out of the wine-shop into the street, out of the street into a court-yard, out of the court-yard up a steep staircase, out of the staircase into a garret, – formerly the garret where a white-haired man sat on a low bench, stooping forward and very busy, making shoes. (Book the Second, Ch. 15)

It seems quite hard to account for the success of this moment in conventional literary terms. One way of doing so is by invoking a recent trend in studies of Dickens in which his work is seen as having anticipated literary modernism; this is how the point is made by John Sutherland in a standard reference work on Victorian fiction: 'His dense thematic compositions, striking use of imagery, rhetoric and dramatic device advanced fiction technically to the threshold of modernism'.[23] The link from modernism to film theory and history opens up a complex area of debate: for some, the connection between what is proto-modernist and proto-filmic is strong; others see the origins of cinema as far removed from early twentieth-century modernism. If, anachronistically, the language of cinematic editing is applied to this passage it is possible to arrive at a more convincing account of its interest. The visual and linguistic rhythm of the short paragraph beginning with 'Out' does not *have* to be seen as an anticipation of cinema; it is simply that the language of montage is the most illuminating way of accounting for its peculiar strengths, which can be read as an example of what Eisenstein refers to as 'cinematic laconism'.[24] He goes on to make a similar point concerning the last chapter of the same novel: Eisenstein begs to be 'excused ... for having found in him [Dickens] even – a "dissolve". How else could this passage be defined'.[25] He asks a question which Dickens answers for him with irresistible force:

> Along the Paris streets, the death-carts rumble, hollow and harsh. Six tumbrils carry the day's wine to La Guillotine ... Six tumbrils roll along the streets. Change these back again to what they were, thou powerful enchanter, Time, and they shall be seen to be the carriages of absolute monarchs, the equipages of feudal nobles, the toilettes of flaring Jezebels, the churches that are not my father's house but dens of thieves, the huts of millions of starving peasants! (Book the Third, Ch. 15)

The dissolve occurs at the moment when the tumbrils melt into carriages filled with aristocratic gangsters and their molls and even, with characteristic visual inventiveness, into churches and peasant huts. A different and extended example is provided by *Bleak House*:

Ada sat at the piano; Richard stood beside her, bending down. Upon the wall, their shadows blended together, surrounded by strange forms, not without a ghostly motion caught from the unsteady fire, though reflected from motionless objects. Ada touched the notes so softly, and sang so low, that the wind, sighing away to the distant hills, was as audible as the music. The mystery of the future, and the little clue afforded to it by the voice of the present, seemed expressed in the whole picture.

But it is not to recall this fancy, well as I remember it, that I recall the scene. First, I was not quite unconscious of the contrast in respect of meaning and intention between the silent look directed that way, and the flow of words that had preceded it. Secondly, though Mr. Jarndyce's glance, as he withdrew it, rested for but a moment on me, I felt as if, in that moment, he confided to me – and knew that he confided to me and that I received the confidence – his hope that Ada and Richard might one day enter on a dearer relationship. (Ch. 6)

The passage begins with what would be for some an echo of the source of all philosophy and even film itself, Plato's cave, a claim that will be explored in the next chapter. Almost as strong as the scene's visual power – flickering shadows generated by firelight – is its ability to embody a sense of music and of the wind. As in the extract from *A Tale of Two Cities*, the rhythms in this passage are inseparable in their evocation of sight and sound. The 'whole picture', its *mise en scène*, is a visual and aural web in which the 'close ups' of human faces, with their interchange of unspoken meanings, is perfectly consistent within its own medium but seems, almost magically, to invite transference to another. In trying to account for the power of this moment, I am again conscious of the dangers of falling into the 'if Dickens were alive today' trap. But it is hard to avoid the sense that one is in the presence here of a screenplay, although a screenplay of genius. It is amazingly elliptical, an interplay of shadows, sounds and glances in which meaning is implicit and so operating in ways that can convincingly be described as cinematic.

Is it reasonable, then, to be discussing pre-cinematic fiction and film in this way, even though interesting things occur when we look at Dickens through the lens of a form that he knew nothing about? Ian Christie seems to think so when he argues that Jules Verne, Rider Haggard and 'many other popular writers created ... a cinematic vision before the invention of motion pictures, a space and time machine of the imagination'.[26] In some ways what I am suggesting here is akin to T. S. Eliot's notion of a tradition in which the introduction of a great new work into the field of literature does not merely enable us to take a fresh look at canonical figures but actually creates changes in the art-works of the past. The shock of the new causes a seismic shift in the landscape of past greatness that almost forces works of canonical status to be radically re-examined. Given Eliot's own reliance on *Our Mutual Friend* in the gestation of *The Waste Land*, there is certainly nothing wrong with looking at an earlier work in the light of a later one; indeed, Eliot's poem may alert us to sexual undercurrents which are undeniably present in the novel but which stand out in clearer detail through the process of reading back over time. In this case, what might be called double vision is still operating within the same form, but it may seem a different matter to compare aesthetic forms that are so widely different as the novel and film. To do so involves looking at human culture as a whole, a bold enterprise, but not an altogether unproductive one if it is controlled by a feeling for evidence and a sense of what is appropriate in comparing one form, as well as one period, with another. A small segment of Dickens's own experience suggests that this aim is not entirely futile. In the section on Venice in his *Pictures from Italy*, Dickens refers to 'a crowd of objects' which would suddenly appear and then just as quickly 'dissolve, like a view in a magic lantern':[27] a clear example of his willingness to record impressions through a medium other than the one in which he had achieved such fame.

It is at this point that the full implications of my title come into play. If Dickens does dream cinema it becomes possible to suggest that his work played some part, however small, in the cultural and material movements and transformations that eventually made it possible. Thus the conceptual framework of the enterprise begins to come into focus. One of my basic assumptions is that it is not merely interesting to engage with large-scale social and cultural phenomena, but that it may even be possible to offer explanations of them. By explanation here I do not intend anything deterministic or, even, causal; contingency rather than necessity is clearly the order of the day. The origins of cinema is one of the most highly debated topics in the history of technology and culture. For the purposes of this book, it is enough to say that most experts agree that something that might as well be called film made its appearance in France, Britain and America towards the end of the nineteenth century. In trying to account for this we are presented with a mass of explanatory material. Concentrating on film as a technical invention, it can be seen as one of the outcomes of the technological inventiveness of the

Industrial Revolution. Although not driven by steam, as Charles Babbitt wished had been the case for his early version of the computer, it clearly belongs within the realm of discovery associated with the daguerreotype and photography. If we concentrate on film as a popular amusement then it seems to belong to the stream of nineteenth-century spectacular entertainments of which the panorama, the diorama and – more controversially for the earliest beginnings of cinema – stage melodrama formed a part.

This book takes these factors into account and discusses them in detail later. But I also wish to raise the question of consciousness as part of the progression towards film. An obvious example of the relationship between consciousness and social change is the supposed alteration in concepts of time brought about by the new conditions of work in factories, the introduction of railway timetables, and so on. Concepts of time were internalised by those who worked to the imperative of the factory whistle rather than the rhythms of nature. Is it possible to see links between changes in urban life, consciousness and the appearance of film if, for example, we think about such phenomena as the introduction of street lights, plate glass windows in shops, and new intensities of movement in the urban scene related to huge increases in the number of city dwellers? What may result from their appearance is an intensification of changes in the sense of the self, and of others, that might be presumed to follow from the widespread access to mirrors and reflections in the nineteenth century compared to earlier periods. What does it mean for people to have direct access to a reflection of their own appearance? On a larger scale, what does it mean for people to be conscious of themselves, assuming that they were self-conscious in this way, surrounded by an unprecedented number of others in a well-lit urban environment in which it is impossible for them to avoid reflections of themselves and their fellow beings? A key aspect of these speculations is that the description of a new kind of environment, such as that just sketched, was taking place in the context of new forms of movement. Urban theorists have argued convincingly that radical changes to London and Paris, such as Nash's creation of Regent Street and Haussmann's boulevards, served among other ends new forms of pedestrian traffic flow. It has been suggested that these new street patterns encouraged, enforced even, an intensity of movement which served the dual purpose of discouraging loitering – which might lead to rioting or other forms of political activity anathema to the authorities – while at the same time encouraging the window-shopping which, in the nineteenth century, became an essential prelude to an increase in purchasing.

It seems reasonable to suggest that these changes in seeing – opening the way to the concept of the gaze – and movement formed part of the general social and cultural sub-structure that helped to make film possible. But how is Dickens to be inserted into all of this and, specifically, into the genesis of film? The first point to make is that Dickens participated fully in the urban experiences to which I've just been referring. Indeed, he was one of the very first to be consciously aware of them. Along with Poe – in 'The Man of the Crowd', for example – and Baudelaire, Dickens is sensing and recording these changes in the urban environment at the very moment when they are coming into existence. It is worth remembering that Dickens was born in 1812 and that his observational powers were fully developed, that he was in fact what Baudelaire calls a 'kaleidoscope gifted with consciousness',[28] by the time he was twenty (as early as 1832). This use of a somewhat mechanical image for Dickens's mental life is justified by the observation of the urban sociologist, Georg Simmel, that 'interpersonal relationships in big cities are distinguished by a marked preponderance of the activity of the eye over the activity of the ear'.[29] The point is reinforced by a leading Dickens scholar, Philip Collins, in his suggestion that 'by the pre-Raphaelite times' Dickens 'was being compared ... to a taker of daguerreotypes, sun-pictures, photographs', so much so that this had become a 'frequent image in Victorian novel-criticism'.[30] Dickens makes this point himself in one of his letters: 'I walked from Durham to Sunderland, and made a little fanciful photograph in my mind of Pit-Country ... I couldn't help looking upon my mind as I was doing it, as a sort of capitally prepared and highly sensitive plate. And I said, without the least conceit ... it really is a pleasure to work with you, you receive the impression so nicely'.[31] Such passages suggest that Dickens can be regarded as being at ease in living at what might be described as the cutting edge of his world. This is the Dickens who insisted his wife should take the then controversial choloroform in giving birth and who celebrated triumphantly the ease in suffering it brought her, the man who was thrilled by railway travel and who delighted in what seemed to him the magical possibility of getting to Paris in eleven hours. And although not a photographer himself, Dickens took a keen interest in the process on the occasions when he was being photographed. It is not entirely surprising, then, that he is willing to see his own observational powers in these apparently mechanistic terms.

However, it is one thing to show that Dickens was *au fait* with the technology of his own day, but quite another to try to account for his role in the appearance of cinema – its genesis, rather than simply the ways in which it developed – especially when the telling of stories began to be an important feature of the new medium. Developments of this kind have already been analysed, with the comprehensiveness of genius, in Eisenstein's essay 'Dickens, Griffith and the Film Today'.[32] The essay is a brilliant piece of literary criticism which shows, definitively, that Dickens creates in his writing a technique that Eisenstein calls parallel montage. In other words, in extended scenes as well as in the larger structure of his novels, Dickens alternates between different threads of narrative interest, focuses of emotion, characters, and so on, by means of something that can only be described as a kind of editing. Eisenstein demonstrates that this is a key feature of such films as D. W. Griffith's *The Birth of a Nation* and *Intolerance*, and that Griffith acknowledged that he learned this technique from his absorption in Dickens's novels, both as written texts and in their theatrical adaptations. And so Dickens's role in the ongoing development of early cinema is demonstrated with magisterial force.

This is fine as far as it goes, but I clearly want to go a bit further. The chapter will therefore end by setting out my own hypothesis in more detail as a preparation for the chapters that follow. The aim of this book is to tell a story about Dickens's role in the emergence of film, a narrative of consciousness across different media and across time. Central to the enterprise is the stress on consciousness as fluid, a constantly changing phenomenon, existing in an interactive relationship with external reality, influenced by, but also influencing, the social milieu of which it is a part. It is possible to demonstrate, with some real attention to evidence, that an increased speed of movement is a feature of life in the second half of the nineteenth century. This is essentially an urban phenomenon and relates to those changes in street patterns, lighting and reflections that I referred to earlier. We know that the urban world was a key ingredient in Dickens's imaginative universe, not merely at the level of subject matter, or journalistic copy, but in providing a kind of energy without which he found it very difficult to work. For example, Dickens wrote a great deal of *Dombey and Son* while he was abroad, and debated the various merits of different places to live in Switzerland. He settled on Lausanne: 'in case I should find, when I begin to write, that I want streets sometimes'.[33] He later considered the possibility of moving to Paris because it will be 'just the very point in the story when the life and crowd of that extraordinary place will come vividly to my assistance in writing'.[34] However, Dickens is not simply a reflector of this process of urban transformation, his work actually contributes to it, at the level of consciousness, by actualising changes almost as they are occurring, both in the detail of his writing and in the larger structures of his novels. Baudelaire is yet again indispensable here, with his obsessive ideal' of a 'poetic prose', what he sees as a 'child of the experience of giant cities, of the intersecting of their myriad relations'.[35] There could hardly be a more apt description of novels such as *Little Dorrit*, *Bleak House* and *Our Mutual Friend*. But works such as these do not simply reflect reality, they *constitute* reality, however minimally, at the level of consciousness. In other words, they help to bring into being the world that is assisting their own creation. In a complex process of artistic transmutation, Dickens absorbs into his imagination significant and representative developments in the world around him. Giving these developments literary form makes them accessible to readers who may have been less conscious of the changes taking place in their surroundings. During the process of creation, these developments become explicable to Dickens himself, not merely to his audience, and are thus able to become a part of the texture of fictions that exert an influence on their world as well as reflecting it. To take an example from another form, one of the earliest essays on photography is by Wiertz, of whom Benjamin claims that 'although he did not foresee, [he] at least demanded, montage as the agitational utilisation of photography'.[36] In other words, Wiertz dreamed, to use my terminology, the possibility of movement inherent, but as yet invisible, in photography. Dickens and Wiertz thus provide specific illustrations of one of Benjamin's larger statements about the Industrial Revolution: 'To the form of the new means of production, which to begin with is still dominated by the old ... there correspond images in the collective consciousness in which the new and the old are intermingled'.[37]

Finally, I suggest that although Dickens was not conscious of cinema itself, he was aware of some of the crucial conditions that were going to aid its appearance. He writes to a friend while staying in Paris, that he must 'picture' his apartment on the Champs Élysées 'with a moving panorama always outside, which is Paris in itself'[38] and it is this combination of light and, above all, movement that I want to emphasise. Writing in 1851, Dickens refers to some sad and shocking aspects of London life as 'shadows of the great moving picture'.[39] Part of the significance of this phrase becomes clearer six years later in a letter to Macready. They have been discussing the kinds of entertainment that they think are best suited to the needs of ordinary working people, and

Macready has recommended a way of making it easier for them to see exhibitions of paintings. Dickens replies: 'But they want more amusement, and particularly (as it strikes me), *something in motion*, though it were only a twisting fountain. The thing [that is, looking at paintings] is too still after their lives of machinery'.[40] It is possible to describe the kind of moving experience Dickens may have had in mind in a description of an illustration of 1829 by Ackermann: an image of a 'Fountain Surrounding a Marble Statue at the Colosseum, Regent's Park' consisting 'of a circle of jets d'eaux throwing a veil of water high into the air. This fell onto the centre on a mass of shells, corals, and mosses. A dial of shells near the top of the fountain revolved continuously. Beautiful prismatic effects were produced when the sun shone on it'.[41]

I do not wish to claim that Dickens's comments are a prophetic insight, a direct foreshadowing of film, the form of entertainment and art that would ease the hardships of millions. The urge towards movement is a widespread feature of the culture of the nineteenth century, as we can see from an advertisement for a mechanical picture in a handbill of 1815: 'Painting is one of the attractive arts cultivated by the ingenuity of man; but in order to complete the pleasure to be derived from it, it's necessary that motion should be imparted to the Sublime Scenery it copies'.[42] Nonetheless, Dickens's letter reveals, at the very least, his awareness of some of the pressures and opportunities that lead to the advent of cinema. This combination of changes in technology and consciousness are described by a scholar of advertising and urban spectacle: 'The purveyors of spectacle were astonishingly inventive about astonishing the early Victorian public. Over the years they cooked up various combinations of lighting, sound, scene painting, transparencies, cutout scenery, models, lanterns, projections, dioramas ... The primary result ... was to institute a continual escalation of representation'.[43] This continual escalation of representation is the same as my fluidity of consciousness but in another form, specifically in relation to the movement towards cinema. This movement might be expressed through what Bergson refers to as 'the uninterrupted humming of life's depths'. Bergson believes that most of us, most of the time, have 'no interest in listening'[44] to this uninterrupted humming, but it is a function of genius to do so. One of the myriad possibilities humming away in the nineteenth century is the eventual emergence of cinema and Dickens's hearing is sufficiently acute to be aware of this, in however unformulated a way. A historian of warfare, John Keegan, clarifies this point by remarking that he is not going to attempt to show how the First World War was caused, but rather the conditions that made it possible.[45] Similarly, I am not trying to suggest that Dickens caused cinema, but that he was one of the conditions that made it possible, a claim that returns me to Benjamin's wonderful observation that Dickens was a dreamer who participated in the 'dream in which every epoch sees in images the epoch which is to succeed it'.

Notes

1 The lines are Prospero's from Shakespeare's *The Tempest*, IV. i. 156–7.
2 Benjamin, Walter, *Charles Baudelaire: a lyric poet in the era of high capitalism*, trans. Harry Zohn, London: Verso, 1997, p. 159. The aphorism, adapted from Michelet, is used by Benjamin on numerous occasions.
3 Cowie, Peter, *The Cinema of Orson Welles*, London: The Tantivy Press, 1978, title page.
4 Vidal, Gore, *Hollywood*, London: Abacus, 1994, pp. 22–5.
5 Benjamin, Walter, 'The Work of Art in an Age of Mechanical Reproduction', *Illuminations*, trans. Harry Zohn and ed. Hannah Arendt, Glasgow: Fontana, 1973, pp. 223–4.
6 Manvell, Roger, *Shakespeare and the Film*, London: J. M. Dent & Sons, 1971, p. 59.
7 Similar moments may be engendered through manipulating video tape, and the possibilities opened up by interactive technology are clearly momentous; perhaps it is the writer's age that leads him to find a special charm in the older form.
8 Callow, Simon, *Orson Welles: the road to Xanadu*, London: Jonathan Cape, 1995, p. 385.
9 Kaplan, Fred, *Dickens and Mesmerism: the hidden springs of fiction*, Princeton, NJ: Princeton University Press, 1975, p. 217.
10 House, M., Storey, G. and Tillotson, K., *et al.* (eds.), *The British Academy Pilgrim Edition of The Letters of Charles Dickens*, Vols. 1–12, Oxford: Clarendon Press, 1965–2002; 17 April 1860, Vol. 9, p. 236.
11 15 March 1858, *Letters of Dickens*, Vol. 8, p. 531.
12 Ray, Robert B., 'Mystery Trains', *Sight & Sound*, London: British Film Institute, November 2000, p. 12.
13 Ray, 'Mystery Trains', p. 12.
14 Benjamin, *Illuminations*, p. 251.
15 Benjamin, *Illuminations*, pp. 251–2.
16 Benjamin, *Illuminations*, p. 239.
17 Letter from Dickens to his publishers, Bradbury and Evans, 8 May 1844, *Letters of Dickens*, Vol. 4, p. 121. For commodity fictions see Feltes, Norman, *Modes of Production of Victorian Novels*, Chicago: University of Chicago Press, 1986, p. 9.
18 Smith, Grahame, *Charles Dickens: a literary life*, Basingstoke: Macmillan Press Ltd, 1996, pp. 28–9.
19 I have decided to exclude a discussion of the illustrations of Dickens's novels. This is partly because the topic has been dealt with in detail by several major scholars, but also because my study focuses on the movement of visual imagery in Dickens's prose rather than static visual images. In addition, there is evidence that Dickens lost interest in the illustration of his books after the publication of *Little Dorrit*. This point is also made by Anne Hollander when she claims that 'in England the pressure of language was keener; and Dickens's later novels ... showed themselves more and more independent of illus-

tration, as Dickens himself took on the job of viualization'. See Hollander, Anne, *Moving Pictures*, New York: Alfred A. Knopf, 1989, p. 332.

20 Bazin, André, *What is Cinema? Essays selected and translated by Hugh Gray*, Vol. 1, Berkeley, Los Angeles: University of California Press, 1967, p. 72.
21 Anon., 'The Late Charles Dickens', *Illustrated London News*, 18 June 1870, Vol. LVI, p. 639.
22 This world is evoked splendidly in Schlicke, Paul, *Dickens and Popular Entertainment*, London: Allen and Unwin, 1985.
23 Sutherland, John, *The Longman Companion to Victorian Fiction*, Harlow, Essex: Longman, 1988, p. 186.
24 Eisenstein, Sergei, *Film Form: essays in film theory*, ed. and trans. Jay Leyda, London: Dennis Dobson Ltd, 1977, p. 212.
25 Eisenstein, *Film Form*, p. 213.
26 Christie, Ian, *The Last Machine: early cinema and the birth of the modern world*, London: BBC Educational Developments, 1994, p. 27.
27 Dickens, Charles, 'An Italian Dream', in Schwarzbach, F. S. and Ormond, Leonee (eds.), *American Notes And Pictures From Italy*, London: Everyman, 1997, p. 362.
28 Baudelaire, Charles, *The Painter of Modern Life, and other essays*, ed. and trans. Jonathan Mayne, London: Phaidon Press, 1964, p. 9.
29 Benjamin, Walter, *Charles Baudelaire: a lyric poet in the era of high capitalism*, trans. Harry Zohn, London: Verso, 1977, p. 38.
30 Collins, Philip, *Dickens: the critical heritage*, London: Routledge, 1971, p. 6.
31 24 September 1858, *Letters of Dickens*, Vol. 8, p. 669.
32 Eisenstein, *Film Form*.
33 13 or 14 June 1846, *Letters of Dickens*, Vol. 4, p. 560.
4 22 June 1946, *Letters of Dickens*, Vol. 4, p. 569.
35 Benjamin, *Charles Baudelaire*, p. 69.
36 Benjamin, *Charles Baudelaire*, pp. 162–3.
37 Benjamin, *Charles Baudelaire*, p. 159.
38 21 October 1855, *Letters of Dickens*, Vol. 7, p. 724.
49 22 March 1851, *Letters of Dickens*, Vol. 6, p. 327.
40 3 August 1857, *Letters of Dickens*, Vol. 8, p. 399.
41 Hyde, Ralph, *Panoramania! The art of the 'all-embracing' view*, London: Trefoil Publications in association with Barbican Art Gallery, 1988, p. 88.
42 Altick, Richard, *The Shows of London*, Cambridge, Mass.: Belknap Press, 1978, p. 198.
43 Richards, Thomas, *Advertising and Spectacle 1851–1914: the commodity culture of Victorian England*, London: Verso, 1991, p. 56.
44 Douglass, Paul, 'Bergson and Cinema: friends or foes?', in Mullarkey, John (ed.), *The New Bergson*, Manchester: Manchester University Press, 1999, p. 210.
45 Source unidentified.

2 Machines and things: seeing and being seen

Touch is the most demystifying of all senses, different from sight, which is the most magical.[1]

We might as well begin at the beginning, with Plato:[2]

'Picture men in an underground cave-dwelling, with a long entrance reaching up towards the light along the whole width of the cave; in this they lie from their childhood, their legs and necks in chains, so that they stay where they are and look only in front of them, as the chain prevents their turning their heads round. Some way off, and higher up, a fire is burning behind them, and between the fire and the prisoners is a road on higher ground. Imagine a wall built along this road, like the screen which showmen have in front of the audience, over which they show the puppets ... picture also men carrying along this wall all kinds of articles which overtop it, statues of men and other creatures in stone and wood and other materials; naturally some of the carriers are speaking, others are silent'.

'A strange image and strange prisoners,' he said.

'They are like ourselves,' I answered. 'For in the first place do you think that such men would have seen anything of themselves or of each other except the shadows thrown by the fire on the wall of the cave opposite to them?'

'How could they,' he said, 'if all their life they had been forced to keep their heads motionless?'

'What would they have seen of the things carried along the wall? Would it not be the same?'

'Surely.'

'Then if they were able to talk with one another, do you not think that they would suppose what they saw to be the real things?'

'Necessarily.'

'Then what if there were in their prison an echo from the opposite wall? When any one of those passing by spoke, do you imagine that they could help thinking that the voice came from the shadowy wall passing before them?'

'No, certainly not,' he said.[3]

The dangers of starting with one of the founding passages of Western philosophical thought are obvious, inviting as it does so many avenues for speculation. However, it is a defining characteristic of great thought to make itself open to a generous range of uses as well as interpretations. Given the aims of this book, the link to the visual aspect is obvious. Prisoners in their chains may constitute an enforced audience, but there they sit nonetheless, watching what they take to be images of life itself, but is only a passing show of shadows cast by men carrying inanimate representations of the animate, the carriers safely hidden from view. And what a show it must seem to the poor devils trapped there, because the pictures they assume to constitute reality are accompanied by the sounds of speech and, presumably, of passing feet: in short, the talkies, moving pictures with sound. It is also a source of amused satisfaction that Plato's words suggest that the teasing complexity of his thought has its origins in one of the commonplace entertainments of his own day, the puppet show which, if not as old as time, is clearly as old as ancient Greece.

The passage can also be related to another commonplace of human existence, our need to seek out knowledge of the world through sight. Plato's cave-dwellers represent this basic mode of comprehension *in extremis*. Chained into immobility, sight and, to a lesser extent, hearing are their sole means of accessing the world outside their cave, a world whose insubstantiality would be instantly revealed if they were allowed to touch what they saw. The centrality of this source of knowledge, to the sighted, is revealed by the phenomenon of facial recognition, in animals just as much as in babies. Why is it that the baby being cooed to, the cat being stroked, gaze so raptly into another face rather than, say, the elbow or any other part of their holder's anatomy? The contact of eyes is crucial to such wordless communication, opening up the mutuality of seeing and being seen at the most basic human and, even, animal level.

Again, a wealth of material presents itself for speculation and discussion at this point. But choices have to be made in the light of the major aim of this chapter: to present a descriptive account, for those who need it, of the visual devices that are referred to so frequently throughout this book. A way into the field is provided by an observation of Paul Virilio's: 'The moment they appeared on the scene, the first optical devices ... profoundly altered the contexts in which mental images were topographically stored and retrieved, the *imperative to re-present oneself*.[4] Although Virilio's point is similar to arguments about changes in nineteenth-century consciousness that have been touched on in Chapter 1 already, and will be taken further in the next chapter, his claim may seem a little strong in relation to what amounts to centuries of recreating the external world through visual mechanisms. Virilio himself is somewhat vague as to chronology at this point and it is not clear whether he realises just how early these optical devices made their appearance. He lacks, of course, the assistance provided by Laurent Mannoni's *The Great Art of Light and Shadow*,[5] a monumental work which recounts the history of optical devices in comprehensive detail. Mannoni charts, for example, the appearance of the camera obscura, one of the most influential of all visual devices in the thirteenth century, although it was also known of in antiquity. Did Virilio's 'imperative to re-present oneself' begin as early as the thirteenth century? It is difficult to answer the question at this stage in the argument, although Mannoni's comments on his own work suggest that an underlying and unifying aim lies beneath his descriptions of the optical toys, visual entertainments and scientific devices that he charts with such detailed care: 'there was one overriding godlike desire: to recreate life, to see a human alter ego, either hand-painted or chronophotographed, living and breathing on the screen,'[6] a dream he sees as being fulfilled in 1895, with the first public demonstration of what is generally accepted as a true cinematic experience.

This grand narrative is questioned in Tom Gunning's rightly laudatory introduction to the book: 'Mannoni sets out here not a simple pedigree or genealogy for cinema, but a whole complex and neglected visual culture, one of whose forms became the movies in the twentieth century'.[7] What Gunning is challenging is the notion of the inevitability of cinema's appearance, the vision of chronological progression in which each new device joins the ranks of others over the centuries, marching towards the apotheosis of film to which all have contributed. In other words, he is arguing that the emergence of film is contingent rather than necessary, one visual possibility among many, and not the deterministic culmination of forces with only one end. Similarly, Virilio's *'imperative'* implies a degree of self-conscious awareness appropriate to the gradual accumulation of visual experience over the centuries, climaxing – one is tempted to suggest – in the nineteenth century, rather than occurring at the 'moment' when the 'first optical devices' made their appearance. Something more modest seems indicated by this fascination with the visual, a human desire for reciprocity of the kind suggested by my example of the infant and the adult, the natural capacity to see joined by the perhaps culturally created need to be seen. If this is an image of love at the human level, it may also stand for the desire to feel at home in one's world, the delighted surprise engendered by the human capacity for image-making, for mirror-like reflections, the consolatory sense that we are not alone. To see ourselves in the company of others, surrounded by the minutiae of daily existence, seems to guarantee an escape from solipsism and provides the pleasure generated by any kind of mechanically created visual amusement, from the kaleidoscope to the wide-screen feature film. The colours, shapes and patterns of the kaleidoscope are an obvious source of delight, but a more deeply felt response is created by the human ingenuity displayed in producing illusions of reality, and it is this pleasure in seeing our world reproduced that will provide a linking thread in what follows, a series of sketches of the visual devices that play their part in forming the vibrant visual world into which Dickens was born. Kate Flint remarks that in *Pictures from Italy* 'Dickens is especially fascinated with the act of seeing'.[8] Flint has her own explanation for this fascination on Dickens's part; what follows may provide another.

The camera obscura

One reason for the longevity and importance of the camera obscura is that its effects can occur without the intervention of an apparatus of any kind, especially in conditions of bright sun-light. If a small gap is made, or occurs by chance, into a fully darkened space, whatever is outside the gap will be projected into that space onto the wall opposite the gap, the image appearing upside down and back to front. The phenomenon was known to Aristotle and it seems likely that it was discovered at an early stage that the introduction of a white surface between the image and the wall – a sheet, for example – would improve its quality although with a consequent loss in size the closer the surface was held to it. A number of thirteenth-century scientists, including the Englishman Roger Bacon, constructed mechanisms for capturing the phenomenon and, by as early as the sixteenth century, the Italian, Giovanni Battista della Porta, had constructed an enter-tainment based on it: 'Della Porta's show foreshadowed the magic lantern projections of the following century. But comparing them from a present-day viewpoint, the Italian camera obscura appears almost superior to the lantern, whose hand-painted glass slides could not offer the complete illusion of this scenic device. Della Porta's images, projected into the room by the crystal lenses and the mirror used since 1558, showed real actors, who moved in front of scenery to the sound of accompanying music.'[9]

The camera obscura was subject to numerous technical improvements over the centuries although it failed to become a public entertainment on the scale of, say, the magic lantern. Its development took two major directions, the first an important contribution to painting. Portable cameras obscura in box form provided painters with a detailed and stable picture of external reality. Indeed, in '1679 the architect and scientist Robert Hooke built a transportable apparatus for landscape painters and ... both amateurs and professionals – among them Canaletto – were using it for topographical painting'.[10] The second major direction was the introduction of camera obscura rooms which combined entertainment and education. A variation of this development can still be enjoyed in Edinburgh, where it has been amusing citizens and visitors for over 150 years. The device projects, by a system of lenses, a moving image of people and objects in the proximity of the camera obscura. I myself can testify to the delight induced in audiences by a visual experience that might seem very small beer compared to the wonders of today's IMAX cinemas. There is no question that the images produced by the Edinburgh camera do look amazingly cinematic, but the relationship of the device to the appearance of film is the focus of a debate in the history of visual technology, a major contribution to which is Jonathan Crary's *Techniques of the Observer*.[11] David Robinson argues that 'the camera obscura is the essential element of photography; the technology of the magic lantern remains intact in even the most sophisticated cinema projector'.[12] In this statement Robinson suggests that, in the words of his own essay, there have been '300 years of cinematography'; in other words, the camera obscura begins a process, taken up by other devices over the centuries, which leads with a kind of inevitability to film. Crary challenges this on the grounds that the observer of, or in, the camera obscura perceives the world from a fixed standpoint which is uninflected by his/her observation of it. Developments in the early nineteenth century, including research into the phenomenon of the after image ('the privileging of the afterimage allowed one to conceive of sensory perception as cut from any necessary links with an external referent'[13]) mean for Crary that 'the corporeal subjectivity of the observer, which was a priori excluded from the concept of the camera obscura, suddenly becomes the site on which an observer is possible. The human body ... becomes the active producer of optical experience'.[14] For my purposes, the value of sketching this debate lies in one of its conclusions, Crary's desire to delineate 'an observing subject who was both a product of and at the same time constitutive of modernity in the nineteenth century'.[15] This is precisely the position I wish to ascribe to Dickens in, for example, his relationship with the emerging metropolis of Victorian London where he is both an observer of transformations in urban life at the very moment when they are occurring and, simultaneously, a contributor to images of the urban through the creative power of the imagined cities of his fiction.

The magic lantern

The magic lantern may not have been a mass entertainment on the scale of the cinema of the 1940s and 1950s, but by the nineteenth century it permeated all aspects of life, as child's toy and family past-time, in addition to contributing publicly to education and recreation on a large scale. For Gunning the magic lantern is clearly an epoch-making intervention in the history of visual technology in being 'the first medium to contest the printed word as a primary mode of information and instruction'.[16] Although subject to incessant modification and improvement over the centuries, in its classic form the magic lantern consisted essentially of a box made of wood, metal or even cardboard; in a darkened room it projected, by means of a light source, pictures painted on glass slides on to a white surface, normally a screen, but perhaps a wall or even, as Mannoni points out, 'white leather' in the eighteenth century.[17] Those who have seen Bill Douglas's film *Comrades* (1986) will have discovered one of the most fascinating aspects of the magic lantern's history: the role of the travelling lanternist who, carrying his lantern on his back, spread its magic throughout town and country. There is ample evidence that through displaying his show in the streets or in people's homes the travelling lanternist exposed significant numbers of people to the wonders of visual technology. Skilled operators were able to create the illusion of movement for their audiences at least as early as 1713, as we can see from Jonathan Swift's comment: 'I went afterwards to see a famous moving Picture'.[18] The sheer beauty, excitement, and interest of magic lantern shows ensured that the device took its own small place in the activities fostered by the Industrial Revolution, so that by the nineteenth century slides and lanterns were being produced on a large scale, employing thousands of people. The firm of W. & F. Newton, for example, had no fewer than 150,000 subjects in its slide catalogue.[19] It is hard to underestimate the impact of this mass production on the emotional and imaginative lives of people in the nineteenth century. Mannoni touchingly evokes the possible effect of some of the still-existing relics of the period when they first appeared: 'These objects, if they have been well preserved, still convey some emotional impact. It is easy to imagine the wonder of a nineteenth-century child opening the cardboard box to discover the Lanterne Riche, for example, which was 55 cm high in its large model and decorated in a riot of colours: a truly luxurious present which deserved its adjective "magic"'.[20]

For those who have not experienced a well-presented magic lantern show, as is made possible by Turin's magnificent Museo Nazionale del Cinema, the device probably seems to inhabit the same world as mistaken views of silent cinema, grotesquely flickering figures rushing dimly about in a context of funereal quiet, although only older readers could have any associations with the device itself. For them the magic lantern probably evokes the mind-numbingly solemn instruction of a church hall slide-show, 'illustrated' by images that bore only a farcical connection to the thrills of the cinema that they no doubt wished they were attending instead. But Fred Guida's evocation, in his study of visual adaptations of Dickens's *A Christmas Carol*, suggests why a visit to the magic lantern show may have generated all the pleasure associated by film goers at the thought of a 'night at the pictures':

Improvements in painting techniques and materials resulted in images of astonishing complexity and beauty, and ... by the mid-nineteenth century advancements in still photography made it possible to project actual photographic images that had been fixed on glass slides ...In this context – the context of motion – the most obvious weapon in the magic lanternist's arsenal was the mechanical slide ... [which] enabled windmills to turn and children on swings to swing ... Chromotope slides produced spectacular kaleidoscopic effects and ... tank slides produced swirling masses of moving colour ... The familiar pan or panning shot ... was easily achieved by pulling (slowly and smoothly!) a long horizontal slide through the projector ... Similarly, the use of two projectors made it possible to cut directly from one slide to the next in much the same way in which a film ... cuts from one shot to another.[21]

We can add to this list of delights the magic lantern's capacity to create so-called 'dissolving views' in which, by means of mechanical improvements, slides slowly merged into each other. This was a major attraction of one of London's most popular shows later in the nineteenth century:

the Poly's [the Polytechnic Institution, Regent Street, London] breath-taking and ingenious 'dissolving view' entertaintments ... featured exquisite, hand-painted slide images executed by and presented by Henry Langdon Childe and his associate, Mr Hill. Each new show was premiered either at Christmas or at Easter-time, and was full of humour. Most were based on traditional stories like *Robinson Crusoe* or *Bluebeard*, and latterly included strong elements of Harlequinade. At other times of the year the theatre would be given over to more descriptive presentations, such as views of the eruption of Vesuvius or an account of a voyage to the North Pole. All incorporated impressive optical effects and transformations produced by the interplay of up to four massive lanterns, projecting onto a giant screen, beyond which were stationed an army of sound-effect operators.[22]

The magic lantern was dispersed throughout all levels of society in the eighteenth and nineteenth centuries, and the affection in which it was held may explain its adoption as a metaphor to evoke the richness of urban life. For Voltaire, in a passage which anticipates Dickens, 'the life of Paris disperses all one's ideas, one forgets everything, one is diverted only momentarily by everything in that great magic lantern, where all the pictures pass as rapidly as shadows'.[23] This relationship between the magic lantern and the city was also seized upon by Lady Blessington in relation to London in *The Magic Lantern; or, Sketches of Scenes in the Metropolis*, published as early as 1822.[24] Another aspect of the magic lantern's deep and widespread influence is that most of the major pioneers of British cinema in its earliest, 'visionary'[25] phase were steeped in the magic lantern, a fact that will be pursued in the next chapter in relation to Thomas Bentley and Cecil Hepworth. Turning to Dickens himself, we find numerous references to the device, in his life as well as the work. It clearly figured vividly in Dickens's childhood as well as that of his own children. One anecdote evokes this world of boyish fun with Dickens's injunction to the servant: '"Now, Mary, clear the kitchen, we're going to have such a game". Then in would come George Stroughill [a boyhood friend] with his magic lantern, and there would be a spirited acting out of plays'.[26] The excitement of such moments is echoed in a letter describing the preparations for his son's Twelfth Night party, a spectacular occasion even by Dickens's standards: 'I have provided a Magic Lantern and divers other tremendous engines of that nature'.[27] This may have been the event remembered by Thackeray's daughter Annie as 'a "shining" party that seemed to go "round and round" in an enchanted way. She and her younger sister Minnie ... were lost in a blur of music, streams of children ... radiant confusion',[28] an experience which seems to echo the pleasures generated by the magic lantern at its joyful best.

Given the role played by the magic lantern in Victorian culture, and in Dickens's life, it is hardly surprising to find it being used in a number of ways in his novels. One result of the young David Copperfield's mild dissipation when he first arrives in London is his 'dim recollection of having seen her [Agnes] at the theatre, as if I had seen her in a pale magic lantern' (Ch. 25). In *Martin Chuzzlewit*, the absurdly pontifical Mr Pecksniff is described at one point as 'Placid, calm, but proud. Honestly proud. Dressed with peculiar care, smiling with even more than usual blandness, pondering on the beauties of his art [architecture] with a mild abstraction from all sordid thoughts, and gently travelling across the disc, as if he were a figure in a magic lantern' (Ch. 35). He is on his way, it turns out, to lay the foundation stone of a new grammar school designed not by himself, as he claims, but by his pupil, Martin. Dickens's travel book, *American Notes*, provides another variation on how the magic lantern influenced perception:

These stumps of trees are a curious feature in American travelling. The varying illusions they present to the unaccustomed eye as it grows dark, are quite astonishing in their number and reality. Now, there is a Grecian urn erected in the centre of a lonely field; now there is a woman weeping at a tomb; now a very commonplace old gentleman in a white waistcoat, with a thumb thrust into each arm-hole of his coat; now a student poring on a book; now a crouching negro; now, a horse, a dog, a cannon, an armed man; a hunch-back throwing off his cloak and stepping forth into the light. They were often as entertaining to me as so many glasses in a magic lantern, and never took their shapes at my bidding, but seemed to force themselves upon me, whether I would or no; and strange to say, I sometimes recognised in them counterparts of figures once familiar to me in pictures attached to childish books, forgotten long ago. (Ch. 14)

Finally, there is the example of 'Tackleton the Toy-merchant' from *The Cricket on the Hearth* who 'despised all toys'. As a result, 'his soul perfectly revelled' in the creation of monstrous objects liable to frighten the daylights out of any normal child, even to the extent of losing money 'by getting up Goblin slides for magic-lanterns, whereon the Powers of Darkness were depicted as a sort of supernatural shell-fish, with human faces'. (Chirp the First.) It would be unwise to make too firm a pattern of these references, but it does seem as if Dickens is manipulating the faintly negative aspects of the device as a shadowy reflection of reality by associating it with insobriety, deception, the fanciful play of imagination at dusk, and a toy maker who loathes toys and presumably, by extension, children.

But perhaps the most suggestive mention of the device is in a letter he wrote in 1846 in which Dickens complains of his difficulty writing *Dombey and Son* while he is living in Switzerland in the relatively small city of Lausanne. The burden of this complaint, rooted in his separation from London, is the 'absence of streets'. The point is important enough to be worth quoting in more detail as Dickens explains that his speed of writing is impeded by 'the absence of streets and numbers of figures. I can't express how much I want these. It seems as if they supplied something to my brain, which it cannot bear, when busy, to lose. For a week or a fortnight I can write prodigiously in a retired place ... and a day in London sets me up again and starts me'. But, 'the toil and labour of writing, day after day, without that magic lantern is *IMMENSE!!*'[29] The urban metropolis of the nineteenth century is for him an immense play of shadows, a huge spectacle in which every possible kind of contrast – luxurious mansions and rotting slums, bodies clothed in high fashion or disintegrating rags, appetites sated on the richest of foods or barely satisfied by the meanest of scraps – are projected onto the screen of his imagination. The cities of his mind, Paris and London, are rooted in the observable realities of his experience of them but, simultaneously, take on mythic status, an almost Expressionist drama of heightened contrasts, distorted settings, the 'unreal city' of T S Eliot. Dickens needs this show desperately to recharge his creative energies, the electricity that seems to flow into him through those nightly hauntings of the empty streets as well as his companionable association with the crowds thronging to theatres and other public entertainments, including the magic lantern itself.

The phantasmagoria

Phantasmagoria, and panorama, have passed into the language partly because, as Altick remarks, the 'available fund of comparisons was inadequate to describe the unprecedented sensations ... [of] travelling on the railway or watching a train go by' or other 'perceptions and effects new in human experience'.[30] In other words, the entertainments these words derive from were not merely pastimes; they helped people to relate to some of the new things that were happening around them and which existed outside any known terms of reference. The phantasmagoria was, in fact, a rather simple modification of the magic lantern that used back projection so that audiences were not conscious of the lanterns that were the source of what they were seeing. Given this apparently uncanny absence of the means by which its illusions were created, the phantasmagoria was able to specialise in the supernatural and conjure up, seemingly out of nowhere, skeletons, spirits, ghosts and so on. However, its key distinguishing feature was the ability to enact the effect of 'images appearing to approach and recede from the spectator'.[31] This assault on the audience's nerves is caught perfectly by Dickens in *The Old Curiosity Shop* in the impact of the vile, yet wonderfully energetic, Quilp on the innocent Kit: 'Quilp said not a word in reply, but walking so close to Kit as to bring his eyes within two or three inches of his face, looked fixedly at him, retreated a little distance without averting his gaze, approached again, again withdrew, and so on for half-a-dozen times, like a head in a phantasmagoria'. (Ch 48) There are many examples of the phantasmagoric in Dickens's writing in the more general sense, none more extraordinary than his memory of a:

certain desolate open-air Morgue that I happened to light upon in London, one day in the hard winter of 1861, and which seemed as strange to me, at the time of seeing it, as if I had found it in China ...

Towards that hour of a winter's afternoon when the lamp-lighters are beginning to light the lamps in the streets a little before they are wanted, because the darkness thickens fast and soon, I was walking in from the country on the northern side of the Regent's Park – hard, frozen and deserted –when I saw an empty Hansom cab drive up to the lodge at Gloucester Gate, and the driver with great agitation call to the man there: who quickly reached a long pole from a tree, and, deftly collared by the driver, jumped to the step of his little seat, and so the Hansom rattled out at the gate, galloping over the iron-bound road. I followed running, though not so fast but that when I came to the right-hand Canal Bridge, near the cross-path to Chalk Farm, the Hansom was stationary, the horse was smoking hot, the long pole was idle on the ground, and the driver and the park-keeper were looking over the bridge parapet. Looking over too, I saw, lying on the towing-path with her face turned up towards us, a woman, dead a day or two, and under thirty, as I guessed, poorly dressed in black. The feet were lightly crossed at the ankles, and the dark hair, all pushed back from the face, as though that had been the last action of her desperate hands, streamed over the ground ... So dreadfully forlorn, so dreadfully sad, so dreadfully mysterious, this spectacle of our dear sister here departed! A barge came up, breaking the floating ice and the silence, and a woman steered it. The man with the horse that towed it, cared so little for the body, that the stumbling hoofs had been among the hair, and the tow-rope had caught and turned the head, before our cry of horror took him to the bridle. At which sound the steering woman looked up at us on the bridge, with contempt unutterable, and then looking down at the body with a similar expression – as if it were made in another likeness from herself, had been informed with other passions, had been lost by other chances, had had another nature dragged down to perdition – steered a spurning streak of mud at it, and passed on.[32]

Two elements of this disturbing scene might be regarded as phantasmagoric in the more technical sense, the dead woman 'with her face turned up towards us' and the contemptuous steering woman looking 'up at us on the bridge'. But the phantasmagoria truly resides in the vividness of this pitiless recording of a total absence of human fellow-feeling, a moment from the life of the city captured in nightmarish detail and recorded without a shred of sentiment on the part of the onlookers.

The panorama

With the panorama we enter the world of one of the most exciting and influential of all the visual entertainments of the past, an experience now beyond recall in a way that is not true of the magic lantern. That a contemporary recreation of the true panorama experience would be expensive as well as elaborate is made clear from the description offered in a historical dictionary of architecture of 1832:

Panorama: The terms sounds as though it should belong exclusively to the language of painting, for it combines two Greek words to signify *complete view*. This is obtained by means of a circular background on which a series of aspects are drawn and then rendered, uniquely, by a series of separate paintings ... this ... makes an architectural work of the painter's field of activity. The name panorama, in fact, refers both to the edifice on which the painting is hung and to the painting itself.[33]

In other words, at its best the panorama involved the combination of a huge, 380 degree (circular) painting in a specially constructed physical setting. Paul Virilio completes the picture with his description of such a building as:

a rotunda with daylight entering from above, the rest of the building remaining dark. Viewers were led into the centre along long, dark corridors so their eyes would adjust to the dark and register the light on the painting as natural. Coming on to a raised amphitheatre in the middle of the rotunda in the dark, viewers had no idea where the light was coming from. They could not see either the top or the bottom of the building, offering no beginning or end, in fact no boundary whatever. It was like being on a mountain with the view obstructed only by the horizon.[34]

The origins of the panorama are fairly clear. An Englishman, Robert Barker, dreamed up the idea, which he patented in 1787, in Edinburgh. Venues were quickly erected for the new attraction, one of the most famous being the Coliseum, purpose-built in the Regent's Park area of London, which held varied and successful shows. In an early example, a panorama of the city itself was constructed from a series of sketches made from the top of St Paul's Cathedral in the early 1820s, an enterprise undertaken in conditions of sometimes hair-raising danger. A link can be made again with the Industrial Revolution as spectators were lifted to the viewing galleries in London's first passenger lift. The panorama was an instant success and it is easy to see why. Contemporaries testify to the wonder of what seemed to them a magical experience, transporting them to views of great cities, famous battles, exotic locations of such beauty and realism that they could hardly believe that they were facing an illusion. In the words of one spectator, you 'are obliged almost to reason with yourself ... that it is not nature, instead of a work of art'.[35] Indeed, there are stories of viewers putting out their hands to touch objects which they believed were three-dimensional despite the fact that they had been painted on a flat surface. These apparently unsophisticated responses are explained by Ruskin's praise of landscapes by Thomas Seddon, whose 'primal object is to place the spectator, as far as art can do, in the scene represented, and to give him the perfect sensation of its reality, wholly unmodified by the artist's execution'.[36] The nature of representation had been examined critically by Coleridge earlier in the nineteenth century in his discussion of *trompe-l'oeil*. His central point perhaps is the disappointment experienced when the illusory object is found not to be real. The whole function of a plaster apple, say, is to convince us that it is the thing itself, unlike the fruit depicted in a still life. In Caravaggio's *Boy with a Basket of Fruit* (1593–4), for example, we are amazed by the artist's power to make his apples (and everything else) *seem* like the real thing, but we are under no illusion as to their status as objects reproduced by paint. On the other hand, we may reach out to the *trompe-l'oeil* apple with the intention of eating it! We are thus full of a possibly amused wonder at the craftsman's ability to make such a lifelike object but, as with the solution to a murder mystery, once the truth is revealed the object loses all its resonance. Looking forward, the phrase 'wholly unmodified by the artist's execution' is suggestive of later debates on the so-called invisibility of classic Hollywood cinema, in which the techniques which create staggering illusions of reality are hidden from view. Despite the wonder and excitement created by the panorama and its widespread popularity in Europe and America, it may have been doomed because it lacked the continuity and staying power of art leaving it vulnerable to the next visual attraction that came along. This is the position taken by Wordsworth in Book VII of *The Prelude*, 'Residence in

London', his brilliant evocation and analysis of the impressions
made by the city on a mind nurtured in rural tranquillity. Like
any tourist, he soaks up the sensory richness of the urban world:

those sights ... that ape
The absolute presence of reality,
Expressing, as in mirror, sea and land,
And what earth is, and what she has to show.
I do not here allude to subtlest craft,
By means refined attaining purest end,
But imitations, fondly made in plain
Confession of man's weakness

Wordsworth is clearly suspicious, not of the art which represents
the external world through an act of creative engagement, but of
mechanical copying of 'all that the traveller sees'[37] of any particular location.

However, the panorama continued to be successful for many
years. It enjoyed two major phases of popularity, between 1800
and 1830, and then from the late 1870s when new venues were
constructed in London, Paris, Brussels and St Petersburg. One
sign of this long-continued interest was the rapidity with which
the form passed into consciousness in a number of ways; its rapid
acceptance into the language is an example of this, as Altick has
pointed out. Amusing evidence is also provided by the description
of the popular shows of the monologist, Charles Matthews, as
'Matthews-oramas'.[38] That this fad was not restricted to the United
Kingdom is demonstrated by a sardonic passage from Balzac's *Le
Père Goriot*:

Now the resident and daily boarders dropped in one after another,
exchanging greetings and the meaningless remarks that pass for wit
among certain classes of Parisians ... The recent invention of the
Diorama, which had carried optical illusion one stage further than
the Panorama, had led in some studios to the pleasantry of talking
'rama', and a young painter who frequented the Maison Vauquer
had inoculated the boarders there with the disease.
  'Well, Monsieur-r-r Poiret,' said the Museum official, 'how is your
little healthorama ... It's desperately chillyorama ... Aha! here comes
a fine souporama'.[39]

Another sign of the times was the aim of the *Illustrated London
News*, as stated in its introductory number in 1842: 'to keep
continually before the eye of the world a living and moving
panorama of all its actions and influences'.[40] This reference to
moving panoramas is a reminder that they were frequently
adapted, for use in the theatre say, by being mounted on rollers
so that audiences were provided with the illusion of a huge back-

drop passing before them. Another innovation was to present a moving panorama in a suitable hall with a commentary on the events being presented; the most famous British example is Albert Smith's account of the ascent of Mont Blanc which he gave some 2000 times. The success of such ventures was due at least in part to the quality of the commentary which, far from being simply a dull lecture, was a total performance enlivened by jokes, music and song, poetry and so on. A final sign of the panorama's influence can be seen in painting, the form from which in a sense it originated. Alexander Wagner, who painted a famous panorama *Rome in the Year 312 AD*, used some of the same techniques in his salon work, for example *The Chariot Race* in the Manchester City Art Gallery which is 'packed with spectacle, drama, action, and emotion. The image is almost three-dimensional: the chariots seem to charge through the canvas and over one's head'.[41]And the almost unimaginably vast settings in the paintings of the Victorian John Martin, such as his *Joshua Commanding the Sun to Stand Still*, have an emphatically panoramic quality.

The diorama

Although both the panorama and the diorama continued side by side throughout much of the nineteenth century, the panorama was eventually challenged by this new form. Its scenic illusionism carried the representation of reality to yet another stage, partly by introducing movement. In the traditional panorama, spectators made their own way round the spectacle; in the diorama they were moved through it, the first example being that created by one of the greatest figures in the history of photography, Daguerre, who:

turned his *Diorama* construction in the rue Samson ... into a *veritable sight travel machine* ... In this structure, which was built in 1822, *the viewers' room was mobile* and spun round like a one-man-operated merry-go-round. Everyone found themselves carried around past all the paintings on show without apparently having to move a muscle ... We are ... interested here in ... Daguerre the lighting engineer, the master technician, whose application of the image to an architectural construct used absolutely realistic and totally illusory time and movement.[42]

Light does indeed seem to have been a key feature of the diorama's magic although, again, it is difficult for us to grasp just how wonderful the experience was to its viewers – although wonderful it evidently was. For Balzac, 'It is the marvel of the century', while a less famous contemporary thought that 'nature could not do it better'.[43] The novelist Thackeray felt that the view from a mountain summit in the theatre was 'so like nature' that he felt in danger of falling.[44] Subtle effects of stage lighting, changes from day to night and spring to summer, the splendour of dissolves from scene to scene – all contributed to visions of dreamlike beauty which, among other uses, 'became the leading spectacular events in the annual Christmas pantomimes at Covent Garden and Drury Lane ... in the 1820s and 1830s'.[45] One last example, which highlights the varied nature of so many nineteenth-century shows, is provided by the editors' footnote in the sixth volume of Dickens's letters and concerns 'Albert Smith's *The Overland Mail*, "A Literary, Pictorial, and Musical Entertainment" ... As dioramic pictures of the Suez to Cairo section of the route, painted by William Beverly, were displayed, Smith accompanied them with an entertaining narrative, including songs, anecdotes and impersonations'.[46] A direct link between Dickens and the diorama is provided by Fred Guida who points out that no less than three separate adaptations of *A Christmas Carol* appeared in theatres simultaneously on 5 February 1844: 'Interestingly, we are told that a ... production ... that was staged one week later incorporated a Diorama in its depiction of at least some of Scrooge's ghostly visions ... it may well be the first occasion on which an audio-visual medium was employed in telling or adapting Dickens's story'.[47]

Panoramas, dioramas and Dickens

Dickens was in the thick of this world of visual entertainment and instruction, even more than he had been with the magic lantern. As spectator, we find him writing a review in 1848 of what he called 'The American Panorama', the work of John Banvard, which constituted 'the largest painting in the world ... exhibited by unrolling it from immense cylinders. It portrayed c. 3000 miles of river scenery, accompanied by Banvard's running commentary ... Exhibited ... in New York and Boston, then London, with immense success'.[48] Dickens followed up his review with a letter: 'I ... cannot refrain from saying that I was in the highest degree interested and pleased by your picture'.[49] Again, Dickens informs one of his close friends, the painter Maclise, that 'I want to see the panorama of the Nile' which, if he did, he would have found to be a moving panorama modelled on the success of Banvard although taking the form of a transparency (not unlike a vast photographic slide) 'acclaimed by critics, especially for its interior of Abu Simbel by torchlight, and a sandstorm overtaking a caravan in the desert'.[50] At a directly personal level, one of his more intimate relationships was with Clarkson Stanfield, his beloved Stanny, who began his career as a scene painter at the Theatre Royal, Drury Lane where he famously created, with others, the series of moving panoramas for their Christmas pantomimes in the 1820s and 1830s which was referred to earlier in this chapter. In the words of a contemporary, 'only those who have seen these really stupendous works can form any idea of the inventive talent and skill developed in them. They opened the eyes of the mixed audience of a theatre to the beauties of landscape painting ... and ... led to a permanent advance and improvement in the scenic decoration of our theatres'.[51] Stanfield was elected to the Royal Academy in 1835, and thereafter he only worked on scene painting when asked to do so by close friends such as Dickens. He contributed to some of Dickens's most striking theatrical productions, including *Every Man in his Humour* in 1845, *The Lighthouse* in 1855, and *The Frozen Deep* in 1857. In addition to painting panoramic scenes for the theatre, Stanfield was also a diorama artist in his day and so through him Dickens had direct professional contact with two related and dominant forms of Victorian visual entertainment.

It is, then, hardly surprising to find that Dickens's work contains a number of references to these two devices, particularly the panorama, at the level of detail as well as in relation to the vast architecture of the novels as a whole. In *David Copperfield*, Mr Micawber refers at one point, with his usual delightful pomposity, to '"the diversified panorama of human existence"' (Ch. 49), while Martin Chuzzlewit finds the wilderness of the United States he has been tricked into investing in to be a 'darkening panorama' (Ch. 23). One of the essays that make up *The Uncommercial Traveller* records the narrator's experience of being called to a London inquest on the death of an infant: 'In a kind of crypt devoted to the warehousing of the parochial coffins, and in the midst of a perfect Panorama of coffins of all sizes, it [the corpse] was stretched on a box'.[52] More interesting than these local instances, however, is a topic that will be explored in detail in Chapter 9, the way in which, having found a place in the language, the panoramic concept returns as a governing metaphor in the structure of Dickens's major fictions. *Bleak House*, *Little Dorrit* and *Our Mutual Friend* can be regarded as panoramic representations of Victorian society and so it seems as if Paul Virilio's claim can, after all, be validated, although in ways that he might not have had in mind directly. There is a sense in which these later novels by Dickens can be understood as obeying an imperative to re-present Victorian society to itself, as long as we remember that they are fictional constructs which help to create a vision of nineteenth-century society as much as reflect it. An interesting perspective is provided by Lynne Kirby when she remarks that 'the link between both the panorama and the diorama and the railroad, as well as with later photography and cinema, appears most clearly in the kinds of discourse generated around the "panoramic perception" of train travel'.[53] My only disagreement here would be the tendency towards a grand narrative in Kirby's work, in which the railway is seen as an explanatory be-all and end-all, especially in relation to the appearance of film. My point has been that panoramic perceptions can be found at work in numerous aspects of nineteenth-century life; railway travel is only one among many. The panorama itself was clearly one of those inventions which opened people's eyes, in more ways than one, by helping them to grasp, for example, that the urban world presented itself as a panoramic spectacle once the clue provided by the panorama experience had been absorbed. And if the panorama can be seen as a vastly elaborated visual toy along with the host of others developed in the nineteenth century such as the Mutoscope and Kinetescope, the film projector may be regarded as the most elaborate toy of all, as long as it is not read as the *culmination* of what had gone before. The theory of persistence of vision has become a controversial area in scientific debate, but the collaboration of mind and body with segments of celluloid passing intermittently through a mechanism is still required to produce the grand illusion of movement and colour that is modern cinema.[54] And this remains as much a cause of wonder and delight as earlier visual entertainments were to their viewers.

Pierce Egan, who was a popular novelist in the nineteenth century, provides a useful postscript to this discussion in his *Life and London*.[55] The narrator offers 'what he calls a "*camera obscura*" view of the city' with the '"invaluable advantages of SEEING and not being seen"'.[56] For Deborah Nord this represents a 'combination of the need to repress and the desire to represent in Egan'[57] and she goes on to apply the idea to Dickens who, in her view, 'turns the camera on [in the *Sketches by Boz*] and keeps it running, hoping to capture movement, above all, and to show how a variety of types occupy the same urban space'.[58] These are interesting formulations and relevant to the issues discussed in this chapter, but both contain a hint of passivity in which the role of the creative mind is displaced in favour of an almost Andy Warhol-like registering of unmediated surfaces. The emphasis in

the following chapters will be different. I shall be taking up the
clue provided by Orson Welles's definition of cinema: his claim
that 'a film is never really good unless the camera is an eye in the
head of a poet'.[59] In other words, the camera is not simply a
recording apparatus in creative film-making, but ultimately in
the service of a controlling imagination. Similarly, if the metaphor
of Dickens as camera has any meaning, it can only be found in
his ability to imbue the surfaces he reflects with significance.
Indeed, given that this act of reflection is embodied in the characteristically rich language that we have come to expect of him,
Dickens's engagement with external reality is, by definition,
reciprocal, bestowing meaning on his fictional world in the very
moment of actualising it in words.

Notes

1 Barthes, Roland, 'La nouvelle Citroën', *Mythologies*, trans. Annette
   Lavers, London: Paladin, 1973, p. 97.
2 This chapter arises out of my surprise that writers of the kind of work
   I am attempting frequently make no effort whatever to explain what
   camera obscuras, panoramas, magic lanterns, and so on, actually
   were, and what they could do. The gap is filled here, although the
   detail goes further than the purely practical.
3 This passage is the famous opening of Book VII of Plato's *Republic*,
   trans. A. D. Lindsay, Everyman series, London: J. M. Dent & Sons,
   1935, pp. 207–8.
4 Virilio, Paul, *The Vision Machine*, trans. Julie Rose, London: British
   Film Institute, 1994, p. 4.
5 Mannoni, Laurent, *The Great Art of Light and Shadow: archaeology of
   the cinema*, Exeter: University of Exeter Press, 2000. This is an invaluable work that I gratefully acknowledge in this chapter.
6 Mannoni, *Light and Shadow*, p. xvii.
7 Mannoni, *Light and Shadow*, p. xx.
8 Flint, Kate, *The Victorians and the Visual Imagination*, Cambridge: Cambridge University Press, 2000, p. 145.
9 Mannoni, *Light and Shadow*, p. 9.
10 Chilvers, Ian and Obsborne, Harold (eds.), *The Oxford Dictionary of Art*,
   Oxford: Oxford University Press, 1997, p. 98.
11 Crary, Jonathan, *Techniques of the Observer: on vision and modernity in
   the nineteenth century*, Cambridge, Mass.: MIT Press, 1992.
12 Robinson, David, 'Realising the Vision: 300 years of cinematography',
   in Williams, Christopher (ed.), *Cinema: the beginnings and the future*,
   London: University of Westminster Press, 1996. p. 34.
13 Crary, *Techniques*, p 98.
14 Crary, *Techniques*, p. 69.
15 Crary, *Techniques*, p. 9.
16 Mannoni, *Light and Shadow*, p. xxvii.
17 Mannoni, *Light and Shadow*, p. 33.
18 Mannoni, *Light and Shadow*, p. 121.
19 Mannoni, *Light and Shadow*, p. 289.
20 Mannoni, *Light and Shadow*, p. 285.
21 Guida, Fred, *A Christmas Carol and Its Adaptations: a critical examination of Dickens's story and its productions on screen and television*,

Jefferson, North Carolina: McFarland and Company, Inc., 2000, pp. 51–5.

22 Heard, Mervyn, 'The Magic Lantern's Wild Years', in Williams, *Cinema*, p. 25.

23 Mannoni, *Light and Shadow*, p. 109.

24 Lady Blessington was a lively presence in Regency London, a friend of Dickens and many other celebrities through the salon she presided over in her town house in St James's Square. She was the author of numerous novels, travel books and other forms of popular entertainment, now all forgotten.

25 Burch, Noël, *Life to those Shadows*, trans. Ben Brewster, London: British Film Institute, 1990, p. 91.

26 Johnson, Edgar, *Charles Dickens: his tragedy and triumph*, revised and abridged. Harmondsworth: Penguin Books Ltd., 1952, p. 19.

27 House, M., Storey, G. and Tillotson, K., *et al.* (eds.), *The British Academy Pilgrim Edition of The Letters of Charles Dickens*, Vols. 1–12, Oxford: Clarendon Press, 1965–2002; 31 December 1842, Vol. 3, p. 416.

28 Johnson, *Charles Dickens*, p. 390.

29 *Letters of Dickens*, 30 August 1846, Vol. 4, p. 612.

30 Altick, Richard, *The Shows of London*, Cambridge, Mass.: Belknap Press, 1978, p. 219.

31 Mannoni, *Light and Shadow*, p. 138.

32 Dickens, Charles, 'Some Recollections of Mortality', *The Uncommercial Traveller*, Ch. 18.

33 Virilio, *Vision Machine*, p. 144.

34 Virilio, *Vision Machine*, p. 144.

35 Altick, *Shows*, p. 149.

36 Hyde, Ralph, *Panoramania! The art of the 'all-embracing' view*, London: Trefoil Publications in association with Barbican Art Gallery, 1988, p. 29.

37 Wordsworth, William, *The Poetical Works of Wordsworth*, ed. Thomas Hutchinson, London: Oxford University Press, 1950, pp. 540–1, ll. 232–59.

38 Hyde, *Panoramania!*, p. 173.

39 de Balzac, Honoré, *Le père Goriot*, trans. Marion Ayton Crawford as *Old Goriot*, Harmondsworth: Penguin Books, 1959, pp. 74–5.

40 Hyde, *Panoramania!*, p. 38.

41 Hyde, *Panoramania!*, p. 178.

42 Virilio, *Vision Machine*, pp. 40–1.

43 Mannoni, *Light and Shadow*, p. 188.

44 Altick, *Shows*, p. 171.

45 Meisel, Martin, *Realizations: narrative, pictorial, and theatrical arts in nineteenth-century England*, Princeton NJ: Princeton University Press, 1983, p. 62.

46 *Letters of Dickens*, 30 May 1850, Vol. 6, p. 107, n. 5.

47 Guida, *Christmas Carol*, n. 4, p. 242.

48 Dickens, Charles, 'The American Panorama', *The Examiner*, 16 December 1848.

49 *Letters of Dickens*, 16 December 1848, Vol. 5, p. 458, n. 2 and 3.

50 *Letters of Dickens*, 22 February 1850, Vol. 6, p. 42 and n. 2.

51 Hyde, *Panoramania!*, p. 146.

52 'Some Recollections of Immortality', Ch. 19.

53 Kirby, Lynne, *Parallel Tracks: the railroad and the silent cinema*, Exeter: University of Exeter Press, 1997, p. 44.

54 New methods of putting the film image before its audience are fast developing and so the process I persist in seeing as magical may be doomed to extinction.

55 There are superficial similarities between Egan and Dickens. *Life in London* appeared in twenty monthly parts during 1820–1 and some of it was illustrated by George Cruikshank, the artist who worked on *Sketches by Boz* and *Oliver Twist*. Its lively, if coarse, picture of Regency life made it popular for a time, especially with young men, but its limitations are obvious, especially in comparison with the genius of Dickens's *Sketches by Boz*.

56 Nord, Deborah, *Walking the Victorian Streets: women, representation and the city*, Ithaca, NY: Cornell University Press, 1995, p. 33.

57 Nord, *Walking*, p. 35.

58 Nord, *Walking*, p. 60.

59 Jones, Alison (ed.), *Dictionary of Quotations*, Edinburgh: Chambers, 1996, 2, p. 1063.

1 A Dickensian moment from *Citizen Kane*

2 The dramatic power of chiaroscuro lighting in *The Magnificent Ambersons*

3 Charlie Chaplin on top of the world

4 Dickens on top of his world

5 Dickens at the time of his second visit to the United States

6 Deep-focus cinematography and the heightening of reality in *Citizen Kane*

7 Dickens bestrides the English Channel

8 An image of the nineteenth-century metropolis by Gustave Doré

9 The delights of the magic lantern

10 A travelling lanternist

11 The psychological power of the dissolve, from *The Magnificent Ambersons*

12 A major venue for the showing of panoramas

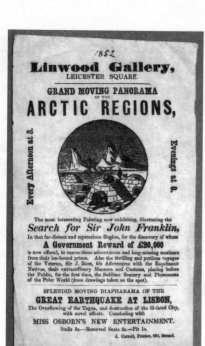

13 A panorama
programme

14 Dickens surrounded
by his characters

Explanations   3

It is only very thoughtless and presumptuous people who can erect
laws and an aesthetic for cinema, proceeding from premises of some
incredible virgin-birth of this art![1]

Many people have posed the question of the origins of cinema; Ian
Christie's formulation is as crisply expressed as any: 'What space
or need was there in the common culture of 1900 that proved so
ready to be filled by this strange new activity?'[2] If the common
culture is expanded to include history in the wider sense, including technology, and if Christie's date is pushed back to 1850, or
even earlier, the issue becomes yet more interesting. Film's
appearance then becomes one of the fascinating puzzles of human
development, an enigma that has been approached from many
different angles, as is amply demonstrated by Thomas Elsaesser:

> early cinema can be considered ... by Burch, Chanan, Musser... to be
> mimetic of certain social, instructional and entertainment forms
> predating the cinema – thus emphasising the historical specificity of
> the cinema experience as well as its continuity with other screen
> practices or spectacle attractions ... on the other hand ... following
> Salt, Brewster, Staiger and Thompson ... the emphasis would be more
> on questions of intelligibility, narrative efficacy and diegetic coherence
> – the cinema as the production of a distinct and unique economy of
> the visible.[3]

Elsaesser proposes a challenging programme involving the systematic study of the origins of cinema. However, proposing a relationship between Dickens and film is daunting enough, bringing
together fields of research that are divided by time as well as form.
Beginning with some of the widely canvassed positions in the
field, my argument will then consider the tendency towards grand

narratives, totalising explanations of the emergence of film whose limitations will clarify the direction I intend to follow.

The distinguished literary scholar, Leon Edel, encapsulates what might be called a classic position in tracing the relations between literature and film when he suggests that: 'Novelists have sought almost from the first to become a camera. And not a static instrument but one possessing the movement through space and time which the motion-picture camera has achieved in our century'.[4] Passing over the historical vagueness of 'almost from the first', the trope has to be seen as unhelpful in its literalism, although one understands precisely what Edel is getting at, and it is only fair to remember that he was writing at a time before film studies had developed into a sophisticated discipline. On the other hand, even if one accepts that narrative is a possibly unifying feature of both forms, that both make use of a 'language' specific to their nature, the passage raises far more questions than it answers: the dissolution of the boundaries between the act of writing and the movement of a physical object that Edel proposes is not easily sustainable. As we saw in the previous chapter, Orson Welles reverses the relationship between literature and cinema with characteristic incisiveness: 'A film is never really good unless the camera is an eye in the head of a poet'.[5] That *is* a metaphor, but one that works. Interestingly, despite all the technical paraphernalia required in the creation of film, Welles places his emphasis on the role of the artist; indeed, the creativity of the artist is internalised in relation to the apparatus, the camera, appropriate to the form chosen.

Another scholar, Alan Spiegel, clarifies what is hazardous about venturing into an examination of film and literature, that it demands knowledge and understanding of two very different fields of enquiry. Spiegel, for example, sees Dickens as slightly marginal in relation to his argument, believing that he 'emerges in the history of the development of concretised form not as a fully conscious exponent of this form but rather as a transitional figure between a pre- and post-Flaubertian manner of presentation ... A thoroughly concretised art does not make comments nor, we need hardly add, does the camera'.[6] Spiegel makes use of the old distinction between telling and showing here but, as far as contemporary scholarship is concerned, it now seems obvious that Dickens is one of the most rigorously dramatising of novelists, especially in his later work, while examination of his letters reveals that he is completely self-consciously aware of this aspect of his formal procedures. In any event, no nineteenth-century and few modern novelists are free from an element of narrative commentary, Flaubert included. Fiction is hardly possible without some degree of telling although, as we shall see in a moment, André Bazin argues that the novel can be every bit as 'objective' as film. Conversely, Spiegel's notion that cinema is incapable of 'making comments', that it is somehow disqualified from subjective intimations of an authorial voice, defies the practice of such major artists as Bergman and Antonioni.

This confusion between the supposed subjectivity of the novel and the objectivity of film is clarified by Bryer's enthusiasm for Dorothy Richardson's experimental novel *Pilgrimage*: 'Then there was the excitement of her style, it was the first time that I realised that modern prose could be as exciting as poetry and as for continuous association, it was stereoscopic, a precursor of the cinema, moving from the window to a face, from a thought back to the room, all in one moment just as it happened in life'.[7] Bryer clearly makes no distinction between the ability of the novel and film to deal with both the inner and outer life, a rejection of rigid demarcations between artistic forms that is echoed in the work of Bazin when, for example, he remarks that 'it is the novel that has discovered the way to raise to the level of an authentic metaphysical significance an almost mirror-like objectivity. What camera has ever been as externally related to its object as the consciousness of the hero of Albert Camus' *L'Etranger?*'[8] Bazin's fearless rejection of the separation of forms, one of the continuing themes of this book, is revealed in the brilliance with which he brings together film, the novel and theatre in his claim that '... the vast majority of images on the screen conform to the psychology of the theatre or to the novel of classical analysis. They proceed from the common sense supposition that a necessary and unambiguous causal relationship exists between feelings and their outward manifestations. They postulate that all is in the consciousness and that this consciousness can be known'.[9] Again, for H.D. (Hilda Doolittle), in the greatest films 'people moved, acted, suffered, we might also say for the first time, not parodies of people, at best ghosts, but spirits ... Thought ... is here for the first time adequately projected'. And there is a clear link between this observation and Eisenstein's 'account of "intellectual montage" as thought made visible'.[10] The aptness of these observations to Dickens is striking. It was once fairly widely held that Dickens's fundamental mode of operation lay in caricature, a near-obsessive preoccupation with surfaces to the exclusion of the inner life. Almost as widely held now, and certainly my position, is the view that Dickens's manipulation of objects, gestures, body language – the full panoply of the external – represents his mode of accessing the unconscious as well as the conscious springs of human behaviour, a method peculiarly appropriate to the urban world which is his central theme. This is how the point is made by Stefan Zweig:

As he himself once said, it is the little things that give meaning to life. He is, therefore, perpetually on the watch for tokens, be they never so slight; a spot of grease on a dress, an awkward gesture caused by shyness, a strand of reddish hair peeping from beneath a wig if its wearer happens to lose his temper. He captures all the nuances of a handshake, knows what the pressure of each finger signifies; detects the shades of meaning in a simile.[11]

This sense of detail as a route into consciousness, combined with Bazin's concept of the unitary nature of art forms, removes the necessity for mechanistic relationships between Dickens and the camera in attempts to analyse the proto-filmic aspects of his work.

Returning to Spiegel, it is clear that his marginalisation of Dickens is rooted in another misunderstanding, this time of the nature of cinema. Because he ignores the aesthetic of long takes and deep focus (significantly, Welles is absent from his index), Spiegel believes that cinema, by its very nature, breaks up spatial unity through montage and so Dickens, for him, is stagy rather than cinematic in using 'theatrical framing and co-ordination of space',[12] a supposed limitation which is, in fact, an apt description of, say, the ballroom scene in *The Magnificent Ambersons*, and many other notable moments in Welles's work. The reverse of Spiegel's position is surely more convincing. The work of creative film-makers such as Fellini and Truffaut renders the subjective/objective distinction between film and the novel meaningless. Similarly, it is impossible to set up montage as a single form of cinematic practice representing the true nature of the form, given that deep focus and long takes represent an equally viable mode of filmic creativity.

There is clearly an overlap between my argument and the work of Edel, Spiegel and others who seek to explore connections between film and literature; on the other hand, recognition of error, where it seems to present itself, is inseparable from any attempt at intellectual enquiry. This is especially the case in the area of monumental explanations of film's emergence, whose totalising narratives offer a single explanatory key. One such account is provided by Anne Hollander's *Moving Pictures*,[13] a book full of interesting observations on, for example, the dominance of black and white images in Western art, and the influence of photography on art history. Hollander argues that because of the dominance of engraving, and other forms of illustration, 'the language of monochrome vision has been the great *lingua franca* of Western art'.[14] The case of photography is even more fascinating as gradually 'the great and not-so-great art of the past ... came to be generally available through *photographic* reproduction. Therefore it, too, entered the general pictorial theatre of popular life'. But this leads to a more problematic conclusion, that the 'history of art eventually "got into the movies" because the reproductive still camera encompassed it first, forcing art to share in the documentary spirit of the new photographic romanticism'.[15] It would be facile to dismiss the importance of fine art as a contributory factor in the emergence of cinema; we have already seen that the large canvases of the Victorian John Martin, such as his *Belshazzar's Feast*, have become a favourite example of the unconscious urging towards film in painting.[16] But Hollander is at once too personal and too general in her claims; for example, in suggesting that:

The art of the past has influenced the movies ... through the undying resonance in their eyes and hearts of the visual imagery of the past. It has come through the following up of old memories and visual habits privately absorbed by the director, designer, or cameraman from prints, photographs, and illustrations, from reproductions and approximations of past art, as well as from actual paintings and earlier movies. Much of this process is unconscious; and so it guarantees the same emotional responses in eventual viewers, unhampered by any conscious recognition of consciously applied effects.[17]

The question of evidence presents itself here in a peculiarly acute form. How, one wonders, could it possibly be demonstrated that this is the case for the generality of film-makers, to say nothing of audiences? Studies have demonstrated that cinematographers have turned to great works and artists of the past in their study of light – Jack Cardiff, for example, has acknowledged the influence of Vermeer – and it is known that John Ford had a particular interest in the painter of the American West, Frederic Remington, but the scope of Hollander's generalisation seems to disqualify verification virtually in principle. In her eagerness to pursue her own thesis, the obvious role of theatre has to be downgraded: 'The power of film comes from being made of endless pictures ... rather than anything like what the theatre does'.[18] But the argument collapses at the point where she claims that a 'future cinema seemed to lurk in these old works'[19] – those of Vermeer and Hals for example – because, as with Spiegel, her conception of the nature of cinema is deeply flawed. Central to her position is the distinction she makes between the Northern and Renaissance strands of European art: the Northern tradition 'led to modern cinema' while the Classical 'led to modern painting'.[20] This divide equates to an art that conceals itself, the Northern tradition *and* film, versus the Renaissance art of display. It goes almost without saying that this is an unbalanced view of cinema, that the opposition between cinematic self-effacement and formal display is as old as the distinction between Lumière and Méliès. This is repeated throughout the history of film, in the invisibility of technique characteristic of classical Hollywood, for example, versus the work of directors such as Welles and Nicholas Roeg who highlight the techniques by which films are constructed in the very process of making them.

If the totalising grand narrative is a cause of unease in such a complicated field, what of Dickens and the dream of cinema? Is this, too, not a single big story? Obviously I hope not, for in suggesting that Dickens does play a role of some kind in the emergence of cinema, the idea of causality is clearly not to be entertained. No one person 'invented' cinema, much less a writer who died in 1870. If Dickens is to be inserted convincingly into the complex of forces at play in cinema's genesis, the problem of methodology presents itself in an acute form. Once again, Benjamin comes to the rescue, firstly in Graeme Gilloch's commentary on his approach: 'There is elaboration rather than development. The cityscapes involve a circling, a continual return to the same loci, the same figures, the same objects, but each time from a different direction, from a shifted vantage-point. In Benjamin's text-as-city, just as in the labyrinth of the modern metropolis, there is continual movement'.[21] Gilloch's point applies as much to this book as it does to Benjamin, in that my argument involves 'elaboration rather than development' in attempting to illuminate its central claim by coming at it from a number of different angles rather than pursuing what Keats refers to in a letter as 'consecutive reasoning'. Similarly, there is 'continual movement' in Dickens's text-as-film as it mimics so effectively 'the labyrinth of the modern metropolis'. The point can be approached in a different but related way through the words of the editors of the new edition of the *Arcades Project*, for whom the work is 'the blueprint for an unimaginably massive and labyrinthine architecture – a dream city, in effect ... a compositional principle at work in the project ... the montage form – with its philosophic play of distances, transitions, and intersections, its perpetually shifting contexts and ironic juxtapositions'.[22] This vision provides a cue for my reading of Dickens in relation to film, that his work is the blueprint of a dream cinema in which montage in all its meanings plays a crucial role.

And so we can see yet another way in which the relationship between Dickens and film is contingent rather than necessary, the evidence for it involving not the linear causality which 'proves' the connection, but rather an examination of the question from a range of possible angles. In short, the undertaking is a complex one but not 'unimaginably massive and labyrinthine'!

Another Benjaminian concept, that of porousness, might be brought into play at this point. Benjamin sees Naples as an example of 'porosity'; that is, as a site marked by its lack of barriers between different activities – for example, the presence of the sacred within the profane, a co-existence of simultaneity rather than overlap in which the two are inextricably bound up with one another in a manner that is ultimately inseparable.[23] In this sense, Dickens might be said to be porous in relation to the innumerable presences in his contemporary world that tend towards the emergence of cinema: panoramas and dioramas, photography, serial fiction, stage spectacle and melodrama. Dickens is completely open towards this range of forces in a way that is democratic and not élitist, so they flow into his work with an ease that in no way conflicts with his manipulation of such material for his own artistic purposes. Any significant piece of Dickens's writing – a passage from a major novel, or the best of the essays that make up *The Uncommercial Traveller* collection – can therefore be seen as examples of Benjamin's monad; that is, fragments which contain traces of the past and present, and which may also contribute to the dream of a cinematic future. This suggests a Dickensian version of what Elsaesser sees as Noël Burch's claim: 'that in order to understand films historically, pre-cinematic and non-cinematic forms of spectacle, storytelling and imaging have to be taken into account: from still photography and picture postcards ... to the influence of the legitimate stage and newspaper cartoons'.[24] Dickens's work is suffused with such material at the level of style and form, in image and metaphor, in symbol, in the complexities of its fictional structure; in short, his work draws on what Peter Ackroyd calls 'the culture of London' – as well as many other sources – amongst whose many attractions 'none [was] more colourful or pervasive than that of the popular print'. Ackroyd continues: 'The city which Dickens ... inherited [was] ... surrounded by music, diverted by illustrations, entertained by songs, haunted by cheap fiction, the whole panoply of London entertainment rolling over him'.[25] This entered his work at every level and made it ready for transmission into whatever imaginative forms his creative spirit chose.

However, if Dickens's work is cinematic, the question still

remains as to how it enters the stream of forces out of which, in its turn, cinema itself will emerge. Benjamin's concept of the dream is again central at this point for, if Dickens dreams cinema, he himself is part of the dream-world of Western culture itself, suffusing it at the level of unconscious assimilation as well as more conventional forms of cultural influence. The sometimes contradictory uses of 'Dickensian' as an adjective in a wide range of discourses – political, social and journalistic – is evidence of the extent to which he infiltrates the culture of the English-speaking world, as is the widespread recognition of what characters such as Scrooge and Fagin stand for, whether or not those who invoke them have actually read the works in which they appear. In addition, Dickens's influence on figures such as Dostoevsky and Kafka is well known, and acknowledged by the writers themselves. Leaving aside the world of high culture, however, the apparently effortless transition of *Oliver Twist* into Lionel Bart's musical, *Oliver!*, suggests the extent to which Dickens occupies a privileged position in the world of popular entertainment, an influence that shows no evidence of decreasing in the twenty-first century. It is hardly going too far, for example, to claim that *A Christmas Carol* reveals Dickens's iconic status in Western and, even, world culture. The ritual of the Christmas transmission of *A Christmas Carol* on television reinforces what one writer refers to as Dickens's 'almost folkloric appeal for Americans',[26] a judgement endorsed by a newspaper at the time of his first visit to the United States which claimed that he 'was read with pleasure over the whole immense extent of the States, from the British dominions on the north, to the glades of Florida, and from the Atlantic cities to the cantonments and barracks on the Mississippi'; indeed, he was read by 'the hunter of buffalo in the wilds ... with a degree of intimacy that only a friend inspires'.[27]

This sense of Dickens as a great popular writer whose presence can be felt at all cultural levels on what is practically the world stage is, I believe, widely accepted. The production of evidence to back up such a large claim, however, is no easy matter. Nonetheless, although the role in the emergence of cinema which I wish to assign to Dickens involves many threads of argument, they have to be grounded in this pervasive presence in his own time and beyond. Without this, the claim could hardly survive sustained attention. What follows is offered as an experiment – restricted to his impact on the world of middle-class and high culture, and within the literary realm – in trying to trace the widespread nature of this assimilation. As at other points in the book, the experiment will involve extended quotation, but the enterprise demands it and at least the reader will have the pleasure of contact with, in this case, Henry James through the medium of his inimitable prose. From a wealth of references we can begin with the detail of James reminiscing about visits to the family dentist, who 'extremely resembles, to my mind's eye, certain figures in Phiz's illustrations to Dickens'. One compensation for these dreaded occasions was provided by 'Godey's Lady's Book, a sallow pile of which ... lay on Joey Bagstock's table for our beguilement while we waited: I was to encounter in ... Dombey and Son that design for our tormentor's type'.[28] This ease of allusion to Dickens's works is reinforced by the passing reference to eating cake in his London tutor's lodgings, the treat 'ushered in by a little girl who might have been a Dickens foundling or "orfling"'.[29]

Seeing the world through Dickens's eyes is more than simply a question of how people such as James are enveloped in a Dickensian typology. London itself is steeped in this inescapable presence, from the first of his several visits until his eventual decision to remain there permanently. For the young boy, 'the London of the 'fifties was even to the weak perception of childhood ... extraordinarily the picture and the scene of Dickens'.[30] Much later, in 1869, James writes:

I didn't go ... to Craven Street for rooms, but I did go ... for atmosphere ... The precious effect in the case of Craven Street was that it absolutely reeked, to my fond fancy, with associations born of the particular ancient piety embodied in one's private altar to Dickens ... it was just that the whole Dickens procession marched up and down, the whole Dickens world looked out of its queer, quite sinister windows – for it was the socially sinister Dickens ... rather than the socially encouraging or confoundingly comic who still at that moment was most apt to meet me with his reasons. Such a reason was just that look of the inscrutable riverward street, packed to bleakness with accumulations of suffered experience.[31]

Such passages offer a justification for the dream methodology of this study. Inner and outer worlds coalesce in a vision of individuals and of the city helplessly enmeshed in the parameters created, accepted and almost universally disseminated by the power of Dickens's writing as the vehicle of *his* vision. James's rendering of his response to external reality as 'the whole Dickens world' is his own perception, but it inhabits the same range of responses as popular films of, say, the 1940s, which invariably see London as shrouded in a 'Dickensian' fog at moments of sinister intent.

James's complex relationship with Dickens might be crystallised in two moments pregnant with significance, his childhood experience of a family reading and his meeting, however brief, with Dickens in 1867. The first touchingly encapsulates what we can assume was a not uncommon experience in the bourgeois world to which Dickens contributed so richly. However well known to some, the story requires repetition:

The whole question dwells for me in a single small reminiscence ... that of my having been sent to bed one evening ... as a very small boy, at an hour when, in the library and under the lamp, one of the elder cousins from Albany, the youngest of an orphaned brood of four, of my grandmother's most extravagant adoption, had begun to read aloud to my mother the new, which must have been the first, instalment of David Copperfield. I had feigned to withdraw, but had only retreated to cover close at hand, the friendly shade of some screen or drooping table-cloth, folded up behind which and glued to the carpet, I held my breath and listened. I listened long and drank deep while the wondrous picture grew, but the tense cord at last snapped under the strain of the Murdstones and I broke into the sobs of sympathy that disclosed my subterfuge. I was this time effectively banished, but the ply then taken was ineffaceable. I remember indeed just afterwards finding the sequel ... beyond my actual capacity; which took a few years to grow adequate – years in which the general contagious consciousness, and our own household responses not least, breathed heavily through Hard Times, Bleak House and Little Dorrit.[32]

The touching little story is suffused with a charm that echoes uncannily the exquisite comic delicacy of the opening chapters of *David Copperfield* itself, but James also generalises the importance of the serial experience of fiction that we know was duplicated in households less rarefied than the James establishment:

With which mild memories thus stands out for me too the lively importance ... of the arrival, from the first number, of the orange-covered earlier Cornhill [a famous Victorian periodical] ... Is anything like that thrill possible today ... these appearances, these strong time-marks in such stretches of production as that of Dickens ... had in the first place simply a genial weight and force, a direct importance, and in the second a command of the permeable air and the collective sensibility, with which nothing since has begun to deserve comparison. They were enrichments of life, they were *large* arrivals, these particular renewals of supply ... These various, let alone numerous, deeper-toned strokes of the great Victorian clock were so many steps in the march of our age, besides being so many notes, full and far-reverberating, of our having high company to keep.[33]

James goes on to remember that his parents spoke similarly of 'the contemporary presence of Scott ... and could take the general civilised participation in the process for a sort of basking in the light of distinction'.[34]

This is more than simply the story of one man's (and a great writer's at that) involvement with Dickens. James is speaking for a generation and a culture here. In doing so, he throws invaluable light on the social as well as the personal experience of reading serial fiction, particularly Dickens's, as being inextricably bound up with daily processes of ordinary living – 'the march of our age' – while at the same time offering a shared entertainment which had its own measure of challenge as well as relaxation: 'our having high company to keep'. And however personal it was to James himself, a similar degree of social significance can be seen in his imperishable evocation of his extremely brief encounter with the great man himself, a moment that still vibrates with tension and excitement after more than 130 years, conveyed as it is in the expressive contortions of James's writing:

So that on the evening I speak of at Shady Hill it was as a slim and shaken vessel of the feeling that one stood there – of the feeling in the first place diffused, public and universal, and in the second place all unfathomably, undemonstrably, unassistedly and, as it were, unrewardedly, proper to one's self as an already groping and fumbling, already dreaming and yearning dabbler in the mystery, the creative, that of comedy, tragedy, evocation, representation, erect and concrete before us there as in a sublimity of mastership. I saw the master – nothing could be more evident – in the light of an intense emotion, and I trembled, I remember, in every limb, while at the same time, by a blest fortune, emotion produced no luminous blur, but left him shining indeed, only shining with august particulars ... the offered inscrutable mask was the great thing, the extremely handsome face, the face of symmetry yet of formidable character, as I at once recognised, and which met my dumb homage with a straight inscrutability, a merciless *military* eye, I might have pronounced it, an automatic hardness, in fine, which at once indicated to me ... a kind of economy of apprehension.[35]

The element of stylistic excess in this passage is surely a measure of the importance of the occasion for James both as passionate reader of Dickens and as budding writer, an importance well summed up by Fred Kaplan: 'Dickens represented the European literary artist in his fullest embodiment, the writer successfully acknowledged as the representative of both art and life, as a presence, a personage, a figure of the fullest measure, the artist both practising his art and standing prominently in the forefront of the social relationships that were an important part of what defined the culture in which he lived'.[36] The final word on the range and depth of this influence can, however, be entrusted to James himself: 'How tremendously it had been laid upon young persons of our generation to feel Dickens, down to the soles of our shoes, no more modern instance that I might try to muster would give, I think, the least measure of'.[37]

In an amusing passage in *David Copperfield*, David refers to being saturated in Dora as a way of trying to express the degree of his love for her; I have used Henry James as a test case to demonstrate the extent to which Dickens saturated the inner lives of individuals and of their culture in his own time and, by implication, later. How to proceed further in this process is, again, a question of methodology. Evidence can be brought to bear from a myriad of sources, in popular as well as high culture, to demonstrate that Dickens, almost to the same extent as Shakespeare, occupies an iconic position in Western experience and beyond.[38] The almost continuous adaptation of his work at the beginning of the twenty-first century suggests that there is no diminution in the width or depth of his influence. To justify this in evidential terms runs the risk of swamping the reader in detail which is exhausting as well as exhaustive, but the topic is important enough to justify a few more examples. A series of letters written during Dickens's second visit to America in 1867 and 1868 testifies to the range and depth of his popularity, even allowing for some authorial exaggeration. He says of the New York stage, for example, that 'comic operas, melodramas, and domestic dramas prevail all over the city, and my stories play no inconsiderable part in them', that they 'are doing Crickets, Oliver Twists, and all sorts of versions of me' and that nothing 'is being played here scarcely that is not founded on my books ... I can't get down Broadway for my own portrait'.[39] This last point could take us into yet another area of Dickens's fame and influence, the extent to which he was photographed in the later stages of his life and how, with earlier forms of illustration, this contributed to his instant recognisability; there are a number of instances of him being stopped in the street by passing strangers who offered thanks for the effect his work had had on their lives.

It is clear that this range and depth of influence had a major impact on the development of cinema at the level of adaptation. As Usai points out, by 1909 'films from his works were common enough for *The Motion Picture Herald* to describe an early programming idea initiated by "several enterprising exhibitors in the East"': 'Once every two or three months they set aside one week for pictures based upon the works of well-known writers. For instance, they advertise "A Week with Dickens" and get their exchanges to reserve all the pictures they can secure in that line'.[40] Another aspect of his role in cinema can be illustrated in the almost uncanny relationship to Dickens of two pioneers of

British cinema, Thomas Bentley and Cecil Hepworth, whose careers overlap in their work on him. Bentley (c.1880–1950), a somewhat shadowy figure, originally trained as an engineer but later worked in music hall and on the stage as an impersonator of Dickens characters, a tradition that began in Dickens's lifetime and has continued into the present in the work of Miriam Margolyes and Simon Callow. Bentley entered the film world in 1910, became a director and specialised in adaptations of Dickens, including a short film entitled *Leaves from the Book of Charles Dickens* (1912) in which he 'portrayed a number of Dickensian characters';[41] silent versions of *Oliver Twist* (1912) and *The Adventures of Mr Pickwick* (1921); and, in 1934, a sound version of *The Old Curiosity Shop*. Cecil Hepworth (1874–1953) is better known, partly because of his memoirs, *Came the Dawn*, and the fact that his *Rescued by Rover* (1905) is one of the classics of early British cinema. As he explains, Hepworth also had his creative roots in the world of popular entertainments spawned by Dickens, in his case the magic lantern:

My father was a popular lecturer when I was a youngster and one of my greatest joys was to go with him and work his 'Dissolving Views' for him. His most successful lecture was The Footprints of Charles Dickens in which I gloried, and heard over and over again ... So when Thomas Bentley presented himself to me as a 'great Dickens character impersonator and scholar' my heart naturally warmed to him and I was readily receptive when he offered to make a Dickens film for me. In the end he made several, but I think *Oliver Twist* was the first ... and it marked the beginning ... of a Dickens series.[42]

Hepworth and Bentley went on to make an adaptation of *David Copperfield* in 1913. This was something of landmark as it was the first British eight-reel feature film, according to Michael Pointer,[43] and so in the region of 70 minutes long. The opening credits include the statement 'Arranged by Thomas Bentley (The Dickensian Character Actor) In the actual scenes immortalised by Charles Dickens'. We know from Hepworth that Bentley's topographical realism was sometimes taken to absurd lengths: 'I remember the joyful glee with which he recounted how he had managed to secure *in the picture* the fascia board ... saying that it was "the house immortalised by Dickens as the house of Miss Betsey Trotwood". I do not think he ever understood why I received this news with so little enthusiasm'.[44] Despite such naive literalism, the film is not without its successes. The Peggotty boathouse is an effective creation and contains a lively evocation of its family life, with Mrs Gummidge in the background, followed by a neat little 'love scene' on the beach between David and Em'ly. It is worth noting that the 'Barkis is willin'' episode, en route to Yarmouth is not filled out with any explanatory titles, presumably on the assumption that it will be familiar to audiences. However, after the detail of a coach arriving at an inn, filled with the bustle of activity, changing of horse cloths, and so on, followed by a vigorous classroom *mêlée* at Dr Strong's school, the film settles for a largely linear exposition of the novel's plot. The darker side of the book is elided as, by way of a title, David becomes part of the Micawber world, after only a glimpse of life in the blacking factory. Details such as Mr Micawber's punch-making are carried off with a flourish and an apt sense of ceremonial on his part. David's painful journey to his Aunt Betsey is the occasion for scenic shots of the Kent countryside and the White Cliffs of Dover, something of a travelogue in fact, but a real opportunity for spectacular effects is missed in the feeble evocation of the storm which leads to the deaths of Steerforth and Ham. Indeed, one wonders if such a moment would not often have been better achieved on the stage than it is here, given the wonders of Victorian theatrical machinery. The film as a whole, then, does possess some apt attention to detail, especially in real-life settings, but it has little sense of character, apart from Micawber. Even allowing for the amplitude provided by its length, it turns eventually into hardly more than a dutiful plod, one thing following another with no indication of the novel's thematic complexity.

This small excursion into the early years of British cinema, illuminating Dickens's place in the proto-cinematic dreamscape of the nineteenth century and beyond, is reinforced by a description of Chaplin, at an early stage in his career, by one of the Eight Lancashire Lads, a clog dancing group: 'He was a great mimic [as was Dickens, one might note] but his heart was set on tragedy. For weeks he would imitate Bransby Williams in 'The Old Curiosity Shop' wearing an old grey wig and tottering with a stick, until we others were sick of him'.[45] The realism of Bentley and Hepworth, as well as Chaplin, has its place in my cinematic dreamscape, although the kind of dreaming I am more interested in is suggested by a fascinating little passage from Eisenstein's memoirs: 'When I look at myself in complete privacy, the image that most readily springs to mind is that of ... David Copperfield'.[46] This level of inwardness is akin to that shown by Truffaut in *Fahrenheit 451* (1966) where the fireman hero, whose task is to burn books, discovers reading through his stumbling attempts to articulate the opening lines of *David Copperfield*. Why Eisenstein and Truffaut turn to Dickens and to this novel in particular, Dickens's own favourite, becomes clear from its opening chapter, one of the most profound initiations into consciousness in literature, as its mysterious first sentence may remind us: 'Whether I shall turn out to be the hero of my own life, or whether that station will be held by anybody else, these pages must show'. If Eisenstein and Truffaut can be seen, at these moments, to be dreaming film through Dickens, perhaps the form itself can be seen as having been dreamt by 'Dickens' – by which I mean the totality of his texts read through the spectacles, clarifying not distorting, of cinema.

Two premises lie at the heart of this book: the assertion that Dickens's work is proto-cinematic and the claim that he is sufficiently important to the private and public life of nineteenth-century culture, widely defined, for his dreamlike anticipation of the form to be a significant factor in the emergence of film. If the focus is placed on the second of these points, the conclusion to this chapter will hardly come as a surprise. The large-scale 'explanation' of the role of Dickens in the emergence of cinema proposed in the preceding pages is, of course, the subject matter of the remainder of this book. As with Benjamin's project, my Dickens dreamscape 'involves a circling, a continual return to the same loci, the same figures, the same objects, but each time from a different direction, from a shifted vantage-point'. Through the use of a variation of 'montage form' the chapters of this book accumulate in such a way as to make the basic premise of the study clear. In doing so, they adhere to Graeme Gilloch's description of the relationship between Benjamin's Arcades Project and the city. Gilloch's 'central argument is that the experience of the metropolis itself is self-consciously embedded in the formal properties of the text'. The project itself is thus 'city-like'; that is, not 'text-about-city' but 'text-as-city'.[47] By the same token, Dickens is for me cinema-like, text-as-film, if one takes a sufficiently inclusive view of the nature of cinema.

Notes

1 Eisenstein, Sergei, *Film Form: essays in film theory*, ed. and trans. Jay Leyda, London: Dennis Dobson Ltd, 1977, p. 232.
2 Christie, Ian, *The Last Machine: early cinema and the birth of the modern world*, London: BBC Educational Developments, 1994, p. 8.
3 Elsaesser, Thomas (ed.) with Barker, Adam, *Early Cinema: space, frame, narrative*, London: British Film Institute, 1990, p. 409.
4 Edel, Leon, 'Novel and Camera', in Halperin, John (ed.), *The Theory of the Novel: new essays*, New York: Oxford University Press, 1974, p. 177.
5 Jones, Alison (ed.), *Dictionary of Quotations*, Edinburgh: Chambers, 1996, 4, p. 1063.
6 Spiegel, Alan, *Fiction and the Camera Eye: visual consciousness in film*

and literature, Charlottesville: University of Virginia Press, 1976, p. 36.

7 Donald, J., Friedberg, A. and Marcus, L. (eds.), Close Up 1927–1933: cinema and modernism, London: Cassell, 1998, pp. 152–3.

8 Bazin, André, What is Cinema? Essays selected and translated by Hugh Gray, Vol. 1, Berkeley, Los Angeles: University of California Press, 1967, p. 64.

9 Bazin, What is Cinema?, p. 62.

10 Donald, Close Up, pp. 99 and 102.

11 Eisenstein, Film Form, pp. 209–10.

12 Spiegel, Camera Eye, p. 39.

13 Hollander, Anne, Moving Pictures, New York: Alfred A. Knopf., 1989.

14 Hollander, Moving Pictures, p. 33.

15 Hollander, Moving Pictures, p. 440.

16 Meisel, Martin, Realizations: narrative, pictorial, and theatrical arts in nineteenth-century England, Princeton, NJ: Princeton University Press, 1983, p. 22.

17 Hollander, Moving Pictures, p. 5.

18 Hollander, Moving Pictures, p. 4.

19 Hollander, Moving Pictures, p. 31.

20 Hollander, Moving Pictures, p. 14.

21 Gilloch, Graeme, Myth and Metropolis: Walter Benjamin and the city, Cambridge: Polity Press, 1997, p. 20.

22 Benjamin, Walter, The Arcades Project, trans. Howard Eiland and Kevin McLaughlin, Cambridge, Mass.: Belknap Press, 1999, p. ix.

23 Gilloch, Benjamin and the city, p. 34.

24 Elsaesser, Early Cinema, p. 407.

25 Ackroyd, Peter, Dickens, London: Guild Publishing, 1990, pp. 91–2.

26 DeBona, Guerric, 'Dickens, the Depression and MGM's David Copperfield', in Naremore, James (ed.), Film Adaptation, London: Athlone Press, 2000, p. 108.

27 DeBona, 'Dickens', p. 106.

28 James, Henry, Autobiography, ed. Frederick W. Dupee, London: W. H. Allen, 1956, p. 39.

29 James, Autobiography, p. 172.

30 James, Autobiography, pp. 171–2.

31 James, Autobiography, p. 572.

32 James, Autobiography, pp. 68–9.

33 James, Autobiography, pp. 251–2.

34 James, Autobiography, p. 252.

35 James, Autobiography, p. 389.

36 Kaplan, Fred, Henry James: the imagination of genius, London: Hodder & Stoughton, 1992, p. 80.

37 James, Autobiography, p. 388.

38 For Dickens's role as a 'media personality' in his own day see Smith, Grahame, 'Dickens's Public: adulation and constraint', Ch. 6, in Charles Dickens: a literary life, Basingstoke: Macmillan Press Ltd, 1996.

39 House, M., Storey, G. and Tillotson, K., et al. (eds.), The British Academy Pilgrim Edition of The Letters of Charles Dickens, Vols. 1–12, Oxford: Clarendon Press, 1965–2002; 15 December 1867, 24 December 1867, 30 December 1867, Vol. 11, pp. 512, 521, 527.

40 Usai, Paolo Cherchi, The Griffith Project, Vol. 2: Films Produced in January–June 1909, London: British Film Institute, 1999, p. 120.

41 Guida, Fred, A Christmas Carol and Its Adaptations: a critical examination of Dickens's story and its productions on screen and television, Jefferson, North Carolina: McFarland and Company, Inc., 2000, p. 73.

42 Pointer, Michael, *Charles Dickens on the Screen: the film, television, and video adaptations*, Lanham, MD: The Scarecrow Press, Inc., 1996, p 31.
43 Pointer, *Dickens on the Screen*, p. 31.
44 Pointer, *Dickens on the Screen*, p. 31.
45 Robinson, David, *Chaplin: his life and art*, New York: McGraw-Hill, 1989, p. 30.
46 Eisenstein, Sergei, *The Memoirs of Sergei Eisenstein*, ed. Richard Taylor and trans. William Powell, London: British Film Institute, 1996, p. 18.
47 Gilloch, *Benjamin and the city*, p. 94.

4   London as labyrinth – Paris as panorama

It was the best of times, it was the worst of times ... it was the season of Light, it was the season of Darkness.[1]

The response of Dickens's contemporaries to the visual qualities of his work, suggested by Philip Collins,[2] is developed in comprehensive detail by David Paroissien:

As early as 1839, Richard Ford was writing in the *Quarterly Review* that 'Boz sketches localities, particularly in London, with marvellous effect; he concentrates with the power of the camera lucida'; by the middle of the century, the metaphor had become an essential part of the critics' vocabulary. Hence George Eliot's praise of Dickens's facility of copying 'with the deliberate accuracy of a sun-picture'; R H Hutton's definition, in part, of Dickens's genius as 'a power of observation so enormous that he could photograph almost everything he saw'; and H F Chorley's comment that 'Dickens possess[ed] the immediate power of daguerrotype'.[3]

This is fascinating on a number of counts. It demonstrates how completely at ease his readers felt with the visual technologies of their own day, even though some of them were still only in the course of being developed. In purely literary terms, we know that critics were prepared to discuss Dickens in relation to such writers as Shakespeare, Cervantes, Fielding and Scott, but one is bound to be impressed by the fact that they often seek to account for his special qualities in relation to devices which were, many of them, only recent outcomes of nineteenth-century technology. Such readers may have sensed something new in Dickens's work that could only be accounted for satisfactorily by consideration of the new world of representation.

This chapter explores the aesthetic bearings of these responses by developing further the overlapping and interconnected interests sketched in Chapter 1: the city and its streets; the role of light in the urban environment; visualisation as a key element in Dickens's imaginative life; and movement in the urban scene. My general aim is to suggest links between these phenomena and Dickens's artistic vision as well as his creative practice. The ultimate object is to take my reading of the genesis of cinema in relation to Dickens a stage further. The connections between urban experience and Dickens's creative processes are, of course, well known, but they have been given a brilliant inflection by Michael Hollington in his article, 'Dickens the Flâneur'.[4] Hollington's major purpose is to place Dickens in the context of *flânerie* as a way of illuminating the form of his novels. By developing these ideas he is, it goes without saying, drawing on the tradition of the heightened observation of the urban stroller initiated crucially by Baudelaire and developed so perceptively by Walter Benjamin.

As a starting point, we could begin with passages from Baudelaire's *The Painter of Modern Life* which relate to Dickens's narrative technique, the spark of creative energy leaping across the apparent differences between the two. Baudelaire is speculating on the entry into the crowd of the presence that he rather grandiosely calls the 'lover of universal life', a process which causes Baudelaire to liken this lover 'to a mirror as vast as the crowd itself; or to a kaleidoscope gifted with consciousness'. He is, Baudelaire suggests, 'an "I" with an insatiable appetite for the "non-I," at every instant rendering and explaining it in pictures more living than life itself, which is always unstable and fugitive'.[5] The links to Dickens at this point are obvious. His writing has seemed to many critics to have precisely this dreamlike quality, a heightening and exaggeration of reality which has the effect of making the books appear to be more real than reality itself. In other words, the vividness and detail of Dickens's writing can create a response akin to that of leaving the cinema only to find the outside world flat and colourless. This quality is quite compatible with the notion of his novels as giant mirrors capturing the panoramic variety and intensity of urban life in a process of reflection cum creation, providing that we accept its essentially distorting nature and function. Dickens's appetite for life, people, incident, every facet of urban experience is quite clearly insatiable, but rooted also in another aspect of the *flâneur*, the Keatsian negative capability that enables him to observe and record with a kind of loving objectivity. A striking example of Dickens's ability to lose himself in the life of people and objects is provided by his response to Lady De Lancey's account of her husband's death at the Battle of Waterloo: 'I am husband, wife, dead man and living woman, Emma and General Dundas, doctor and bedstead, – everything and everybody ... all in one'.[6]

How can we explain this similarity of attitude and response between Dickens and Baudelaire? It is not, clearly, a matter of influence. Rather, it seems to relate to some pervasive movements in consciousness that are coming into being as a direct result of urban experience. As Hollington suggests, Dickens too is a *flâneur* because the whole bias of his consciousness makes him excitedly responsive to the metropolis at the very moment when it is coming into existence. We have seen in Chapter 2 how important streets were to Dickens in the writing of *Dombey and Son*, but he clearly experienced this need almost from the very beginning of his career. As early as 1841 we find him wandering the streets of London after working on *Barnaby Rudge* 'searching for some pictures I wanted to build upon'.[7]

It is, of course, possible to follow this preoccupation with the urban experience of London throughout Dickens's entire career. At one level, it might be seen as a facet of what his biographer and friend, John Forster, calls his 'profound attraction of repulsion',[8] if only in relation to the diversity and richness of subject matter provided by the appearance of new forms of living in the urban environment. That this subject matter came to him in a special kind of way is suggested by an insight of Charles Lamb's from his essay 'A Complaint of the Decay of Beggars in the Metropolis': 'Among her shows, her museums, and supplies for ever-gaping curiosity (and what else but an accumulation of sights – endless sights – is a great city; for what else is it desirable?)'.[9] This focusing of the urban experience on the visual, on what Baudelaire calls the 'vast picture gallery which is London or Paris',[10] is suggestive in a number of ways, especially in returning us again to the central insight of the urban sociologist, Georg Simmel, for whom 'interpersonal relationships in big cities are distinguished by a marked preponderance of the activity of the eye over the activity of the ear'.[11] Simmel's claim is a large one although evidence for it might be found, for example, in the increasing importance of the static rendering of facets of city life through the intervention of photography.

From another angle altogether, there is a similarity with the theatrical tableaux that were such a feature of nineteenth-century theatre, those moments when the characters would freeze into stasis under the pressure of high emotion or at the play's end. Once again, Benjamin brings together a number of differing, but related, phenomena in commenting on the German Romantic writer E. T. A. Hoffmann's desire to 'initiate his visitor into the "the principles of the art of seeing". This consists of an ability to enjoy *tableaux vivants*'.[12] In other words, the enjoyment of tableaux *vivants* is akin to registering the spectacle of city life as a series of moments which express some aspect of urban experience with representative force.

Dickens's preoccupation with a special kind of visualisation occurs in numerous ways, light-hearted as well as serious. For example, he closes a letter to his actor friend Macready in 1841 with an appropriately theatrical finale: 'Drink my health in my absence – wish well to Barnaby ... and ... do not – curse me. With that cue for slow music and closing in with a picture, [tableau at fall of curtain] I ring down the envelope'.[13] The visual is present much later in Dickens's career in a quite different way, in the very special range of sights that are embodied for us in the essays collected as *The Uncommercial Traveller* (in, say, 'On An Amateur Beat'):

Walking faster ... I overturned a wretched little creature, who, clutching at the rags of a pair of trousers with one of its claws, and at its ragged hair with the other, pattered with bare feet over the muddy stones. I stopped to raise and succour this poor weeping wretch, and fifty like it, but of both sexes, were about me in a moment, begging, tumbling, fighting, clamouring, yelling, shivering in their nakedness and hunger. The piece of money I had put into the claw of the child I had overturned was clawed out of it, and was again clawed out of that wolfish gripe, and again out of that, and soon I had no notion in what part of the obscene scuffle in the mud, of rags and legs and arms and dirt, the money might be.[14]

Questions might be posed about the implications of the animal imagery on display here, but what is not in question is the power of the hallucinatory I/eye to render experience with overwhelming force. The letters also are rich in scenes of transcendent horror, at the moment in 1853 when Dickens strayed into the Borough of Southwark, for example: 'In a broken down gallery at the back of a row ... [of horribly decaying houses] there was a wan child looking over at a starved old white horse who was making a meal of oyster shells. The sun was going down and flaring out like an angry fire at the child – and the child, and I, and the pale horse, stared at one another in silence for some five minutes as if we were so many figures in a dismal allegory'.[15]

This is a sight with a vengeance, a moment of Blakean, visionary horror in which the random ingredients of the cityscape are held in a temporary, and potentially meaningful, stasis by the eye of the observer. Deborah Nord may have such moments in mind in her reference to the 'panoramic view and the sudden, instructive encounter with a solitary figure'[16] of urban experience, although Dickens's meeting is less directly instructive than Words-worth's encounter with the blind beggar on the streets of London in Book 7 of *The Prelude*, which provokes a meditation on questions of identity and our knowledge of one another in the impersonal whirl of the city. The power of Dickens's 'On An Amateur Beat', in its writing as well as in its vision of the world, is rooted in an intensity of perception which was an essential part of his make-up, but which was also related, by onlookers and by Dickens himself, to nineteenth-century technology. Close friends testified to what Macready, in a well-known phrase, called his 'clutching eye'[17] and this is reinforced by Forster's tribute to Dickens's 'unrivalled quickness of observation, the rare faculty of seizing out of a multitude of things the thing that is essential'.[18] But this clutching eye was more than a psychological and physiological tic, as it were. Dickens himself suggests its connection with his creativity in fascinating comments from the beginning and the end of his career. The link is made unmistakably clear in Dickens's letter to Forster of 1841, writing of his pain at the death of his sister-in-law, Mary Hogarth:

Of my distress I will say no more than that it has borne a terrible, frightful horrible proportion to the quickness of the gifts you remind me of. But may I not be forgiven for thinking it a wonderful testi-mony to my being made for my art, that when, in the midst of this trouble and pain, I sit down to my book [*Oliver Twist*], some beneficent power shows it all to me, and tempts me to be interested, and I don't invent it – really do not – *but see it*, and write it down ... It is only when it all fades away and is gone, that I begin to suspect that this momentary relief has cost me something.[19]

Nearly twenty-five years later, the same processes are at work as he struggles with his last completed novel: 'Tired with Our Mutual Friend, I sat down to cast about for an idea, with a depress-ing notion that I was, for the moment, overworked. Suddenly, the little character that you will see and all belonging to it, came flashing up in the most cheerful manner, and I had only to look on and leisurely describe it'.[20] A final example of this special faculty in Dickens might be his comment on *A Tale of Two Cities*: 'I am at work, and see the story in a wonderful glass'.[21] As we have already seen in the passage from *American Notes* quoted in Chapter 2, glasses are the painted slides which were such an essential part of the apparatus of that major form of Victorian entertainment and instruction, the magic lantern.

One wonders if this creative mindset in Dickens is merely a

mental habit or whether it is explicable in more general terms. A way forward is provided by a gifted contemporary, G. H. Lewes, a writer not always in complete sympathy with Dickens but who, in one passage, sees him as 'Gifted with an imagination of marvellous vividness ... He was a seer of visions; and his visions were of objects at once familiar and potent ... in no other sane mind ... have I observed vividness of imagination approaching so closely to hallucination ... what seem preposterous, impossible of observation to us, seemed to him simple fact'.[22] Lewes's insight offers an opportunity to move from what might be called the personal side of Dickens's creativity to the technological, a process in which a number of apparently disparate threads – the city and its streets, walking, and the looking which is an inseparable part of walking – begin to form some kind of pattern, a move facilitated by the remarks of another contemporary, John Hollingshead: 'His walks were always walks of observation, through parts of London that he wanted to study. His brain must have been like a photographic lens, and fully studded with "snapshots" of the whole kaleidoscope of Metropolitan existence'.[23] It is clear that Dickens's own response to photography was by no means unambiguous, as in his dislike of 'the multiplication of my countenance in the shop windows' in 1856.[24] But this did not prevent him from displaying a sympathetic understanding of and respect for the daguerreotype in a letter of 1852 to his friend, Miss Burdett Coutts: 'The Artist who operated [John E Maynall] is quite a Genius in that way, and has acquired a large stock of very singular knowledge of all the little eccentricities of the light and the instrument ... Some of the peculiarities inseparable from the process – as a slight rigidity and desperate grimness are in it [his portrait], but greatly modified. I sat five times'.[25]

What these passages suggest is that Dickens was a writer of a rather special kind. His remarks on the death of Mary Hogarth seem especially relevant with their stress on seeing and then writing down. It is impossible to say what came first here, Dickens's innate, if that is what it is, capacity to 'see' imagined experience which he then translated into written language, or a prompting towards this kind of visualisation from the urban sights by which he was surrounded from such an early age and which marked his inner life so indelibly. This is clearly a chicken and egg question, although one to which Stephen Bann offers a helpful explanation in his suggestion that in this area Dickens is drawing on modes of perception and spectatorship made available to him by such devices as the panorama: 'I am arguing for a particular subjective investment in the extensive visual prospect to which the bourgeois novelist – the nineteenth-century man of letters who is familiar with the contemporary developments of spectacle – can lay claim'.[26] But it is also unmistakably clear that the city, that is London, was at least initially a primary source of his imaginative energy, affecting his work at the level of form as well as subject matter. Both are encapsulated in one of Dickens's key words, 'labyrinth', to which he recurs continuously in his attempts to capture the essence of the metropolis. It is surely significant that in fastening on this word, rich in classical associations, Dickens is identifying a term pregnant with the sense of movement. The original labyrinth was, of course, constructed by Daedalus for King Minos of Crete as a place from which no one could escape, the home of the monstrous Minotaur. Theseus did, however, penetrate to the heart of the labyrinth, killed the Minotaur and, with the help of the thread of Ariadne, found his way out again. Some of this dark background is present in Dickens's frequent use of the word as a way of crystallising his sense of the city, a representative example being the sombre moment in *Dombey and Son* when 'good Mrs Brown' releases the captive Florence into the wilderness of London: 'At length, Mrs Brown, issuing forth, conducted her changed and ragged little friend through a labyrinth of narrow streets and lanes and alleys, which emerged, after a long time, upon a stable yard, with a gateway at the end, whence the roar of a great thoroughfare made itself audible' (Ch. 6). This is a not untypical use of the trope; a more extended passage concerns Todgers's, from *Martin Chuzzlewit*:

You couldn't walk about in Todgers's neighbourhood, as you could in any other neighbourhood. You groped your way for an hour through lanes and by-ways, and court-yards, and passages; and you never once emerged upon anything that might be reasonably called a street. A kind of resigned distraction came over the stranger as he trod those devious mazes, and, giving himself up for lost, went in and out and round about and quietly turned back again when he came to a dead wall or was stopped by an iron railing, and felt that the means of escape might possibly present themselves in their own good time, but that to anticipate them was hopeless. (Ch. 9)

Such brilliantly funny and perceptive writing is itself labyrinthine, its prose enacting the sinister farce of attempting to find one's way out of such a serpentine puzzle. And the whole passage is imbued with a sense of movement, although movement baffled, retarded, repulsed. But, in a moment from *Barnaby Rudge*, the urban maze is as filled with light and sound as it is with movement:

And now, he approached the great city, which lay outstretched before him like a dark shadow on the ground, reddening the sluggish air with a deep dull light, that told of labyrinths of public ways and shops, and swarms of busy people. Approaching nearer and nearer yet, this halo began to fade, and the causes which produced it slowly to develop themselves. Long lines of poorly lighted streets might be faintly traced, with here and there a lighter spot, where lamps were clustered round a square or market, or round some great building; after a time these grew more distinct, and the lamps themselves were visible; slight, yellow specks, that seemed to be rapidly snuffed out one by one as intervening obstacles hid them from the sight. Then sounds arose – the striking of church clocks, the distant bark of dogs, the hum of traffic in the streets; then outlines might be traced – tall steeples looming in the air, and piles of unequal roofs oppressed by chimneys: then, the noise swelled into a louder sound, and forms grew more distinct and numerous still, and London – visible in the darkness by its own faint light, and not by that of Heaven – was at hand. (Ch 3)

This is the city as spectacle, man-made not to say unnatural, its halo not the sign that this is the City of God but an optical illusion, its light not that of the moon and stars, but rendered 'visible in the darkness by its own faint light'. And, in being manufactured, it seems almost superfluous to insist on its cine-matic flow and vividness, its sense of coming more and more into close-up, in sound as well as image. Such a passage validates one of this book's central tenets, that in dreaming the metropolis Dickens gains access to one of the city's own dreams – that of cinema.

But the nightmare, too, is never far from Dickens's rendering of the urban world. One of the most striking examples is the moment when Oliver, after his rescue by Mr Brownlow, is recap-tured in the streets by Nancy and, above all, Sykes:

Weak with recent illness; stupefied by the blows and the suddenness of the attack; terrified by the fierce growling of the dog, and the brutality of the man; overpowered by the conviction of the bystanders that he really was the hardened little wretch he was described to be; what could one poor child do? Darkness had set in; it was a low neighbourhood; no help was near; resistance was useless. In another moment he was dragged into a labyrinth of dark narrow courts, and was forced along them at a pace which rendered the few cries he dared to give utterance to, unintelligible. It was of little moment, indeed, whether they were intelligible or no; for there was nobody to care for them, had they been ever so plain. (Ch. 15)

What could be more richly suggestive than the newly cosseted Oliver, well dressed and with money in his pocket, being 'over-powered by the conviction of the bystanders that he really was the hardened little wretch he was described to be?' And so this moment becomes the dream of Freud as much as the dream of cinema. In being dragged back through the labyrinth to Fagin, Oliver is being returned to the darkest terrors of abandonment and deprivation, a loss of identity sufficient to make him believe that he *is* the evil-doer the onlookers take him for, onlookers who forge yet another link between Dickens, the city and cinema. Early photographs and the illustrations of Doré, to use only two examples, reveal a London teeming with humanity, a world in which nothing can go unobserved although it may be ignored. Early film, whether in its manifestation as a cinema of attractions (that is, as a factual record of daily events) or in the work of Chaplin, also records the urban scene under the pressure of hordes of humanity. Similarly, almost all moments of crisis in Dickens command an audience, especially when they are in a comic vein. The revelation that Mr Bounderby in *Hard Times* is not a self-made man occurs in his house, but in the presence of a crowd of Coketowners who have rushed in from the street, while the Samson-like cutting of the hair of the Patriarch, Mr Casby, in *Little Dorrit* is achieved to 'the sound of laughter in Bleeding Heart Yard, rippling through the air and making it ring again' (Book the Second, Ch. 32). That this theme of the city as a place of sometimes voyeuristic onlookers is taken over by the cinema is demonstrated by a moment in King Vidor's *The Crowd* of 1927 in which neighbours press into a tenement room to see the body of a child run over in the street.

These themes – the city as dream and nightmare, its sounds and movements, its oscillations between light and dark, its pre-figuring of cinema – are present everywhere in Dickens's work, but his last completed novel, *Our Mutual Friend*, provides a parti-cularly rich example. Length precludes a full-scale examination of the text from this point of view. However, a number of dazzling sequences might act as a summation of this part of my argument. Mirrors are a metaphorical staple of film technique and one of the most striking examples is Kane's emergence from the wreckage of his wife's bedroom only to be reflected to infinity, it seems, by the mirrors he steps in front of. Dickens constantly displays his skill in manipulating mirrors, as in the Veneering dinner-party scene early in *Our Mutual Friend*, a passage of such length and complexity that it must be abbreviated:

The great looking-glass above the sideboard, reflects the table and the company. Reflects the new Veneering crest, in gold and eke in silver, frosted and also thawed, a camel of all work ... Reflects Veneering; forty, wavy-haired, dark, tending to corpulence, sly, mysterious, filmy – a kind of sufficiently well-looking veiled-prophet, not prophesying. Reflects Mrs Veneering; fair, aquiline-nosed and fingered, not so much light hair as she might have, gorgeous in raiment and jewels, enthusiastic, propitiatory, conscious that a corner of her husband's veil is over herself. Reflects Podsnap ... Reflects Mrs Podsnap ... Reflects Twemlow ... Reflects charming old Lady Tippins on Veneering's right; with an immense obtuse drab oblong face, like a face in a tablespoon ... Reflects Eugene, friend of Mortimer; buried alive in the back of his chair, behind a shoulder ... Lastly, the looking-glass reflects Boots and Brewer, and two other stuffed Buffers interposed between the rest of the company and possible accidents. (Book the First, Ch. 2)

This self-reflexive *tour de force* of controlled satirical anger ensures that we relate to these largely nightmarish figures at at least two removes, through the distancing of Dickens's ironic prose and then because our contact with them is via their reflections only. Indeed, in the case of Lady Tippins there is an implied third level in the fact that her reflected visage does in any case look like 'a face in a tablespoon'. One keynote is struck by the description of Veneering as 'filmy' – wavering, insubstantial, depthless – and so are they all, at least on this first viewing. If Eugene is, with a note of sinister near-prophecy, 'buried alive in the back of his chair', this is akin to the condition of the others, buried in the mirrored reflections which are their only reality, yet another example of the novel's ability, like that of film, to convey meaning via indirection rather than through narrative commentary.

Mirrors and reflections are intimately related to the camera I/ eye which is in turn connected to the gaze and voyeurism, again staples of cinema and again amply present in this text. The upper-class Eugene pursues the illiterate, beautiful working-class Lizzie by eventually seeking her out in the streets – the world of Hitchcock's *Vertigo* comes instantly to mind – but his first real sighting of her is through the window of her father's sordid hut:

He could see the light of the fire shining through the window. Perhaps it drew him on to look in. Perhaps he had come out with the express intention ... She had no other light than the light of the fire. The unkindled lamp stood on the table. She sat on the ground, looking at the brazier, with her face leaning on her hand. There was a kind of film or flicker on her face, which at first he took to be the fitful firelight; but, on second look, he saw that she was weeping. A sad and solitary spectacle, as shown him by the rising and falling of the fire.

The complexity of Eugene's responses is revealed in the same chapter, in an exchange with his dearest friend, and double, Mortimer:

'I'll take a peep through the window,' said Mortimer.
'No, don't!' Eugene caught him by the arm. 'Best not make a show of her'. (Book the First, Ch. 13)

The whole episode constitutes a brilliant reinforcement of my argument. Despite his disclaimer, a 'show' is precisely what Lizzie has just been to Eugene, and an erotically charged one at that. Just as in the cinema, Eugene's gaze is unmodified by any sense of propriety because he is unseen, while Lizzie's own gaze is directed at the source of heat and light – an obvious metaphor for passion. Like Veneering, she too is filmy, but in a quite different way, her dreamlike insubstantiality an unconscious invitation to desire. Eugene must have to stare hard to see that the 'flicker on her face' is caused not by 'the fitful firelight' but by weeping. This tear-induced flicker is similar to the effect produced on the spikes of the Marshalsea Prison by the crying of Little Dorrit: 'New zigzags sprung into the cruel pattern sometimes, when she saw it through a burst of tears' (Book the First, Ch. 24), moments that can hardly fail to evoke memories of one of cinema's magical moments, the effect of drooping eyelids on a window blind in *Man with a Movie Camera* and with it Vertov's reinforcement of the intimacy between eye and lens, the I/eye at the heart of film.

Riches of this kind are to be found everywhere in the novel, as in an extraordinary evocation of animate and inanimate London:

It was a foggy day in London, and the fog was heavy and dark. Animate London, with smarting eyes and irritated lungs, was blinking, wheezing, and choking; inanimate London was a sooty spectre, divided in purpose between being visible and invisible, and so being wholly neither. Gaslights flared in the shops with a haggard and unblest air, as knowing themselves to be night-creatures that had no business abroad under the sun; while the sun itself, when it was for a few moments dimly indicated through circling eddies of fog, showed as if it had gone out and were collapsing flat and cold ... the whole metropolis was a heap of vapour charged with muffled sound of wheels, and enfolding a gigantic catarrh. (Book the Third, Ch. 1)

Oh for a cinematic genius to transfer this to the screen with a flick of a magic wand! It would of course take all the resources of film, to say nothing of talent, to convey the paradox at work here, that the inanimate city is every bit as living as its animate inhabitants. The gaslights' self-conscious awareness that they should not be operating in daylight mirrors, at the level of street life, the cosmic unnaturalness of the extinction of the sun, a world so out of joint that London itself is afflicted by a disgusting *human* condition. What Laura Marcus argues for in twentieth-century fiction has surely happened here: 'Through the production of fiction as film, these modernist writers sought to remove from the scene the omniscient author ... In so doing, they transcribe a ghostly realism, a spectral mimesis, which anticipates Christian Metz's characterisation of the film image as signifying the "presence of an absence"'.[27] Dickens's starting point is a fact real enough for Victorian London, its regular enveloping in near-impenetrable fog, but the act of writing translates this mundane reality into a ghostly and spectral city haunted by the absence of the good we associate with the City of God. The passage embodies another essential feature of cinema, the objectification of people and the animation of objects. It might indeed stand as a *locus classicus* of the uncanny, with its animism and anthropomorphism. Like *Our Mutual Friend*, Dickens's late, great fiction – *Bleak House*, *Little Dorrit*, *Great Expectations* – is not closed and hegemonic, but open and eager for interpretation, self-reflexive; its narrators are not omniscient, but puzzled and questioning, haunted by ghosts and spectres. The absence they circle endlessly round is, in the last analysis, contradiction, the irresolvable tensions of capitalism and the schisms in Dickens's inner world caused, at least in part, by his transition from abandoned working boy to self-made bourgeois success.

One final example of the novel's 'grand comprehensive swoop of the eye' (Book the First, Ch. 8) will have to suffice, the parody of the *flâneur* reported in Eugene's terrible punishment of the self-made schoolmaster, Bradley Headstone, for daring to desire the woman he desires, a torment daringly enacted in dialogue rather than narrative:

'Then soberly and plainly, Mortimer, I goad the schoolmaster to madness. I make the schoolmaster so ridiculous, and so aware of being ridiculous, that I see him chafe and fret at every pore when we cross one another. The amiable occupation has been the solace of my life, since I was balked in the manner unnecessary to recall [Lizzie's disappearance]. I have derived inexpressible comfort from it. I do it thus: I stroll out after dark, stroll a little way, look in at a window and furtively look out for the schoolmaster. Sooner or later, I perceive the schoolmaster on the watch; sometime accompanied by his hopeful pupil [Lizzie's brother]; oftener, pupil-less. Having made sure of his watching me, I tempt him on, all over London. One night I go east, another night north, in a few nights I go all round the compass. Sometimes, I walk; sometimes, I proceed in cabs, draining the pocket of the schoolmaster who then follows in cabs. I study and get up abstruse No Thoroughfares in the course of the day. With Venetian mystery I seek those No Thoroughfares at night, glide into them by means of dark courts, tempt the schoolmaster to follow, turn suddenly, and catch him before he can retreat. Then we face one another, and I pass him as unaware of his existence, and he undergoes grinding torments. Similarly, I walk at a great pace down a short street, rapidly turn the corner, and, getting out of his view, as rapidly turn back. I catch him coming on post, again pass him as unaware of his existence, and again he undergoes grinding torments. Night after night his disappointment is acute, but hope springs eternal in the scholastic breast, and he follows me again to-morrow. [In the hope of discovering Lizzie's whereabouts, of which Eugene himself is ignorant.] Thus I enjoy the pleasures of the chase, and derive great benefit from the healthful exercise. When I do not enjoy the pleasures of the chase, for anything I know he watches at Temple Gate [Eugene and Mortimer's rooms] all night.' (Book the Third Ch. 10)

I remarked earlier on the labyrinthine quality of a particular passage – a reinforcement of content and form characteristic of Dickens's best work – and a quality shared by this sadistic outburst. It also helps us to see that the novel itself is labyrinthine, a hugely complex interweaving of event and character marked by uncanny coincidences and ghostly presences for which the urban setting is the perfect spectral equivalent. As Bradley's enforced pursuit of Eugene finds itself blocked by dead-ends, endlessly turning on itself through a maze of passageways and courts, so the city-as-text and the text-as-city perfectly reinforce Borges's famous description of *Citizen Kane*, adapting Chesterton, as 'a labyrinth with no centre'.[28] For the fact is that Eugene knows as little of Lizzie's whereabouts as does Bradley, who is following him in the desperate hope of finding her. Eugene may in some sense have the upper hand, but he and Bradley are yet another example of the doubles that proliferate throughout the novel in their shared ignorance. The 1998 BBC television adaptation of the novel did its best to convey the echoing desolation of this episode – within the limits of the form and the production values available – but it cries out for transference to the large screen, although not because of any deficiencies in Dickens's presentation of it. In other words, a novel such as *Our Mutual Friend* can be seen to exist on two levels: as a great and totally self-sufficient work of art in its own right and as a dream of the form to come as though, again uncannily, film were lurking within the text as a ghostly, spectral presence.

We have seen, then, that Dickens fastened hungrily on the streets of London as a source of subject matter, and as a form, from the beginning of his career, as early as *Sketches by Boz*, in fact. But there came a moment when he began to turn against the city which had nurtured him as a writer so deeply: 'London is a vile place, I sincerely believe. I have never taken kindly to it since I lived abroad. Whenever I come back from the Country, now, and see that great heavy canopy lowering over the housetops, I wonder what on earth I do there, except on obligation'.[29] Living abroad meant a number of different things and places for Dickens, but one crucial strand of his foreign experience was Paris, the city with which he identified most strongly after London, and so it becomes possible to trace Dickens's 'cinematic' response to *two* great urban centres.

As with his rather mixed reactions to photography – or, at least, being photographed – Dickens's first impressions of Paris were by no means unambiguous. Forster tells us that he was 'almost frightened' by 'the brilliancy and brightness' of the city on his first visit in 1846.[30] Even the excitement generated by his stay on the Champs Élysées in the mid 1850s is tempered in a number of ways. The astonishing quantity of mud in the streets, for example, seemed more reminiscent of the London of *Bleak House* than the City of Light. But, despite these reservations, the general impression of Dickens's involvement with Paris during his six-month stay in 1855–6 is overwhelmingly positive, of a city which is "extraordinarily gay, and wonderfully improving".[31] And there could hardly be a stronger testimony to Dickens's love of Paris than his association of it with his adored *Arabian Nights* in that 'the Genius of the Lamp is always building Palaces in the night' in it.[32] These impressions of the city cannot be disentangled from the pleasure Dickens took in his apartment on the Champs Élysées, above all in the view from its windows which, as was noted earlier, he told his right-hand man of business, W. H. Wills, that he 'must picture ... with a moving panorama always outside, which is Paris in itself'.[33] Dickens's association of Paris with the panorama began as early as 1847: 'I have been seeing Paris – wandering into Hospitals, Prisons, Dead-houses, Operas, Theatres, Concert Rooms, Burial-grounds, Palaces, and Wine shops. In my unoccupied fortnight of each month' [that is, the two weeks when he is not writing his current serial number] 'every description of gaudy and ghastly sight has been passing before me in a rapid Panorama'.[34] This preoccupation may help to explain Peter Ackroyd's interesting claim, although it is one that demands qualification, about the closeness of Paris to 'Dickens's own vision of the world'. It seems clear that Paris fulfilled what Ackroyd calls Dickens's 'own needs for light and brilliancy'[35] as we saw in the letter just quoted which links Paris to the *Arabian Nights* and which, in full, amusingly expresses a double-sided response to the city; the 'Genius of the Lamp' may be 'always building Palaces in the night', but 'he charges for them in the article of rent, in a manner altogether Parisian and not in the least Arabian'.[36]

Dickens's fascination with both London and Paris is yet another example of one of the inveterate tendencies of his imagination, that of reading the world in terms of dualities which, although contrasting, are not necessarily oppositional in the binary sense. For example, it is not sensible to claim either that London and Paris are in conflict in Dickens's imagination or that one is privileged over the other. But it is feasible to suggest that the City of Darkness and the City of Light occupy positions roughly similar to the oppositions introduced in the opening of *Little Dorrit*: 'There was no wind to make a ripple on the foul water within the harbour, or on the beautiful sea without. The line of demarcation between the two colours, black and blue, showed the point which the pure sea would not pass; but it lay as quiet as the abominable pool, with which it never mixed' (Book the First, Ch. I). One way of suggesting an analogy between this passage and the cities of Dickens's mind is, then, through the images of labyrinth and panorama. As I have shown, Dickens's fictional London is figured continually as a maze, a Piranesi-like confusion of alleys, steps and courts which mirror the mysteries of social and personal life suggested by, for example, *Bleak House* and *Our Mutual Friend*. The panorama that Dickens discovered in Paris reinforces Ackroyd's suggestion that in it 'the world is turned into a spectacle',[37] but so it is also, surely, in London, although a spectacle of a different kind. If Ackroyd is right in claiming that Paris fulfilled Dickens's 'own needs for light and brilliancy', we could argue that London fulfilled his equally strong need for darkness and confusion. This relationship between home and abroad is epitomised in the contrast between the London Sunday evening of the third chapter of *Little Dorrit* – 'gloomy, close, and stale'(Book the First, Ch. III, p. 26) – and an image of Paris specially illuminated to celebrate the return of troops from the Crimean War, which brings into play the brilliance of Dickens's favourite Italian cities: 'It looked in the dark like Venice and Genoa rolled into one, and split up through the middle by the Corso at Rome in the carnival time'.[38] Another way of putting this opposition is in terms of the contrasting uses of the concept of spectacle in urban theory. London is more akin to spectacle as used by Situationists such as Guy Débord; that is, a process in which all human life, leisure as much as work-time, is consumed by the relentless saturation of the city, in all its aspects, in commodities and commodification.[39] Parisian spectacle, on the other hand, is the word used in its less ideological sense, connoting the varied theatrical richness and display of the urban parade. In this sense, the carnivalesque at its most positive is never far off.

Dickens's constant identification of Paris with panoramas associates it with the popular visual entertainments he refers to so frequently, and which were applied to him by others. For example, a section of his travel book, *Pictures from Italy*, is entitled 'A Rapid Diorama'. Again, on a more personal level, Dickens's American friend Kate Field evokes the transitions from one passage to the next in his public readings in America as 'one turn of the kaleidoscope',[40] moving the audience from the horrible creatures hovering over Scrooge's corpse to something quite different. For Sala, the city itself became a kaleidoscope under Dickens's walking gaze: 'looking seemingly neither to the right nor the left, but of a surety looking at and into everything – now at the myriad aspects of London life, the ever-changing raree-show, the endless roundabout, the infinite kaleidoscope of wealth and pauperism, of happiness and misery, of good and evil in this Babylon'.[41] Such a passage reminds one that the contrast between London and Paris I am suggesting is a tendency rather than an absolute. Even the dark world of *Our Mutual Friend* is lightened by the pleasures enjoyed by the Boffins in their newly acquired wealth:

Having been hard at work in one dull enclosure all his life, he had a child's delight in looking at shops. It had been one of the first novelties and pleasures of his freedom, and was equally the delight of his wife. For many years their only walks in London had been taken on Sundays when the shops were shut; and when every day in the week became their holiday, they derived an enjoyment from the variety and fancy and beauty of the display in the windows, which seemed incapable of exhaustion. As if the principal streets were a great Theatre and the play were childishly new to them, Mr and Mrs Boffin ... had been constantly in the front row, charmed with all they saw and applauding vigorously. (Book the Third, Ch. 5)

Although the stress on the child-like quality of the Boffins' response introduces a hint of ironic detachment into the passage's celebratory tone, this more positive note on London is struck as early as *Sketches by Boz* where the experience of riding an omnibus is rendered as one of kaleidoscopic changeability, in contrast with coach travel: 'Now, you meet with none of these afflictions in an omnibus; sameness there can never be. The passengers change as often in the course of one journey as the figures in a kaleidoscope, and though not so glittering, are far more amusing'.[42] Care is needed in making the London–Paris distinction, but it remains meaningful and establishes the manifold nature of Dickens's spectral dream of the future: labyrinthine London is full of movement, panoramic Paris is suffused with light; both are essential ingredients of cinema.

London and Paris make it clear that Dickens was profoundly affected by movement and light in the urban scene and we have seen how important movement was to his creative life – that is, his need for streets as a stimulus to writing. An amazing little passage from *Pictures from Italy* also makes clear how deeply it answered needs within his inner life. This is how he praises Genoa, where he lived for the best part of a year ('Genoa and its Neighbourhood'):

It is a place that 'grows upon you' every day. There seems to be always something to find out in it. There are the most extraordinary alleys and by-ways to walk about in. You can lose your way (what a comfort that is, when you are idle!) twenty times a day, if you like; and turn up again, under the most unexpected and surprising difficulties. It abounds in the strangest contrasts; things that are picturesque, ugly, mean, magnificent, delightful, and offensive, break upon the view at every turn.

The exclamation mark seems to indicate that even Dickens himself finds his need to lose his way a little bizarre. Whatever its origins, it clearly fulfils a profound longing. Light, too, is another pheno-menon through which he experienced life most deeply. This responsiveness can be followed in a number of varied, but inter-connected, ways; in his feeling for stage lighting, in his own productions as well as those of others, for example: a production of Gounod's *Faust* in Paris was 'remarkable for some admirable, and really poetical, effects of light. In the more striking situations, Mephistopheles surrounded by an infernal red atmosphere of his own, Marguerite by a pale blue mournful light. The two never blending'.[43] It was not the vanity of Sir Walter Elliot in Jane Austen's *Persuasion* that led Dickens to bathe in light the chalet where he wrote in the garden of his home, Gad's Hill: 'I have put five mirrors in the Swiss chalet (where I write) and they reflect and refract in all kinds of ways the leaves that are quivering at the windows, and the great fields of waving corn, and the sail-dotted river'.[44] The reflection and refraction we see here are vastly different from that in the Veneering dinner-party scene; it seems, rather, an explicit echo of one of Dickens's favourite writers, the Tennyson of 'The Lady of Shallot', a link which suggests that these reflections and refractions are a metaphor for the relationship between art and reality (a stimulus to Dickens's creativity as well as the satisfaction of a psychic need).[45]

We can return, at this point, to Paris as panorama by remem-bering yet again that Dickens wishes Wills to picture the apartment on the Champs Elysées 'with a moving panorama always outside, which is Paris in itself', a reminder that will allow us to examine this combination of light and movement in more detail. Benjamin again has something pertinent to say concerning connections between urban life and seeing as a new kind of experience amongst the crowds that thronged the city: '... once the eyes had mastered this task of dealing with the spectacle of a lively crowd they welcomed opportunities to test their newly acquired faculties. This would mean that the technique of Impressionist painting, whereby the picture is garnered in a riot of dabs of colour, would be a reflection of experiences with which the eyes of a big-city dweller have become familiar'.[46] Another observation is relevant here, one that gives me an opportunity to fuse a number of different insights together into a moment of coherence, Dickens's reference to some aspects of London life as 'shadows of the great moving picture'. It is part of my argument that in using this image of the city as a moving picture Dickens is operating within a tradition of viewing the city as a visual spectacle. In taking an example from Charles Lamb, a writer he immensely admired and by whom he was certainly influenced, we become aware of a general shift in consciousness that had been under way long before the middle of the nineteenth century: 'Often, when I have felt a weariness or distaste at home, have I rushed out into her crowded Strand, and fed my humour, till tears have whetted my cheek for unutterable sympathy with the multitudinous moving picture, which she never fails to present at all hours, like the scenes of a shifting pantomime'.[47] There is the sense of a more than personal movement of mind at work here and I don't in the least wish to isolate Dickens from such a 'general and gregarious advance of intellect', as Keats calls it.[48] My aim is, rather, to demonstrate his specific awareness, within a general context, of the pressures and opportunities leading towards the advent of cinema. His contribution could be expressed in a number of different ways, but what I have concentrated on here are the insights made possible to Dickens by his being, like Baudelaire, 'a kaleidoscope gifted with consciousness' who reads the city as labyrinth and panorama, a generator of movement and light which saturates the content and form of his work at every level while simultaneously prefiguring film.

If cinema is to be understood as a provisional end-point of a series of steps, at least some of which are rooted in technology, it becomes yet another child of the Industrial Revolution and those words of Benjamin we have already looked at can take on a new resonance: 'To the form of the new means of production, which to begin with is still dominated by the old ... there correspond images in the collective consciousness in which the new and the old are intermingled'.[49] Another passage shows how such abstractions may be actualised in concrete detail: 'Tireless efforts had been made to render the dioramas, by means of technical artifice, the *locus* of a perfect imitation of nature ... they foreshadowed, via photo-graphy, the moving-picture and the talking-picture'.[50] However, it is one thing for the cultural critic, brilliant as he may be, to make these connections after the event; it is quite another for this to be done by contemporaries in hinting at that which had not yet come into existence. Of these, Dickens was among the most perceptive for his insights into the nature of the modern city and his ability to transform these insights into images of the metro-polis that haunt his pages, from the briefest of sketches to novels which can only be described as immense. Since, as I have argued, the city itself dreams cinema, this is yet another way in which Dickens's work gives form to the shadow which still lacked substance at the time of his death in 1870.

Notes

1 These are the opening lines of Dickens's *A Tale of Two Cities*, published in 1859.
2 As we have seen in Chapter 1.
3 Paroissien, David, 'Dickens and the Cinema', *Dickens Studies Annual*, Vol. 7, Carbondale, Illinois: Southern Illinois University Press, 1980, p. 78.
4 Hollington, Michael, 'Dickens the Flâneur', *The Dickensian*, Vol. 77, 1981.
5 Baudelaire, Charles, *The Painter of Modern Life, and other essays*, ed. and trans. Jonathan Mayne, London: Phaidon Press, 1964, pp. 9–10.
6 House, M., Storey, G. and Tillotson, K., *et al.* (eds.), *The British Academy Pilgrim Edition of The Letters of Charles Dickens*, Vols. 1–12, Oxford: Clarendon Press, 1965–2002; 16 March 1841, Vol. 2, p. 235. A friend, Basil Hall, had sent Dickens the manuscript of Lady De Lancey's account of her daily life between 8 June 1815 and 26 June, when her husband died from wounds received at the Battle of Waterloo.
7 *Letters of Dickens*, 16 March 1841, Vol. 2, p. 234.
8 Forster, John, *The Life of Charles Dickens*, London: J. M. Dent & Sons, 1927, Vol. 1, p. 14.
9 Lucas, E. V. (ed.), *The Works of Charles and Mary Lamb*, London: Methuen, 1903, p. 106.
10 Baudelaire, *Painter of Modern Life*, p. 37.
11 Rignall, John, *Realist Fiction and the Strolling Spectator*, London: Rout-ledge, 1992, p. 10.
12 Benjamin, Walter, *Illuminations*, trans. Harry Zohn and ed. Hannah Arendt, Glasgow: Fontana, 1973, p. 175.
13 *Letters of Dickens*, 23 February 1841 (Appendix A), Vol. 7, p. 825.
14 Dickens, Charles, 'On an Amateur Beat', *The Uncommercial Traveller*, Ch. 34.
15 *Letters of Dickens*, 7 January 1853, Vol. 7, p. 2.
16 Nord, Deborah, *Walking the Victorian Streets: women, representation and the city*, Ithaca, NY: Cornell University Press, 1995, p. 21.
17 *Letters of Dickens*, Vol. 3, p. ix.
18 *Letters of Dickens*, Vol. 3, p. ix.
19 *Letters of Dickens*, ? October 1841, Vol. 2, pp. 410–11.
20 *Letters of Dickens*, ? Early November, 1865, Vol. 11, p. 105. The 'little

character' mentioned here is Sophie, Dr Marigold's adopted daughter, from the story *Dr Marigold's Prescriptions*.

21 *Letters of Dickens*, 8 July 1859, Vol. 9, p. 90.
22 Collins, Philip, *Dickens: the critical heritage*, London: Routledge, 1971, p. 571.
23 Collins, Philip, *Interviews and Recollections*, London: Macmillan, 1981, Vol. 2, p. 222.
24 Dexter, Walter (ed.), *The Letters of Charles Dickens*, London: The Nonesuch Press, 1938, Vol. 2, p. 819.
25 *Letters of Dickens*, Vol. 6, p. 834.
26 Bann, Stephen, 'Visuality Codes the Text: Charles Dickens's *Pictures from Italy*', in Bullen, J. B. (ed.), *Writing and Victorianism*, London: Longman, 1997, p. 213.
27 Donald, J., Friedberg, A. and Marcus, L. (eds.), *Close Up 1927–1933: cinema and modernism*, London: Cassell, 1998, pp. 154–5.
28 This heavily used, and often misquoted, passage is identified by David Thompson, in *Rosebud* (see Select bibliography), as occurring in a 1941 article reproduced in 'An Overwhelming Film', in Cozarinsky, Edgardo (ed.), *Borges In/And/On Film*, New York: Lumen Books, 1988, p. 77.
29 *Letters of Dickens*, 9 March 1854, Vol. 7, p. 287.
30 Forster, *Life*, Vol. 1, p. 442.
31 *Letters of Dickens*, 13 October 1853, Vol. 7, p. 163.
32 Dexter, *Letters of Dickens*, Vol. 3, p. 55.
33 *Letters of Dickens*, 21 October 1855, Vol. 7, p. 724.
34 *Letters of Dickens*, 28 January 1847, Vol. 5, p. 19.
35 Ackroyd, Peter, *Dickens*, London: Guild Publishing, 1990, pp. 434, 433.
36 Dexter, *Letters of Dickens*, Vol. 3, p. 55.
37 Ackroyd, *Dickens*, p. 434.
38 *Letters of Dickens*, 1 January 1856, Vol. 8, p. 2.
39 See Débord, Guy, *Society of the Spectacle*, Detroit: Black & Red, 1983.
40 Collins, *Interviews and Recollections*, Vol. 2, p. 255.
41 Collins, *Interviews and Recollections*, Vol. 2, pp. 197–8.
42 Slater, Michael (ed.), *Dickens' Journalism: Sketches by Boz and other early papers 1833–39*, Chapter 16, 'Omnibuses', London: Phoenix, 1996, p. 139.
43 Dexter, *Letters of Dickens*, Vol. 3, pp. 342–3.
44 Dexter, *Letters of Dickens*, Vol. 3, p. 650.
45 Evidence of this can be found in an 1868 letter complaining of the difficulties of coming up with new ideas for the Christmas number of *All the Year Round*: 'I sit in the chalet, like Mariana in the moated grange', *Letters of Dickens*, Vol. 12, p. 167.
46 Benjamin, *Illuminations*, p. 199.
47 Lucas, *Works of Charles and Mary Lamb*, p. 107.
48 Forman, Maurice Buxton (ed.), *The Letters of John Keats*, 4th edition, London: Oxford University Press, 1952, p. 143.
49 Benjamin, Walter, *Charles Baudelaire: a lyric poet in the era of high capitalism*, trans. Harry Zohn, London: Verso, 1997, p. 159.
50 Benjamin, *Charles Baudelaire*, p. 161.

5 The magic carpet of technology

What I want to do ... is to write the poem of modern activity. Hence ... no more pessimism ... [or] the stupidity and sadness of life. Instead, conclude with ... the power and gaiety that comes from its productivity. In a word, go along with the century, express the century.[1]

The horrors of nineteenth-century industrialisation have been described, analysed and criticised in such exhaustive, and exhausting, detail that our image of the Victorian age can become one of unremitting squalor, suffering and degradation. Dickens's later, darker, novels have played a major role in this process: once read, it is hard to forget the fly-blown Marshalsea Prison in which Little Dorrit is born or the filthy Thames that oozes its way through *Our Mutual Friend*. But it is sometimes forgotten that these works too are comic. Moments of fun and gaiety exist even in such sombre contexts and, more importantly perhaps, they are embodied in words which create an exhilarating sense of vitality, an immersion in language that uses the full range of its expressive power. Paradoxically, there is no mimetic connection between the pessimism which is an inseparable feature of the vision at work in the later novels and the medium of expression through which this vision is conveyed. Indeed, if there is a hopeful aspect to works such as *Bleak House*, *Little Dorrit* and *Our Mutual Friend* it is to be found in the energy of Dickens's inexhaustible linguistic virtuosity. It cannot be said, of course, that these books are celebrations of the times in which they were created, but they do fulfil one of Dickens's crucial purposes in writing, the stimulation of the imaginative faculty (what he called fancy) in a utilitarian age. When we look across the full range of his output, it is clear that Dickens is far from utterly at odds with his own time, that he does not share the apocalyptic anxiety that often assails modern commentators, especially in relation to developments in Victorian technology where we are sometimes invited to believe that each new invention – or the refinement of some already existing machinery – was yet another step on the road to alienation and loss of self. Dickens, on the other hand, understood how technology could often enhance human life, whether in entertainment, the speed of travel or, as we have seen, the control of pain.[2] It is amusing to see how fascinated Dickens can be by the artistic uses of technology, as in his long description in a letter to Mark Lemon dated 1856, of a 'novelty' on the Parisian stage 'which I think it worth letting you know of, as it is easily available, either for a serious or a comic interest – the introduction of a supposed electric telegraph'.[3] This chapter will explore two aspects of Dickens's delight in technology, both of which play important roles in the nineteenth-century's dream of cinema.

Pictures to the eye and mind[4]

Mr Booley's travels

In a *Household Words* article of 20 April 1850, 'Some Account of an Extraordinary Traveller', we are introduced to the apparently far from extraordinary Mr Booley:

In person Mr Booley is below the middle size, and corpulent. His countenance is florid, he is perfectly bald, and soon hot; and there is a composure in his gait and manner, calculated to impress a stranger with the idea of his being, on the whole, an unwieldy man. It is only in his eye that the adventurous character of Mr Booley is seen to shine. It is a moist, bright eye, of a cheerful expression, and indicative of keen and eager curiosity.[5]

A little opposition is set up here, in relation to travelling, between Mr Booley's inner and outer man. He seems admirably equipped for journeying in psychological terms, but one wonders how his Pickwick-like frame would stand up to the physical rigours of Victorian tourism, much less exploration. Nothing daunted, however, he closes 'the door of his house behind him at one o'clock in the afternoon of a certain day, and immediately proceeded to New Orleans in the United States of America' where, amongst other sights, he observes the effects of 'the bodies of dead slaves'.[6] He is not alone in these travels:

In this expedition he had the pleasure of encountering a party of intelligent workmen from Birmingham who were making the same tour. Also his nephew Septimus, aged only thirteen. The intrepid boy had started from Peckham, in the old country, with two and sixpence sterling in his pocket; and had, when he encountered his uncle at a point of the Ohio River, called Snaggy Bar, still one shilling of that sum remaining![7]

A little later, the group is joined by 'two Scotch gardeners; several English compositors, accompanied by their wives; three brass founders from the neighbourhood of Long Acre, London; two coach painters, a gold-beater and his only daughter, by trade a stay-maker; and several other working-people from sundry parts of Great Britain'.[8] Mr Booley continues on his journey 'like an opium-eater in a mighty dream', his 'days were all Arabian nights, and he saw wonders without end'.[9] Clearly, our extraordinary traveller is being transported in more ways than one and the source of his magical, dreamlike experiences is cunningly delayed until towards the end of the essay:

'It is very gratifying to me,' said he, 'to have seen so much at my time of life, and to have acquired a knowledge of the countries I have visited which I could not have derived from books alone. When I was a boy, such travelling would have been impossible, as the gigantic-moving-panorama or diorama mode of conveyance, which I have principally adopted (all my modes of conveyance have been pictorial), had then not been attempted'.[10]

It is worth quoting this piece at some length to give the full flavour and tone of Dickens's attitude to this phenomenon, dramatised as it is through Mr Booley's own words. We know that Dickens was interested in the full range of entertainments on offer to the Victorian public, partly because he attended them himself; at this level, there is no distinction between him and the great mass of the people he wrote for. But he also thought deeply about the meaning of these activities for both the personal lives of individuals and the wider health of his society. In Mr Sleary's immortal words, 'People must be amuthed'[11] but for Dickens amusement was the reverse of trivial pastimes, fulfilling as it did a deep human need. He saw a direct link between amusement and imagination, the cultivation of that faculty by popular and high culture alike, without which society and the individuals who make up society are inevitably impoverished.

Dickens's thinking in this field is a link in a chain of positive responses to popular forms of art and entertainment which is still being discussed in current debates about the role of television, and even more advanced developments, in the lives of individuals in a media-saturated environment. Dorothy Richardson's comment about cinema illuminates the continuing process between Dickens's world and ours:

Is there not a certain obscenity, a separation of the inner spirit from the outer manifestation thereof, in regarding pictures we despise and audiences we loftily look down upon in the momentary relationship as we imagine it to exist in the accursed picture-house? Should we not rather set ourselves the far more difficult task of conjuring up the pre-picture outlook on life of those who make no contact with art in any form, and then try to follow out in imagination the result of the innumerable gifts of almost any kind of film, bestowed along with it, unawares, and therefore remaining with the recipient all the more potently: the gift of quiet, of attention and concentration, of perspective? The social gifts: the insensibly learned awareness of alien people and alien ways? The awakening of the imaginative power, the gift of expansion, of moving, ever so little, into a new dimension of consciousness?[12]

This beautifully sympathetic passage does, of course, exaggerate the ignorance of those belonging to the 'pre-picture outlook'. Indeed, taking the word 'picture' in a different sense, a major purpose of this book is to demonstrate the extent to which nineteenth-century culture was immersed in visual experience, but Richardson's point still holds. Richardson's defence of the role of cinema is like an echo of Mr Booley's enthusiastic defence of the panorama:

It is a delightful characteristic of these times, that new and cheap means are continually being devised for conveying the results of actual experience to those who are unable to obtain such experiences for themselves; and to bring them within the reach of the people – emphatically of the people; for it is they at large who are addressed in these endeavours, and not exclusive audiences ... Some of the best results of actual travel are suggested by such means to those whose lot it is to stay at home. New worlds open out to them, beyond their little worlds, and widen their range of reflection, information, sympathy, and interest. The more man knows of man, the better for the common brotherhood among us all.[13]

Finally, the essentially democratic thrust of this celebration of a popular visual entertainment is endorsed by a narrative comment: 'Possessed of good health and good spirits, with powers unimpaired by all he has gone through, and with an increase of appetite still growing with what it feeds on, what may not be expected yet from this extraordinary man'.[14] The complexity of Dickens's response to these issues is mirrored in the delicate irony of the statement 'powers unimpaired by all he has gone through', and the allusion to high culture in the unacknowledged misquotation from *Hamlet* ('appetite still growing by what it feeds on').[15] But there remains no doubt that he regards the experiences provided for Mr Booley by the panorama as in every way life-enhancing.

However, as so often with Dickens, his response to the panorama as a form of popular entertainment is not straightforward. We can note, in passing, that when David Copperfield has his joyful reunion with his old school friend Steerforth 'we went out in a hackney-chariot, and saw a Panorama, and some other sights' (Ch. 20), not a particularly dissipated venture for Steerorth, one would have thought. Rather than dissipation, what Dickens himself fled from was the familiar claim that the panorama was 'pleasingly instructive'.[16] His most extended objection occurs in a piece in *The Uncommercial Traveller* which brings into play the figure of Barlow, the representative for Dickens of the dead hand of mechanically informative 'entertainment': 'Mr Barlow ... invested largely in the moving panorama trade', and having on various occasions identified him ... in the dark with a long wand in his hand, holding forth in his old way', he ... 'systematically shun[s] pictorial entertainment on rollers'.[17] But despite these reservations, Mr Booley has shown us how seriously Dickens can take the panorama as an educative as well as pleasurable entertainment.

The next section demonstrates an engagement deeper even than this, Dickens's use of the panorama as an exploration of visual experience itself.

Pictures from Italy

Turning from the explicit to the implicit use of the panorama in Dickens's work, the best place to begin is with the significantly named *Pictures from Italy*, his travel book of 1846, partly because it encapsulates some of this book's major themes, both in its recourse to visual metaphor and in terms of its wider vision. Indeed, there is a sense in which Dickens can be said to have created his own panorama in its pages. For example, the opening section, 'The Reader's Passport', suggests that the book's audience 'may visit' the places he describes 'in fancy'[18] (p. 299) in a way that is similar to the panorama's ability to open up the world to Mr Booley. In addition, this evocation of pictures from a country Dickens loved so much immediately invests them with a sense of movement, as 'a series of faint reflections – mere shadows in the water' (p. 300). Far from being a conventional piece of travel writing, a genre well established by this time, the book springs to life, using the title of one of its sections, as 'A Rapid Diorama' rather than a purely static series of views. Such is the vitality of Dickens's response to the scenes before him that his panoramic diorama opens out into an imaginatively charged catalogue of some of his major responses to the world. Market-day in one of his party's overnight stops in France is therefore experienced as something essentially theatrical:

The market is held in the little square outside in front of the cathedral. It is crowded with men and women, in blue, in red, in green, in white; with canvassed stalls; and fluttering merchandise. The country people are grouped about, with their clean baskets before them. Here, the lace-sellers; there, the shoe-makers. The whole place looks as if it were the stage of some great theatre, and the curtain had just run up, for a picturesque ballet. And there is the cathedral to boot: scene-like: all grim, and swarthy, and mouldering, and cold: just splashing the pavement in one place with faint purple drops, as the morning sun, entering by a little window on the eastern side, struggles through some stained glass panes, on the western. (p. 308)

Italy becomes a spectacle through Dickens's use of the devices of popular visual entertainment. The squalor and beauty of Genoa, where he settled for a considerable time and which he came to love, is a 'bewildering phantasmagoria, with all the inconsistency of a dream, and all the pain and all the pleasure of an extravagant reality!' (p. 330). When we remember that the key aspect of the phantasmagoria is its illusion of moving towards and then away from the spectator, we gain a heightened sense of how the city threatens to overwhelm Dickens with its paradoxical combination of delights and horrors. As we saw in the previous chapter, the dreamlike immersion in the city, hovering constantly on the edge of nightmare, is a familiar response from Dickens's life and work, above all in relation to London and Paris, the twin poles of his urban experience. This psychic consistency, as it were, is mirrored in the prompting to live in rooms with a view. What is seen from their windows is different, but the urge towards the panoramic is as strong in the move to Dickens's second, and major, residence in Genoa, the Palazzo Peschiere, as the apartment in the Champs Élysées:

It stands on a height within the walls of Genoa, but aloof from the town: surrounded by beautiful gardens of its own, adorned with statues, vases, fountains, marble basins, terraces, walks of orange-trees and lemon-trees, groves of roses and camelias. All its apartments are beautiful in their proportions and decorations; but the great hall, some fifty feet in height, with three large windows at the end, overlooking the whole town of Genoa, the harbour, and the neighbouring sea, affords one of the most fascinating and delightful prospects in the world. Any house more cheerful and habitable than the great rooms are, within, it would be difficult to conceive; and certainly nothing more delicious than the scene without, in sunshine or in moonlight, could be imagined. It is more like an enchanted place in an Eastern story than a grave and sober lodging. (p. 342)

But if Italy is dream and spectacle, panorama and diorama, there is a darker side to Dickens's involvement. In Ferrara for example:

The aspect of this dreary town, half an hour before sunrise one fine morning, when I left it, was as picturesque as it seemed unreal and spectral. It was no matter that the people were not yet out of bed; for if they had all been up and busy, they would have made but little difference in that desert of a place. It was best to see it, without a single figure in the picture; a city of the dead, without one solitary survivor. Pestilence might have ravaged streets, squares, and market-places; sack and siege have ruined the old houses, battered down their doors and windows, and made breaches in their roofs. (p. 360)

Such passages are at least partly a political response to what Dickens, and other like-minded liberals, saw as the degradation of a once splendid civilisation into a backward, fragmented and tyrannised collection of states, but it co-exists with a recognition of the uncanny, constantly prompted by a bloody, if magnificent, past and an often squalid, if charming, present – as in these reflections on the Coliseum:

It is no fiction, but plain, sober, honest Truth, to say: so suggestive and distinct is it at this hour: that, for a moment – actually in passing in – they who will, have the whole great pile before them, as it used to be, with thousands of eager faces staring down into the arena, and such a whirl of strife, and blood, and dust going on there, as no language can describe. Its solitude, its awful beauty, and its utter desolation, strike upon the stranger the next moment, like a softened sorrow; and never in his life, perhaps, will he be so moved and over-come by any sight, not immediately connected with his own affections and afflictions. (p. 397)

All of this amounts to seeing 'the ghost of old Rome, wicked wonderful old city, haunting the very ground on which its people trod' (p. 397), a passage again suffused with what can only be called a sense of the uncanny.

By this stage, it hardly seems going too far to describe *Pictures from Italy* as a cinematic travelogue, especially if the discussion concludes with the section entitled 'An Italian Dream'. As with Mr Booley's travelling by panorama there is a cunningly delayed revelation here in revealing what the dream actually is. The feverish restlessness of this part of the book is brought on, at least partly, by the fact that Dickens 'had been travelling for some days':

resting very little in the night, and never in the day. The rapid and unbroken succession of novelties that had passed before me, came back like half-formed dreams; and a crowd of objects wandered in the greatest confusion through my mind, as I travelled on, by a solitary road. At intervals, some one among them would stop, as it were, in its restless flitting to and fro, and enable me to look at it, quite steadily, and behold it in full distinctness. After a few moments, it would dissolve, like a view in a magic-lantern ... This was no sooner visible than, in its turn, it melted into something else. (p. 362)

Clearly, everything is in movement here, shimmering, evanescent, flickering, dreamlike, drug-induced almost, a moment when that apparently magical effect of the magic lantern, and of the cinema, the dissolve, seems the only way to convey the continuous over-lapping of impressions that invade Dickens's consciousness. The magic lantern had of course reached a high degree of sophis-tication by the time *Pictures from Italy* was written, with its ability to merge one image into another with total fluidity. As a cinematic device, one of which Welles is a master, the dissolve has the ability to effect transitions in time and place while simultaneously evoking unconscious desires. Welles's *The Magnificent Ambersons* provides a striking example in the mirrored reflection of George Minafer looking out at the enforced departure of his mother's lover, an image of 'his imposition of a regime of desire and denial that eradicates Isabel'.[19] (A similar intensity is achieved in the tragic pain which suffuses the face of Agnes Moorehead, overlaid by the indifferent stares of local townspeople.) But the unconscious seems almost to be evoked by Dickens too in phrases such as 'rapid and unbroken succession', 'half-formed dreams', 'a crowd of objects wandered in the greatest confusion through my mind'. At any rate, he is clearly in an appropriate state to find himself 'gliding up a street, a phantom street; houses rising on both sides, from the water, and the black boat gliding on beneath their windows. Lights were shining from some of these casements, plumbing the depth of the black stream with their reflected rays, but all was profoundly silent' (p. 363). Again, the experience is haunting, almost as much for us as it had been for Dickens:

Sometimes, alighting at the doors of churches and vast palaces, I wandered on, from room to room, from aisle to aisle, through labyrinths of rich altars, ancient monuments; decayed apartments where the furniture, half awful, half grotesque, was mouldering away. Pictures were there, replete with such enduring beauty and expression: with such passion, truth and power: that they seemed so many young and fresh realities among a host of spectres ... Then, coming down some marble staircase where the water lapped and oozed against the lower steps, I passed into my boat again, and went on in my dream. (p. 368)

The reader may have noticed by now a peculiar feature of the punctuation in *Pictures from Italy*, its insistent reliance on the colon, a device which here creates a ceaseless flow in the structure of sentences, an almost endless running on of one sight, image, picture into another, a grammatical montage which makes the text a seemingly ceaseless flow. 'The End' is reached with the revelation of the key to the dream, which is saved for the last paragraph when Dickens wakes 'in the old market-place in Verona. I have, many and many a time, thought since, of this strange Dream upon the water: half-wondering if it lie there yet, and if its name be VENICE' (p. 369).

Pictures from Italy as a whole and the Venice section in particular reveal that Dickens finds ways of embodying some of his most important insights through the panorama and other visual devices. As well as being a matchless evocation of the city itself for those who have experienced it, the passages on Venice weave a complex pattern, as I have tried to demonstrate. They are cinematic, not in the superficial sense of painting externally conceived pictures, but in rendering the flux of movement and light in ways that open up the reader's experience as well as Dickens's own. As he wanders through 'labyrinths of ... decayed apartments where furniture, half awful, half grotesque, was mouldering away' he seems to have wandered into his own repressed history while, simultaneously, invading the psychology of the reader. Vision takes on complex layers of meaning here: Dickens's own first experience of the city, recorded in some wonderful letters, is transmuted in his text into a super-charged rendering of an external reality imbued with layers of history that recall Freud's archeologising of the unconscious. At the same time, the hypnotic rhythms of Dickens's prose draw the reader into an uncanny symbiosis so that to close the book is akin almost to the exit from an afternoon visit to the cinema. We emerge from the flickering chiaroscuro of both into a light less real than the one we have been experiencing.

Eleven hours to Paris!

Ian Christie is surely right in suggesting that 'sixty years of railways had prepared people to be film spectators',[20] a judgement that can be verified in a whole numbers of ways. Several recent studies, including Lynne Kirby's *Parallel Tracks*,[21] point out convincing similarities between the position of the railway passenger and the member of a film audience.[22] Despite the speed of the train, both remain in a fixed position observing an ongoing rush of visual impressions and it is no accident that one of the early forms of film entertainment was the so-called Hale's Tours in which audiences sat in mock-ups of railway carriages to look at films that were frequently travelogues shot from moving trains. Those who have seen Ophuls's *Letter from an Unknown Woman* (1948) will remember a primitive precursor of this entertainment in the Viennese fairground to which the experienced lover takes his innocent companion. The young couple sit in a 'railway carriage', an attraction run by an elderly couple, the woman taking the money, the man 'cycling' on an apparatus with pedals and wheels which pulls a moving panorama of European countries past the carriage window. The old man, wearing a uniform cap, blows a whistle and honks a horn in an attempt to complete the illusion of rail travel, the whole episode a charming tribute to, and evocation of, primitive cinema.

Returning to Kirby, she argues that as 'a *perceptual* paradigm, the railroad established a new, specifically modern mode of perception that cinema absorbed naturally'.[23] There is much that is fascinating to ponder on here, although it is questionable if anything occurs 'naturally' in this field, or any other where human input is involved. Again, arguments about the relationship between the movement of trains and such cinematic devices as the tracking shot are well established, but still remain suggestive. However, Kirby also strays into analogies that are less than convincing: 'As a machine of vision and an instrument for conquering space and time, the train is a mechanical double for the cinema and for the transport of the spectator in fiction, fantasy, and dream ... In other words, both the train and the cinema were designed to seduce the public, the patron, the customer'.[24] Few would quarrel with the idea that railways were in an important sense proto-filmic and played their part, along with many other factors, in the eventual emergence of cinema, but at this point the differences seem almost as great as the similarities. However dreamlike the experience of rail travel may be, the images whizzing past outside the carriage window are actually of the real world, and it is hard to see how passengers are being 'seduced' in being transported from point X to point Y.

Railways and cinema are linked, then, but how do they relate to Dickens? *Pictures from Italy* has shown us that he was an inveterate traveller (he made two major trips to America, for example, at the beginning of his first great success and towards the end of his life) and he was interested in the experience of travel itself as movement, not simply in the arrival at a destination. One sign of this is his delight in evoking the physical and psychological texture of travelling, as in the sudden coming to life of a coach as it catches sight, as it were, of 'the first indication of a town', after the monotony of the final stage of a long day:

As if the equipage were a great firework, and the mere sight of a smoking cottage chimney had lighted it, instantly it began to crack and splutter, as if the very devil were in it. Crack, crack, crack, crack. Crack-crack-crack. Crick-crack. Crick-crack. Helo! Hola! Vite! Voleur! Brigand! Hi hi hi! En r-r-r-r-r-route! Whip, wheels, driver, stones, beggars, children, crack, crack, crack; helo! hela! charité pour l'amour de Dieu! crick-crack-crick-crack; crick, crick, crick: bump, jolt, crack, bump, crick-crack; round the corner, up the narrow street, down the paved hill on the other side; in the gutter; bump, bump; jolt, jog, crick, crick, crick; crack, crack, crack; into the shop-windows on the left hand side of the street, preliminary to a sweeping turn into the wooden archway on the right; rumble, rumble, rumble; clatter, clatter, clatter; crick, crick, crick; and here we are in the yard of the Hôtel de l'Ecu d'Or, used up, gone out, smoking, spent, exhausted; but sometimes making a false start unexpectedly, with nothing coming of it – like a firework to the last![25]

This almost Joycean torrent of verbal sound, the extraordinary variations in punctuation and freewheeling disregard for the niceties of sentence structure all contribute to the explosive crescendo of a coach rushing to the end of its journey over a nightmare assortment of bumps, ruts and holes, whip cracking, horses being encouraged, windows as much in danger as people. But Dickens exists on the cusp of that momentous change in human history, the move from transport based on the body, human or animal, to the mechanical. An appropriate example can be found in 'Railway Dreaming'[26] where a major starting point is provided, just as it was for the panorama, by an essay, entitled in this case 'A Flight'.[27] Again, it might be best to let the piece speak for itself. It contains an exquisite delicacy and humour in its delineation of French and English passengers, a quality only demonstrable by lengthy quotation, although its perceptiveness can be seen in the wonderfully observed psychological transition that occurs as the train approaches its destination: 'And now I find that all the French people on board begin to grow, and all the English people to shrink. The French are nearing home, and shaking off a disadvantage, whereas we are shaking it on. Zamiel is the same man, and Abd-el-Kader is the same man [the names are fanciful, of course, not realistic], but each seems to come into possession of an indescribable confidence that departs from us – from Monied Interest, for instance, and from me. Just what they gain, we lose'.[28] But it is the evocation of rail travel that is of most interest and it is worth noting that, at least in this passage, the newer form of transport seems not to lend itself to the virtuoso display we saw in the sights, sounds and physical movement of coach travel:

Ah! The fresh air is pleasant after the forcing-frame, though it does blow over these interminable streets, and scatter the smoke of this vast wilderness of chimneys. Here we are – no, I mean there we were, for it has darted far into the rear – in Bermondsey where the tanners live. Flash! The distant shipping in the Thames is gone. Whirr! The little streets of new brick and red tile, with here and there a flagstaff growing like a tall weed out of the scarlet beans, and, everywhere, plenty of open sewer and ditch for the promotion of the public health, have been fired off in a volley. Whizz! Dust-heaps, market-gardens, and waste-grounds. Rattle! New Cross Station. Shock! There we were at Croydon. Bur-r-r-r! The tunnel.[29]

The vertiginous rapidity with which the world flashes past the spectator – who, paradoxically, is both immobile in his seat and yet rushing at great speed – is the defining characteristic here. The modulation from the idiomatic 'Here we are at Croydon' to 'There we were at Croydon' embodies a new perceptual reality – one, it is worth noting again, that Dickens is recording at its very coming into existence. Compared to the coach, Dickens perceives this mode as a kind of flight and records, with close attention to detail as well as linguistic richness, the ways in which a new method of transport alters our awareness of the external world:

Anon, with no more trouble than before, I am flying again, and lazily wondering as I fly. What has the South-Eastern done with all the horrible little villages we used to pass through, in the *Diligence*? [A coach.] What have they done with all the summer's dust, with the winter mud, with all the dreary avenues of little trees, with all the ramshackle post-yards, with all the beggars (who used to turn out at night with bits of lighted candle, to look in at the coach windows), with all the long-tailed horses who were always biting one another, with all the big postillions in jack-boots – with all the mouldy cafés that we used to stop at, where a long mildewed table-cloth, set forth with jovial bottles of vinegar and oil, and with a Siamese arrangement of pepper and salt, was never wanting?[30]

As always, Dickens makes the connection between a physical process and the mental state it engenders, in this case the lazy wondering over the fact that the new mode of transport has, in the process of annihilating time, apparently destroyed space also or, at least, what it contains. The 'horrible little villages' seem to have disappeared into thin air, and it is worth noting that all of the features associated with the older form of transport are negative: dust, mud, dreariness, mildew are the keynotes of this past. The passage therefore becomes a celebration of the new as well as a psychological record of its effect on both mind and body.

The magic carpet of technology

What had become of the characteristic bodily afflictions of coach travel: 'Where are the pains in my bones, where are the fidgets in my legs?'[31] The nature of this flight is revealed in the concluding passage which records yet more of the mental responses evoked by the rapid transition from one physical location to another:

The crowds in the streets, the lights in the shops and balconies, the elegance, variety, and beauty of their decorations, the number of the theatres, the brilliant cafés with their windows thrown up high and their vivacious groups at little tables on the pavement, the light and glitter of the houses turned as it were inside out, soon convince me that it is no dream; that I am in Paris, howsoever I got here. I stroll down to the sparkling Palais Royal, up the Rue de Rivoli, to the Place Vendôme ... I walk up to the Barrière de l'Etoile, sufficiently dazed by my flight to have a pleasant doubt of the reality of everything about me; of the lively crowd, the overhanging trees, the performing dogs, the hobby-horses, the beautiful perspective of shining-lamps: the hundred and one enclosures, where the singing is, in gleaming orchestras of azure and gold, and where a star-eyed Houri comes round with a box for voluntary offerings. So, I pass to my hotel, enchanted; sup, enchanted; go to bed, enchanted; pushing back this morning (if it really were this morning) into the remoteness of time, blessing the South-Eastern Company for realising the Arabian Nights in these prose days, murmuring, as I wing my idle flight into the land of dreams, 'No hurry, ladies and gentlemen, going to Paris in eleven hours. It is so well done, that there is really no hurry!'[32]

Dickens's flight is, of course, the technological magic carpet of my title and it is typical of the way his mind works that his imaginative response to the most advanced technical resources of his own day should be expressed in terms of dream, with the unfailing recourse to the *Arabian Nights*. In this mood, we might say 'and I read *A Flight*, enchanted!' As with the glittering chiaroscuro and movement of *Pictures from Italy*, it seems almost redundant to point to the cinematic vivacity of this picture of Paris, an Impressionist panorama in which all elements of the scene have stepped out of the canvas into an illusory life of movement.

The passage could, of course, be read differently. Then Paris becomes the site of a Débordian spectacle, of consumerism and commodification run riot; the significantly named Houri is soliciting in more than one sense; and the magical rapidity of Dickens's trip is only made possible by the South-Eastern's ruthless exploitation of its work-force. Dickens was, of course, aware of the darker sides of railway travel: he was himself a victim of a serious accident in 1865 and he argued consistently in both journalism and public statements against the chaotic lack of a centralised structure for the railways. At this point we can move into a very different evocation of railway travel from that embodied in 'A Flight' while not losing sight of the major theme both of this section, and of the chapter as a whole.

The most extended fictional grappling with the railway as a symptomatic aspect of Victorian capitalism occurs in an early masterpiece, *Dombey and Son* (1848), the novel which is often seen as marking Dickens's entry into a more responsible and aesthetically controlled mode of writing. The eruption of the railway system into London, a colossal technical achievement akin to Haussmann's remodelling of the centre of Paris, is recorded in a remarkable passage with an imaginative fervour far removed from journalistic detail:

The first shock of a great earthquake had, just at that period, rent the whole neighbourhood to its centre. Traces of its course were visible on every side. Houses were knocked down; streets broken through and stopped; deep pits and trenches dug in the ground; enormous heaps of earth and clay thrown up; buildings that were undermined and shaking, propped by great beams of wood. Here, a chaos of carts, overthrown and jumbled together, lay topsy-turvy at the bottom of a steep unnatural hill; there, confused treasures of iron soaked and rusted in something that had accidentally become a pond. Everywhere were bridges that led nowhere; thoroughfares that were wholly impassable; Babel towers of chimneys, wanting half their height; temporary wooden houses and enclosures, in the most unlikely situations; carcasses of ragged tenements, and fragments of unfinished walls and arches, and piles of scaffolding, and wildernesses of bricks, and giant forms of cranes, and tripods straddling above nothing. There were a hundred thousand shapes and substances of incompleteness, wildly mingled out of their places, upside down, burrowing in the earth, aspiring in the air, mouldering in the water, and unintelligible as any dream. Hot springs and fiery eruptions, the usual attendants upon earthquakes, lent their contributions of confusion to the scene. Boiling water hissed and heaved within dilapidated walls; whence, also, the glare and roar of flames came issuing forth; and mounds of ashes blocked up rights of way, and wholly changed the law and custom of the neighbourhood. (Ch. 6)

The energy of the writing here, the huge pictorial vividness of the scene taken as a whole, mirrors the forces necessary to bring the railway into existence in reality, and can be read cinematically in at least two ways. The passage resembles, anticipates even, one of those colossal scenes that are such a marked feature of silent cinema in its advanced phase while, at the same time, it could equally be the *set* of such a scene, an ordered chaos littered with the machinery that will bring it to illusory life on the screen. Given that the director D. W. Griffith was a self-acknowledged disciple of Dickens, perhaps the most obvious cinematic example of a scene such as this is his film *Intolerance* (1916), which famously interweaves stories from ancient Babylon, Christ's Judaea, sixteenth-century Europe and early twentieth-century America. Setting is important in all segments of the film, but it is the massive crowd scenes and gigantic sets of the Babylonion episodes which most resemble, despite the distance in historical time, the vast scale evident in *Dombey*. But there is more than simply spectacle at work in *Dombey*'s presentation of the railways; there is also an acknowledgement of the human cost of the destruction that would have been justified in utilitarian terms by Victorian engineers and capitalists. The radical nature of the human intervention involved in such transformations of the urban landscape is partly mirrored as a natural catastrophe, one which, in knocking down houses, is clearly displacing people. Hills have appeared in this chaos, but they, on the other hand, are 'unnatural', made by humankind, not caused by earthquakes. The scene is also imbued with a Piranesi-like confusion, a grotesque foreshadowing of Expressionist bridges leading nowhere (one is reminded of the sets of *The Cabinet of Dr Caligari*), impassable thoroughfares, chimneys like the Tower of Babel, all summed up in the image of 'giant forms of cranes, and tripods straddling above nothing'. Characteristic of Dickens, in the midst of this dreamlike unintelligibility and apparently meaningless confusion, there is the recognition of the social dimensions of this phantasmagoria, that it has 'wholly changed the law and custom of the neighbourhood'. Equally characteristic is the acknowledgement that what is being inflicted on Staggs's Gardens is not, when considered in the larger scheme of things, all bad. In a way that we have come to recognise as typical of Dickens's stylistic manoeuvres, the meaning of this disorder is held back, the delayed message coming with an element of surprise: 'In short, the yet unfinished and unopened Railroad was in progress; and, from the very core of all this dire disorder, trailed smoothly away, upon its mighty course of civilisation and improvement' (Ch. 6).

This dark, or at least mixed, vision of the railway and its possibilities is pursued with a range of insights; for example, the evocation of neighbourhoods 'shy to own the Railroad' which are hovering in the liminal space between old and new worlds where a 'bran-new Tavern ... had taken for its sign The Railway Arms ... and the old-established Ham and Beef Shop had become the Railway Eating House' (Ch. 6). But these are bye-ways too far from the core of this chapter to be explored in detail. What can be pursued fruitfully are the links that exist between the novel's social vision of the railways and the moral atmosphere of its human story. These are brought together in *Dombey*, particularly in Dickens's portrayal of Carker, the manager of Dombey's merchant-capitalist enterprises. Dombey's wife, the fiercely aloof former widow Edith Granger, is shamed by being virtually prostituted to him in marriage by her mother. In a complex act of revenge, she elopes with Carker, whom she despises, to Dijon where he confidently expects their relationship to be consummated, although nothing could be further from Edith's intentions. As with a good deal of the novel's action this intrigue is facilitated by rail travel and its climax is achieved by one of those accidents that were becoming increasingly common in the period.

Rejected by Edith and pursued by Dombey, Carker's state of mind is dramatised in an extended sequence by way of his disturbing obsession with the railway:

Unable to rest, and irresistibly attracted – or he thought so – to this road, he went out and lounged on the brink of it, marking the way the train had gone, by the yet smoking cinders that were lying in its track. After a lounge of some half hour in the direction by which it had disappeared, he turned and walked the other way – still keeping to the brink of the road – past the inn garden, and a long way down; looking curiously at the bridges, signals, lamps, and wondering when another Devil would come by.

A trembling of the ground, and quick vibration in his ears; a distant shriek; a dull light advancing, quickly changed to two red eyes, and a fierce fire, dropping glowing coals; an irresistible bearing on of a great roaring and dilating mass; a high wind, and a rattle – another come and gone, and he holding to a gate, as if to save himself!

He waited for another, and for another. He walked back to his former point, and back again to that, and still, through the wearisome vision of his journey, looked for these approaching monsters. He loitered about the station, waiting until one should stay to call there; and when one did, and was detached for water, he stood parallel with it, watching its heavy wheels and brazen front, and thinking what a cruel power and might it had. Ugh! To see the great wheels slowly turning, and to think of being run down and crushed! ... So in his bed, whither he repaired with no hope of sleep. He still lay listening; and when he felt the trembling and vibration, got up and went to the window, to watch (as he could from its position) the dull light changing to the two red eyes, and the fierce fire dropping glowing coals, and the rush of the giant as it fled past, and the track of glare and smoke along the valley ... He paid the money for his journey to the country-place he had thought of; and was walking to and fro, alone, looking along the lines of iron, across the valley in one direction, and towards a dark bridge near at hand in the other; when, turning in his walk, where it was bounded by one end of the wooden stage on which he paced up and down, he saw the man from whom he had fled [Mr Dombey], emerging from the door by which he himself had entered there. And their eyes met.

In the quick unsteadiness of the surprise, he staggered, and slipped on to the road below him. But recovering his feet immediately, he stepped back a pace or two upon that road, to interpose some wider space between them, and looked at his pursuer, breathing short and quick.

He heard a shout – another – saw the face change from its vindictive passion to a faint sickness and terror – felt the earth tremble – knew in a moment that the rush was come – uttered a shriek – looked round – saw the red eyes, bleared and dim, in the daylight, close upon him – was beaten down, caught up, and whirled away upon a jagged mill, that spun him round and round, and struck him limb from limb, and licked his stream of life up with its fiery heat, and cast his mutilated fragments in the air. (Ch. 55)

Perhaps the most striking feature of this passage is the seamless transition it achieves between the worlds of melodrama and advanced technology. For Dickens, the perfect embodiment of Carker's death wish, in a novel which has the railway as an integral part of its vision, is the train engine in its manifestation of destructiveness, rather than its equally powerful embodiment of civilisation and progress. Dickens uses the railway as part of his melodramatic moral scheme without any sense of strain because, for him, the contrast of melodrama as 'old-fashioned' and the train as advanced would be a binary, and so false, opposition. The story of Dickens's inheritance of melodrama is a complicated one, in which the popular theatre that he both loved and viewed quizzically played a major part, but by the time of *Dombey*, if not earlier, he had made this inheritance entirely his own. Dickens understood that the violent contrasts of melodrama, its reliance on coincidence, and its unexpected connections between people and things made it the perfect vehicle for his fictional exploration of the modern world as it was coming into being, above all in its manifestation in urban life. The metropolis was for him melodramatic in its very nature, as it was for Poe and Baudelaire, and as an earlier London had been for Blake, Wordsworth, Lamb, Hazlitt, De Quincey and others. But it was Dickens alone who, understanding this link between melodrama and the city, had the creative energy to make the 'real' London of the nineteenth century an ever-present setting for the colossal structures of *Bleak House*, *Little Dorrit* and *Our Mutual Friend*. The inclusion of the railway in this urban phantasmagoria as early as *Dombey* is a remarkable achievement since 1848 was the year when the railway was first being laid down all over Britain. Equally striking, I would suggest, is the analogy between *Dombey*'s fusion of melodrama and the urban setting with the blending of these features in the mature phase of early cinema. Just as Griffith provides an obvious example in relation to spectacle, the figure who comes most readily to mind at this point is Charlie Chaplin whose life and work is suffused in Dickensian themes of poverty, sacrifice and regeneration, enacted with a mixture of laughter and tears against the backdrop of an alienating city with its extreme degradation and affluence. Griffith's early short master-pieces bear testimony to Chaplin's fascination with the human possibilities constantly under threat in the city. An extended example can be found in Chaplin's *The Kid* (1921) where the tramp's attempts to assist an illegitimate child in a world of officialdom reminiscent of the Beadle in *Oliver Twist* has a richly detailed slum-life as its backdrop.

A perfect fusion of the qualities I am seeking is provided by King Vidor's *The Crowd* (1927), a 'Dickensian' masterpiece not in the sense of having been directly influenced by Dickens but in demonstrating the pervasiveness of the qualities associated with his genius within popular culture. The city, in this case New York, is present here not as a backcloth, but rather as the medium within which human lives are inescapably played out. Love flowers, and does so touchingly, by means of the essentially urban phenomenon of the blind date which is assisted by the mechanical, but not dehumanising, pleasures of Coney Island. Work is portrayed through the famous panning of the camera up a huge skyscraper. Our protagonist is eventually picked out hunched over what appears to be one desk among hundreds in a vast panorama of alienating labour. The melodrama of city life is acted out through the death of a child run over in the streets, subsequent unemployment, despair and the near destruction of a marriage. After a period of separation, the tiny family – husband, wife and remaining child – are reunited, their precarious stability pictured in their membership of a huge audience being 'amuthed', to use Mr Sleary's term. Cinematic virtuosity and exquisite human detail are the combined hallmarks of this film, displaying simultaneously the full panoply of the city's technological inventiveness and the reliance on a moral scheme which has its roots deep in the melodramatic tradition of which Dickens himself was so important a part.

We have seen in this chapter Dickens's positive response to some of the technological developments of the nineteenth century despite his awareness of the destructive aspects of, for example, the laying down of the Victorian railway system. We know also, from *Hard Times*, that Dickens hated the alienating aspects of the mechanised labour of factories, although the novel does acknowledge the civilising role of the products of this labour. It is also worth remembering that one of the darker novels, *Bleak House*, contains Dickens's most positive portrait of a Victorian industrialist in Mr Rouncewell the iron-master. Dickens's response to technology is, as we would expect, a complex one, but that he could see it as a magic carpet transporting people to worlds of pleasure and knowledge is undeniable. The panorama, railway travel, and Dickens's visually dominated response to Italy all demonstrate his allegiance to aspects of the nineteenth century that would play their part, however small, in the gradual emergence of cinema.

Notes

1 Zola, Émile, *The Ladies' Paradise*, ed. and trans. Brian Nelson, Oxford: World's Classics, 1998, p. ix.
2 I have already noted Dickens's delight in the efficacy of chloroform during his wife's pregnancies.
3 House, M., Storey, G. and Tillotson, K., *et al.* (eds.), *British Academy Pilgrim Edition of The Letters of Charles Dickens*, Vols. 1–12, Oxford: Clarendon Press, 1965–2002; 7 January 1856, Vol. 8, p. 11.
4 A 'picture to the eye and mind' is Dickens's description of an ideal dramatic production, in *Letters of Dickens*, 13 September 1867, Vol. 11, pp. 427–8.
5 Pascoe, David, *Charles Dickens Selected Journalism 1850–1870*, London: Penguin Books, 1997, p. 511.
6 Pascoe, *Journalism*, p. 512.
7 Pascoe, *Journalism*, p. 514.
8 Pascoe, *Journalism*, p. 518.
9 Pascoe, *Journalism*, pp. 516, 517.
10 Pascoe, *Journalism*, p. 519.
11 *Hard Times*, Ch. 6.
12 Donald, J., Friedberg, A. and Marcus, L. (eds.), *Close Up 1927–1933: cinema and modernism*, London: Cassell, 1998, p. 205.
13 Pascoe, *Journalism*, p. 519.
14 Pascoe, *Journalism*, p. 519.
15 The lines in Shakespeare's *Hamlet* read: 'Why, she would hang on him, / As if increase in appetite had grown / By what it fed on' (I. ii. 143).
16 Dickens, Charles, 'Dulborough Town', *The Uncommercial Traveller*, Ch. 12.
17 Dickens, Charles, 'Mr Barlow', *The Uncommercial Traveller*, Ch. 33.
18 In the case of Dickens, Charles, *Pictures from Italy* page references are given to Schwarzbach, F. S. and Ormond, Leonee (eds.), *American Notes And Pictures From Italy*, London: Everyman, 1997.
19 Perkins, V. F., *The Magnificent Ambersons*, BFI Film Classics, London: British Film Institute, 1999, p. 53.
20 Christie, Ian, *The Last Machine: early cinema and the birth of the modern world*, London: BBC Educational Developments, 1994, p. 17.
21 Kirby, Lynne, *Parallel Tracks: the railroad and the silent cinema*, Exeter: University of Exeter Press, 1997.
22 Lynne Kirby acknowledges the influence on her work of Schivelbusch, Wolfgang, *The Railway Journey: trains and travel in the 19th century*, trans. Anselm Hollo, New York: Urizen Books, 1979) whose

insights are applied across the general cultural field of the nineteenth century.

23 Kirby, *Parallel Tracks*, p. 7.
24 Kirby, *Parallel Tracks*, pp. 2 and 36.
25 Dickens *Pictures from Italy*, p. 305.
26 'Railway Dreaming' is the title of a *Household Words* essay by Charles Dickens (10 May 1856)
27 Dickens, Charles, *Household Words*, 30 August 1851, in Pascoe, *Journalism*.
28 Pascoe, *Journalism*, pp. 141–2.
29 Pascoe, *Journalism*, p. 139.
30 Pascoe, *Journalism*, p. 144.
31 Pascoe, *Journalism*, p. 144.
32 Pascoe, *Journalism*, p. 145.

Dickens, theatre and spectacle

There's No Business Like Show Business.[1]

Although this book is telling a story about Dickens's relation to
cinema, it is clear that its narrative is not linear. Rather than a
classic realist text, with its causally connected elements of character, plot and so on, my tale might be described as post-modern, its
ingredients linked by contingency rather than necessity, its time-
scheme shifting between past and present, its narrative circular
and overlapping rather than straightforward. Nowhere is this more
obvious than in the connections between Dickens, theatre and
film where the richness of the materials to hand almost defies
coherent ordering. The areas which demand attention can perhaps
be limited to the following: Dickens's personal involvement with
the stage, including his leading role in a series of amateur theatricals of more or less professional quality; the sheer volume of
dramatisations of his work, in his lifetime and after; and the
saturation of his texts in theatrical elements, at a structural as
well as linguistic level. A key point in what follows is the conviction that, as in his relations with the urban world, Dickens was
not simply a reflector of the theatrical scene, but occupied a
position of reciprocity in which he contributed almost as much as
he took from the form that he loved.

Throughout his life, Dickens wanted to be entertained as well
as to entertain, and the major source of this life-enhancing pleasure
for him was theatre, widely defined; that is, not simply the presentation of plays in our modern sense, but melodrama, circus,
equestrian shows, puppets and marionettes – anything and everything, in fact, which added to the gaiety of life. He was introduced

to these delights as a child – much as later generations were to the cinema and now to television – and for long periods in his life went to the theatre several times a week. Dickens wrote and put on plays as a boy, characteristically taking on the role of impresario, masterminding all aspects of the production. As a young man he prepared very seriously for a stage audition using comic material of his own devising, cancelling at the last moment because of illness. He acted in, and controlled all aspects of, amateur productions of established classics, such as Ben Jonson's *Every Man In His Humour*, as well as contemporary melodramas, *The Frozen Deep* by Wilkie Collins, for example. He also maintained an informed interest in theatre through intimate friendships with figures such as W. C. Macready, the greatest tragedian of the period. And Dickens himself became one of the leading performers and entertainers of his own day in the paid public readings of his work which began in 1858.

The major evidence of Dickens's influence on contemporary theatre is, of course, the sheer volume of dramatisations which, as we have seen, began from the earliest stages of his career. By 1850, for example, at least 240 productions had appeared, which increased to over 350 in the era after his death.[2] Dickens drew from the most popular form of theatre, melodrama, for his own work, an early example being *Nicholas Nickleby* (1839) where Crummles's acting troupe is the object of affectionate mockery. But, in a paradox characteristic of Dickens, the satire of the company's melodramatic excesses exists side by side with the novel's own melodramatic structure and resolution, to say nothing of its language. In other words, Dickens was aware of the absurdities of melodrama while never weakening in his commitment to it as a mode of moral and aesthetic expression. If, however, melodrama was the major genre of Victorian theatre, its central theatrical device was spectacle, and this will form a major topic in the ensuing discussion.

All views of the past are partial and limited, distorted by ideology, myth and misconception, and the late twentieth- and early twenty-first-century responses to the Victorian era are no exception. But one of the benefits of the renewed interest in the Victorian period since about 1950, expressed in major exhibitions of paintings as well as important scholarly work, has been to counter an earlier, almost unformulated, sense of the visual impoverishment of the nineteenth century. Reading Victorian novels, especially those of Dickens, creates the illusion of our immersion in a sensuously vibrant fictional world pulsating with the sights, sounds and smells of a novelistic image of reality.

However, when we turn from fiction to 'reality' itself I believe that responses may have been somewhat different, for reasons rooted in our misunderstanding of nineteenth-century photographic techniques. When we look at Victorian photographs of people, for example, we must be struck by the unsmiling rigidity of pose almost universally associated with such images. This solidity reinforces, and perhaps helps to create, our feeling that the Victorians were somehow dauntingly inflexible, with little of the varied richness we take for granted in images of people in the twenty-first century; as is well known, this inflexible vision of the past is a reflection of a technical feature of Victorian cameras which required extremely long exposure times if the photograph was to come out satisfactorily. It is impossible to maintain a natural-seeming smile and flexible pose for more than a few seconds and so nineteenth-century photographs often present us with representations of patriarchy that comfortably confirm all our worst fears of the horrors of the Victorian family. Similarly, when we look at the earliest cinematic images of people from the late-Victorian or Edwardian period we are usually presented with a ludicrously flat surface of tiny, jerky figures that conveys merely a parody of human existence, a black and white farce that, again, contrasts unfavourably with the dense, highly coloured texture of life captured by modern cinema. It ought to be widely known, although experience suggests it is not, that such visions of the past are usually distorted by two technical failings: poor print quality and projection at the number of frames per second required for sound, rather than silent, cinema. Anyone who has experienced the beauty of so-called silent film projected at the correct speed in a good print, with the appropriate musical accompaniment, will understand how our apparent experience of the past can be limited by purely external features.

My book, along with many others[3] – some of which were pioneering studies – is committed to the view that the nineteenth century was a densely visual epoch in its high art, popular culture and social reality. 'Looking at the world through the medium of pictures ... became a habit in the first half of the nineteenth century',[4] a habit that had an enormous influence on art, entertainment and social life in the late nineteenth and early twentieth centuries. The central purpose of this chapter is to explore one of the most striking visual phenonemona of the nineteenth century, one which incidentally offers perhaps the closest approximation to the full resources of modern cinema, Victorian spectacular theatre.[5] Nothing demonstrates more clearly the centrality of the role of the Industrial Revolution in nineteenth-century life than the constant technological improvements which invested the theatrical experience with a level of spectacular realism that has never been superseded on the stage. These developments were far from controversial in the sense that for much Victorian theatre 'the eye and not the ear was the organ of appeal',[6] to the extent that some critics and theatre-goers felt that language was being sacrificed to spectacle, even in the case of Shakespeare, as a knowledgeable friend of Dickens, Charles Kent, makes clear in his comments on a Shakespearian production:

Archeological knowledge, scenic illusion, gorgeous upholstery, sumptuous costumes, have, in the remembrance of many, been squandered in profusion upon the boards of one of our leading theatres in the getting up of a drama by the master-dramatist. All this has tended, however, only to realize the more painfully the inadequacy of the [acting] powers ... of the whole company to undertake the interpretation of the dramatic masterpiece. The spectacle which we are viewing is ... resplendent; but it is so purely as a spectacle.[7]

The nineteenth-century debate over the nature of theatre and its future is complex, as we can see from the interventions of Dickens, a lover of melodrama and all forms of popular entertainment, but someone capable of taking a wider view in his more reflective moments. In a letter to one of his oldest friends, Dickens wrote: 'On the whole, the Theatres, except in the articles of scenery and pictorial effect, are poor enough ... The most hopeless feature is, that ... they [the actors] have the smallest possible idea of an effective and harmonious whole: each "going in" for himself or herself'.[8] These concerns are reinforced in an interesting correspondence with his fellow writer and friend Bulwer Lytton, to whom Dickens confided many of his thoughts about the art and craft of writing. In his attempts to persuade Lytton to write for the stage, Dickens sets out the ideal relationship between spectacle and drama, that 'all these scenic appliances are subdued to the Piece, instead of the Piece being sacrificed to them'.[9] But the position is then complicated when he urges that there 'never was a time when a good new play was more wanted ... Fechter [a distinguished actor and friend of Dickens] is a thorough artist, and what he may sometimes want in personal force is compensated by the admirable whole he can make of a play, and his perfect understanding of its presentation as a picture to the eye and mind'.[10] Dickens is, then, suspicious of the theatre's domination by empty spectacle, and deeply concerned for dramatic unity in ways that have a suggestive bearing on his conception of his own work but, in the last analysis, a play must succeed as a 'picture', although to the 'mind' as well as merely to the 'eye'. One thread in this book's continuing pattern of argument is that Dickens's novels can be experienced as pictures to the mind, and that this was, in fact, part of his conscious artistic intention.

Clearly, there was a debate about the proper role of special effects in Victorian drama. However, given that 'melodrama and pantomime were creatures of technology',[11] and since the general audience appears to have had a boundless appetite for the spectacle that could be created by stage machinery, this line of development proved unstoppable until challenged by the even greater spectacular realism of sophisticated silent cinema as it developed from about 1910. One possible line of explanation of this appetite for spectacle has the benefit of bringing into alignment some of the apparently disparate elements of my argument by suggesting that the city, spectacle and melodrama were all aspects of a conjunction of feeling that deeply affected consciousness in the period. In his first collection of writings, the *Sketches by Boz*, Dickens writes: 'The getting into a cab is a very pretty and graceful process, which, when well performed, is essentially melodramatic. First, there is the expressive pantomime of every one of the eighteen cabmen on the stand, the moment you raise your eyes from the ground. Then there is your own pantomime in reply – quite a little ballet'.[12] I argued in Chapter 3 that Dickens is aware of the shift from London as the 'town' – to use the former time-honoured expression – into the metropolis at the very moment when this is coming about, in the early 1830s, and that he is not simply a reflector of this process but a contributor to a wider awareness of urban developments through the power of his writing and the breadth of his popularity. In *Sketches* as a whole we can observe how Dickens initiates a tradition of reading the urban experience as drama and spectacle which is sometimes light-hearted and comic. Dickens is not, of course, solely responsible for this vision of the city, but it is one in which he played a major part and which influenced, for example, the development of spectacle in the Victorian theatre. This is how the point is made by an expert in the field, Michael Booth: 'The real achievement of the theatre in this age of cities was to make theatres of the cities themselves. A deliberate artistic and thematic use of the city as a moral symbol and an image of existence, as well as a strikingly visual and human presentation of the realities of its daily living, originates in the theatre ... the attempt virtually to make the city a character in the drama was made and became common practice. The urbanized drama was born'.[13] Plays appeared with titles such as *The Streets of London* (1864), *Lost in London* (1867) and *The Great City* (1867). This is the kind of thing that could be seen in them: 'It is a marvellous example of stage realism, complete in every possible detail ... If anything, it is all too real, too painful, too smeared with the dirt and degradation of London Life, where drunkenness, debauchery, and depravity are shown in all their naked hideousness. Amidst the buying and selling, the hoarse roar of costermongers, the jingle of the piano-organ, the screams of the dissolute, fathers teach their children to cheat and lie, drabs swarm in and out of the public house'.[14] And a contemporary reviewer marvels at the 'union of an exact picture with all the movement and mechanical aids which are appropriate to the scene ... of Charing-cross at midnight ... its groups of rich and poor wending their way to club or garret ... perhaps the most real scene on the stage in London'.[15] Finally, Blanchard Jerrold provides a particularly evocative depiction of the Garrick Theatre in White-chapel in *London: A Pilrimage* (1872):

Gallery, one penny; pit, twopence; boxes, threepence ... The first time we penetrated its gloomy passages, great excitement prevailed. The company were performing 'The Starving Poor of Whitechapel'; and at the moment of our entry the stage policemen were getting very much the worst of a free fight, to the unbounded delight of pit and gallery. The sympathies of the audience, however, were kindly. They leant to the starveling, and the victim of fate; for four out of five understood only too well what hard life in Whitechapel meant: and had spent nights with the stars, upon the stones of London. In this, and kindred establishments, the helper of 'a female in distress' (dismissed from the West End long ago) is sure of his rounds of applause ... It is not in such establishments as the Garrick ... that the ignorant poor learn how to slip from poverty into crime.[16]

Dickens cannot have been the sole influence on this pre-occupation with urban spectacle in the Victorian theatre, although it is inconceivable that a writer of his fame and popularity, whose work is saturated in urban squalor and dramatised to such a great extent, should have played no part in its development. More interesting than the agony of influence, however, is an attempt at comprehension inflected by consciousness. If Victorian art and entertainment are understood as forms of material production in the cultural sphere, then Dickens's work can be seen as part of a continuum that includes the visual phenomena this book focuses on, as well as the more conventional literary contexts out of which the novels were produced. We know that Dickens's peculiar form of serialisation in parts was only made possible by develop-ments in the nature of publishing and distribution in addition to technical developments in engraving and printing.[17] Studies in cultural materialism have familiarised us with the extent to which even works of imaginative genius are not created in an ivory tower, hermetically sealed off from the worlds of commerce, industry and popular culture. And even if it is clear that the special nature of Dickens's art lies in his extraordinary command of language this, again, does not mean that it exists in a realm that has no interactive relationship with the social life of which he was so actively a part. Indeed, given the essentially social nature of language this could hardly be so. However, if all writing, all art, is embedded in the culture and technology of its period, this is true in a rather special sense in the case of Dickens. Serial publication, with its attendant special features of illustration and advertising, gave his work an added proximity to the reality it both reflected and shaped. It is this very closeness to what we still seem to have to call the real world which permits a reconceptualisation of the imagery rightly seen as central to Dickens's achievement as a writer. I want to argue, in fact, that that there is a special kind of imagery, the structural, at work in Dickens's fiction that is distinct from the localised vividness of language that the term usually signifies.

What, then, is structural imagery? The answer lies in an aspect of Dickens's total artistic personality that has been consistently undervalued, although probably less so today than at any point in the past, and this is his capacity for rigorous thought. The view of Dickens as the great entertainer – with all that implies, for good as well as ill – was current in his own time, but reached its most extreme form in the rigorous scrutiny of F. R. Leavis. Leavis's influential study of the novel, *The Great Tradition*, famously relegates Dickens to 'An Analytic Note' on a single book, *Hard Times*, on the grounds that it is only here that he escapes his role as 'the great popular entertainer'.[18] That Leavis is no mere debunker is clear from his judgement that the 'final stress may fall on Dickens's command of word, phrase, rhythm, and image: in ease and range there is surely no greater master of English except Shakespeare'.[19] But his view that Dickens's 'criticisms of the world he lives in are casual and incidental'[20] is the reverse of that offered in this book, and especially this chapter. One kind of evidence for an opposing judgement is provided by the great edition of Dickens's letters[21] which clearly reveals his capacity for independent thought, based on wide reading as well as observation and experience. But it is not this kind of intellectual capacity to which I wish to draw attention. Like many artists, Dickens is also a special kind of thinker, one who thinks, in his case, as a novelist through character, setting, theme and, of course, imagery: his capacity to think in images can be demonstrated through countless examples of the vivid writing that are such a marked feature of his work. One example is the subject of Dickens's article, 'Curious Misprint in the Edinburgh Review', in his magazine *All the Year Round*, which will be discussed in some detail in the final section of this book, the 'Dream Epilogue'. The article focuses on negative criticism of the collapse of the Clennam house in *Little Dorrit*, an event which is anticipated throughout the novel in many small touches of imagery and which reaches its climax only towards the end of this very long book:

In one swift instant the old house was before them, with the man lying smoking in the window; another thundering sound, and it heaved, surged outward, opened asunder in fifty places, collapsed, and fell. Deafened by the noise, stifled, choked, and blinded by the dust, they hid their faces and stood rooted to the spot. The dust storm, driving between them and the placid sky, parted for a moment and showed them the stars. As they looked up, wildly crying for help, the great pile of chimneys, which was then alone left standing like a tower in a whirlwind, rocked, broke, and hailed itself down upon the heap of ruin, as if every tumbling fragment were intent on burying the crushed wretch beneath. (Ch. 31)

This event is watched by Mrs Clennam and the novel's embodiment of good, Little Dorrit; the 'crushed wretch' is Blandois-Rigaud, its embodiment of evil. The significance of what happens here, and which is forecast throughout the novel, is nowhere generalised in abstract statements but, taken in relation to the book as a whole, its meanings are quite evident. The house of Clennam, and all that it stands for in terms of cruelty and repression, has collapsed in on itself, taking the novel's major representative of evil with it. This event constitutes what might be described as the allegorical conclusion to the novel, although the book also has a 'realistic' ending in its closing lines. The revelation of 'the placid sky' which 'parted for a moment and showed them the stars' clearly embodies the triumph of the forces of good over evil, but this abstraction is shown, embodied in the detail of language, rather than being the subject of literal statement. In other words, complex truths about the novel's system of values are conveyed in novelistic rather than, say, philosophical terms.

There is, however, another kind of imagery I wish to explore: the sense, for example, in which novels themselves may be seen as images on a massive scale. The notion that a literary text, even one as long as a novel, can be read as a metaphor or symbol is familiar enough; my own idea is merely an extension of this. In what sense, then, can books such as *Bleak House*, *Little Dorrit* and

Our Mutual Friend be described as images? What can they be said to be images of? They are not, of course, merely uncomplicated reflections of Victorian England, although they have important links to the society from which they emerge – links which are not in the least, to use Leavis's words, 'casual and incidental'. They are, rather, *representations* of external reality in the form of *fictional* worlds, and Dickens's capacity to create these huge structures in such a way as to prevent their collapse into incoherent detail is rooted in his understanding of some of the key defining pressures of industrial, urban capitalism as it was coming into being before his eyes.[22] It is now quite widely accepted that Dickens's friend and mentor, Thomas Carlyle, anticipated Marx's concept of alienation in works such as *Signs of the Times* and *Past and Present*; Dickens learned from Carlyle and added to his insights the fruits of his own experience of society, ideas that he began to formulate as early as his journalistic period, as the writer of *Sketches by Boz*. One possible reading of his last novels is that they present images of a complete fictional society, one that is structured by an understanding of the major social and economic processes at work in Dickens's lifetime. This may explain why, in reading them, we feel immersed in a fictional reality which, in taking account of contradictions at a deep level, also seems capable of illuminating the world from which it emerged and of which it is a mirror, although one distorted by the liberating power of imaginative comprehension. This is why the oddities of Mr Jarndyce in *Bleak House*, for example, are not an example of Dickens's obsession with caricature, but represent the confusions of a good man trying to act benevolently in a fundamentally hostile world. Taken as a whole, these late novels function as structured, fictional images of nineteenth-century England, images structured by the controlling power of Dickens's artistry, a term all-embracing enough to include thought as well as linguistic virtuosity.

Structural imagery can also exist within a text as well as being a way of describing a text as a whole. What I mean by this is that Dickens's novels are studded with major scenes, extended moments, which themselves embody insights rendered specific in language, gesture, movement, the full range of novelistic devices open to him as a writer. The concept may become clearer by way of an example, from *Dombey and Son*. Chapter 47, 'The Thunderbolt', begins with an attempt to be 'just' to Mr Dombey in recognising that he and his wife are an 'ill-assorted couple, unhappy in themselves and in each other, bound together by no tie but the manacle that joined their fettered hands'. In examining whether Mr Dombey's 'master-vice' of pride is 'an unnatural characteristic' the narrative goes on to enquire 'what Nature is, and how men work to change her', and this leads to an examination of the horrors of nineteenth-century poverty which are 'most unnatural, and yet most natural in being so'. These narrative abstractions are followed by a justly famous passage:

Oh for a good spirit who would take the house-tops off, with a more potent and benignant hand than the lame demon in the tale, and show a Christian people what dark shapes issue from amidst their homes, to swell the retinue of the Destroying Angel as he moves forth among them! For only one night's view of the pale phantoms rising from the scenes of our too-long neglect; and from the thick and sullen air where Vice and Fever propagate together, raining the tremendous social retributions which are ever pouring down, and ever coming thicker! Bright and blest the morning that should rise on such a night: for men, delayed no more by stumbling-blocks of their own making, which are but specks of dust upon the path between them and eternity, would then apply themselves, like creatures of one common origin, owing one duty to the Father of one family, and tending to one common end, to make the world a better place!

Not the less bright and blest would that day be for rousing some who never have looked out upon the world of human life around them, to a knowledge of their own relation to it, and for making them acquainted with a perversion of nature in their own contracted sympathies and estimates; as great, and yet as natural in its development when once begun, as the lowest degradation known.

But no such day had ever dawned on Mr Dombey, or his wife; and the course of each was taken.

The imagery in which the collapse of the Clennam house is embodied is an example of a familiar literary device, the image pattern which runs throughout a work with some degree of unifying force. The continual use of the word 'silver' in Conrad's *Nostromo* is a well-known example, as is the imagery of clothes which forms an indirect moral evaluation of Macbeth in Shakespeare's play. At the opposite pole from this is the concept of the text itself as an image, which I have just been examining. The passage from *Dombey* seems to fit into neither category. It is sufficiently large in scale to constitute a major episode in the text, but it is not recurred to, and forms no part of its unifying pattern. It seems to stand apart from the novel in some sense, as though the ongoing movement of language and narrative is halted by this literally fantastic image of a good spirit removing the house-tops. Another way in which the passage seems to present itself as a special case is in relation to its sources in Dickens's creative life. My suggestion is that this structural image not merely flows from the depths of Dickens's artistry but, in doing so, stems also from the vivid world of visual entertainment that I am trying to evoke in this chapter, which is another way of making the point that Dickens is a popular genius whose imagination is inseparable from the forms taken by the social life of his own time. This cry of social compassion, embodied in an image of supernatural power, is evoked from a novelist for whom the city is the setting of his most personal and worked-out responses to human degradation, whether individual or in the mass, the novelist for whom the city is both magic lantern and panorama *or*, and this is a key point, a huge theatrical set on which the most elaborate effects can be worked out in the interests of an exploration of personal and social evil.

It is, clearly, the theatrical implications of this passage that are crucial to my argument for the theatre, like the city, was central to Dickens's life. Given this level of involvement, it would be strange indeed if it failed to exert some influence over his work or, as I have been suggesting, if his work failed to exert some influence over the theatre. It is at any rate obvious that the passage from *Dombey* is suffused in the theatrical. It seems almost to take us into the world of serious pantomime where, with a wave of her wand, the good fairy peforms her magic trick in the interests, not of simple enjoyment, but of moral revelation. The moment therefore finds its place within the nineteenth-century tradition of spectacular visual effects and stage machinery. What could be more theatrical than this dramatic revelation of the evil that lurks within the houses, as well as the lives, of the neglected poor? The passage also embodies some central concerns of the Victorian stage through its reliance on the opposing dichotomies of melodrama. We may seem far removed here from the, to us, absurdities of virginal innocence, hissing villains, and last-minute rescues that we associate with Victorian drama but, at its level of social indignation, exactly the same dualities are being deployed in the struggle between good and evil personified in the 'good spirit' and the 'Destroying Angel'. If the 'good spirit', whisking off the housetops, is an example of serious pantomime, the play of light and dark in the passage is an example of serious melodrama. In other words, the ethical insights at work here cannot be separated from the forms in which the moral atmosphere of Dickens's period struggled towards its own kinds of understanding, a process in which melodrama played a role at the level of high art as well as crude entertainment. On the large scale, this analysis of a specific episode from a single novel suggests a two-way process of dramatisation, with Dickens drawing essential elements of his imaginative life from the theatre while simultaneously contributing to it through the diffusive influence of such popular writings as his personally supervised periodicals, *Household Words* and *All the Year Round*, as well as the novels themselves.

The connection between nineteenth-century theatre and early cinema is a complex and hotly debated issue in contemporary film studies. One of the earliest and best known works is Nicholas Vardac's *Stage to Screen*[23], a pioneering book which has provoked a highly technical response informed by the latest film scholarship, Ben Brewster and Lea Jacobs's *Theatre to Cinema*.[24] My own dissatisfaction with Vardac's position centres on his reduction of the emergence of film to a single explanatory cause, the belief that in the face of stage pictorialism 'the arrival of cinema would appear to have been preordained'.[25] Such a view can only be sanctioned by a limited conception of film itself, as when Vardac remarks that from 'the beginning the cinema was recognised as a highly realistic and representational medium with ...the means of proceeding in the romantic direction many degrees beyond the stage'.[26] It should be enough to point to the contrasting styles of Mèliés and Lumière to demonstrate that film was not inherently realistic and representational from its beginnings; in addition, Vardac himself seems not to question the tensions implicit in his own use of realistic and romantic. I am happy to find myself in agreement with Brewster and Jacobs in their rejection of 'the view that the history of the cinema is one of steady emancipation from theatrical models'.[27] Even more useful is their endorsement that 'with the development of longer films after 1910, theatrical models came back with a force that overwhelmed all of the others except perhaps the literary ones ... in the 1910s the theatre became a storehouse of devices for the cinema, and has remained so'.[28] Taking a specific example, there is a clear line from what might be called the dirty realism of Victorian theatrical depictions of the city into the world of Charlie Chaplin by way of his involvement in Fred Karno's stage company. *The Football Match* provides an example with its 'huge panoramic cloth with a great crowd of people painted on it. The painted figures had loose arms and hats which were activated by electric fans behind a raked ground row. In front of these were supers, with very small people arranged behind larger ones, to produce the effect of perspective'.[29] Chaplin graduated from a theatrical world with its own forms of spectacle, used in the interests of farce, which may have inspired his transition into films in which the comic misadventures of the little tramp are played out in the streets, bars, and markets of the city, a panorama crowded with the dispossessed, and the occasional toff. In this context, it is fascinating to know that, in his final years, Chaplin re-read his favourite Dickens novel, *Oliver Twist*, obsessively. He may have had many reasons for doing so, but one is likely to have been its preoccupation with the melodramatic dualities facing the urban poor in the nineteenth and early twentieth century: the descent into the abyss or salvation into a world of higher things.

There are other forms of stage spectacle than the urban realism we have been looking at so far. An example of what could be seen on the nineteenth-century stage can be found in a description of a London production of *Ben-Hur*, which had first been performed in New York in 1899: 'In this production could be seen a panorama of Jerusalem, and the interior of a Roman galley packed with slaves chained to their oars .... The chief scenic attraction was the chariot race in the arena at Antioch. Here twenty-two horses were used instead of the twelve in New York, although only four chariots could actually race together side by side'.[30] Only four chariots! Developing the hint contained in the Chaplin episode, the direction my argument is now taking may be illustrated by the following:

Between two mountains was the location chosen for the great wall against which Holofernes hurls his cohorts in vain attacks. Eighteen hundred feet long, and broad enough to permit of the defenders being massed upon it, the wall rose slowly until it was a giant's causeway connecting the crags on either side. Within, a city sprang up .... Beyond it, in the valley, was pitched the great armed camp of the Assyrians. In the chieftain's tent alone were hangings and rugs costing thousands of dollars.[31]

Apart from the reference to a wall eighteen hundred feet long, this might well be the set of any one of a number of American or British stage productions from the 1850s on. It is, in fact, a location for Griffith's *Judith of Bethulia* (1914), the film that marked his break into longer, feature-length work from 1908 to 1914 in which he made nearly 500 short films.

My argument can now be summed up in two ways. First, that there is an element of continuity between the technical aspects of nineteenth-century popular entertainment and the cinema, although to some moving film might seem to arrive with the force of a totally revolutionary upheaval. Second, what I have already referred to as the moral atmosphere of some central features of Victorian culture – reliance on melodrama and its attendant sentimentality as devices for embodying the clash of good and evil – was taken over into early cinema as part of its essential inheritance. On a purely practical level, this is not hard to explain since many theatrical practitioners moved into what they saw as the potentially more successful world of the new form of cinema, bringing with them the ways of seeing and feeling that had developed throughout nineteenth-century drama. As we have seen, adaptation entered into cinema in its beginnings through its reliance on already existing texts, especially plays. But these issues can be pursued at a level more interesting than the practical and more convincing, perhaps, than large generalisations. Eisenstein's essay, 'Dickens, Griffith and the Film Today' will be discussed in the next chapter, but at this stage Eisenstein provides an essential link in the chain that connects Dickens, Victorian spectacular theatre, and film when he writes that Dickens defines 'his direct relation to the theatre melodrama. This is as if Dickens had placed himself in the position of a connecting link between the future, unforeseen art of the cinema, and the not so distant (for Dickens) past – the traditions of "good murderous meldodramas"'.[32] Eisenstein makes a further link to Griffith: 'Melodrama, having attained on American soil by the end of the nineteenth century its most complete and exuberant ripeness, at this peak must certainly have had a great influence on Griffith, whose first art was the theatre, and its methods must have been stored away in Griffith's reserve fund with no little quantity of wonderful and characteristic features'.[33]

What seems clear from a comparison of the location of Griffith's film and the passage from *Dombey and Son* quoted earlier is that they are both images of a special kind, huge in scale, and similar to the scenes of urban destruction caused by the introduction of railways that were discussed in the previous chapter. They are therefore part of a continuum that unites technology and popular entertainment, spectacle and high culture; in other words, we are not dealing here with a simple relationship of influence from Dickens to Griffith. The fact is that spectacle was such a widely diffused aspect of Victorian, and to a perhaps lesser extent American, culture that its presence is felt in the city as metropolis, with London as the prime example, in the spectacular range and depth of the novels of Dickens and other nineteenth-century writers, as well as in the theatre. Theatrical spectacle was not simply limited to the grimy urban realism we have already looked at:

The annual autumn drama at Drury Lane, an institution that lasted from the 1880s until after the First World War, offered the most elaborate effects of all, especially in portraying the pleasures, occupations, and public resorts of the upper classes: Derby Day, Ascot ... the Stock Exchange, the House of Commons ... all staged with the full scenic and mechanical resources of Drury Lane, which were considerable.[34]

We can see exactly the same forces at work early in Victoria's reign, in Macready's production of *Coriolanus*, a particularly forceful example given his concern for Shakespeare's text and his desire to avoid empty spectacle at all costs. According to a contemporary review, 'the stage becomes animated with a seemingly countless mob of barbarians ... A whole people are summoned up, and a drama instinct with their life rolls its changes o'er the scene'.[35] In Macready's theatre, as Martin Meisel points out, 'the supernumeraries were directed with as painstaking care as the principals',[36] a practice which points forward to the 'casts of thousands' made up of film extras. Finally, the continuum I am suggesting can be reinforced by a leap into the twentieth century and a completely different genre, Hardy's long dramatic poem, *The Dynasts*, an 'Epic-Drama of the War with Napoleon', published between 1904 and 1908, which Hardy himself described as having the combined effect of both the diorama and panorama.[37] Although not intended for the stage, it stands as one of a number of works with connections to a range of differing forms. In Meisel's words, 'If *The Dynasts* looks forward to *The Birth of a Nation*, it also looks back to the representations of Waterloo and other combats staged at Hardy's beloved Astley's'.[38]

When we remember that Astley's was equally beloved of Dickens, the circle I have been drawing in this chapter seems complete. Dickens's work is clearly spectacular in a number of senses, in addition to my special inflection of structural imagery. His novels are filled with extras, 'the supernumeraries ... directed with as painstaking care as the principals', and occupy the largest possible canvas in terms of setting. The extremes of poverty and wealth exist side by side and overarching this opposition is the life-and-death struggle enacted between the forces of good and evil. *Little Dorrit* is a particularly rich example with its shifting panorama of Marseilles, London, the Alps, Venice, and its suggestive division into two 'Books': 'Poverty' and 'Riches'. And, as we have seen, it has its own explicitly melodramatic figure in the villainous Blandois-Rigaud, who is self-consciously aware of his role to the extent of throwing his cloak over his shoulders and stroking his moustaches with a flourish. The novels are, as I have argued, part of a continuum of spectacle from which they draw and to which they, in turn, make a contribution. But, as with the best of Victorian stage productions – Macready's, for example – their spectacle is far from empty. At this point, we can see Dickens's unique contribution to the tradition of spectacle and melodrama. Structural imagery, as I have defined and analysed it, is an expression of thought as well as the love of making effects on a grand scale. There may be a clue here to the causes of what I see as the relative lack of success in adaptations and versions of Dickens compared with Shakespeare, but this is a topic that will have to wait until the book's final section, its 'Dream Epilogue'.

Notes

1 Title of a 1946 song by Irving Berlin.
2 Bolton, Philip, 'Dramatisations and Dramatisers of Dickens's Works', in Schlicke, Paul (ed.), *The Oxford Reader's Companion to Dickens*, Oxford: Oxford University Press, 1999, pp. 196–7.
3 Perhaps the most striking recent example is Flint, Kate, *The Victorians and the Visual Imagination*, Cambridge: Cambridge University Press, 2000.
4 Booth, Michael R., *Victorian Spectacular Theatre*, London: Routledge, 1981, p. 8.
5 I am aware, of course, of the dangers of falling into essentialism at this point. There are many kinds of cinema other than visual spectacle. On the other hand, the link between Victorian spectacular theatre and the kinds of effects on display in such works as D. W. Griffith's *Birth of a Nation* and *Intolerance* seems undeniable.
6 Booth, *Victorian Spectacular Theatre*, p. 60.
7 Kent, Charles, *Charles Dickens as a Reader*, London: Chapman & Hall, 1872, pp. 11–12.
8 House, M., Storey, G. and Tillotson, K., *et al.* (eds.), *The British Academy Pilgrim Edition of The Letters of Charles Dickens*, Vols. 1–12, Oxford: Clarendon Press, 1965–2002; 1 January 1867, Vol. 11, p. 293.
9 *Letters of Dickens*, 17 September 1867, Vol. 11, pp. 433–4.
10 *Letters of Dickens*, 13 September 1867, Vol. 11, pp. 427–8.
11 Booth, *Victorian Spectacular Theatre*, p. 64.
12 Slater, Michael (ed.), Dickens' Journalism: Sketches by Boz and other early papers 1833–39, Ch. 17, 'The Last Cab Driver, and the First Omnibus Cad', London: Phoenix, 1996, p. 144.
13 Booth, Michael, 'The Metropolis on Stage', in Dyos, H. J. and Wolff, Michael, *The Victorian City: images and realities*, Vol. 1, London: Routledge, Kegan and Paul Ltd, 1973, pp. 211–12.
14 Booth, *Victorian Spectacular Theatre*, p. 221.
15 Booth, 'The Metropolis on Stage', p. 62.
16 Doré, Gustave and Jerrold, Blanchard, *London: a pilgrimage*, New York: Dover Publications, 1872, reprinted 1970, p. 137.
17 See Smith, Grahame, 'Publishers and Serialization', Ch. 2, *Charles Dickens: a literary life*, Basingstoke: Macmillan, 1996.
18 Leavis, F. R., *The Great Tradition*, Harmondsworth: Penguin Books , 1962, p. 251.
19 Leavis, *Great Tradition*, p. 272.
20 Leavis, *Great Tradition*, p. 250.
21 *Letters of Dickens*, Vols. 1–12.
22 These ideas are explored in detail in Smith, Grahame, *Dickens, Money and Society*, Berkeley: University of California Press, 1968.
23 Vardac, Nicholas, A., *Stage to Screen: theatrical method from Garrick to Griffith*, New York: Benjamin Blom, 1968.
24 Brewster, Ben, and Jacobs, Lea, *Theatre to Cinema: stage pictorialism and the early feature film*, Oxford: Oxford University Press, 1997.
25 Vardac, *Stage to Screen*, p. xxv.
26 Vardac, *Stage to Screen*, p. xxvi.
27 Brewster and Jacobs, *Theatre to Cinema*, p. 214.

28 Brewster and Jacobs, *Theatre to Cinema*, p. 214.
29 Robinson, David, *Chaplin: his life and art*, New York: McGraw-Hill, 1989, pp. 74–5.
30 Booth, *Victorian Spectacular Theatre*, p. 72.
31 Geduld, Harry M. (ed.), *Focus on D. W. Griffith*, Englewood Cliffs, NJ: Prentice-Hall, Inc., 1971, p. 76.
32 Eisenstein, Sergei, *Film Form: essays in film theory*, ed. and trans. Jay Leyda, London: Dennis Dobson Ltd, 1977, p. 224.
33 Eisenstein, *Film Form*, p. 226.
34 Booth, 'The Metropolis on Stage', p. 224.
35 Meisel, Martin, *Realizations: narrative, pictorial, and theatrical arts in nineteenth-century England*, Princeton, NJ: Princeton University Press, 1983, p. 228.
36 Meisel, *Realizations*, p. 228.
37 Altick, Richard, *The Shows of London*, Cambridge, Mass.: Belknap Press, 1978, p. 186.
38 Meisel, *Realizations*, p. 216.

the very subject of adaptation has constituted one of the most jejune areas of scholarly writing about the cinema.[1]

This book tells a story about Dickens's relationship to cinema and, like all stories, attempts to fuse together interesting subject matter with a convincing narrative structure. Chapter 1 opens up a dream landscape in which links are made between Dickens and a form which still did not exist at his death. There follows an account of the human fascination with visuality and a descriptive analysis of the scientific devices, toys and popular entertainments which resulted from this preoccupation. Chapter 3 clears the ground theoretically for the whole enterprise, ending with the assertion that the chapters which follow constitute the heart of my claims for Dickens's relationship to film: London and Paris, the panorama and the railway, theatre and spectacle are all analysed as cultural formations which feed into his work, making specific contributions to the proto-cinematic elements in Dickens's writing which lie at the core of the book's argument. Chapter 8 will examine *Little Dorrit* as a case study of a major attempt to transform a novel into film. The final chapter will demonstrate how the conflux of forces discussed in Chapters 4–6 enters into the detail of Dickens's language, above all into the *movement* of his prose and the panoramic nature of his fictional structures. The Epilogue will re-enter the dream landscape of Chapter 1 in bringing together Dickens and his ideal filmic collaborator.

Given the nature of the story I am attempting to tell, the reader will hardly feel surprise that adaptation is not at the forefront of it; on the other hand, it would be quixotic to dismiss the issue from consideration completely. Rather than survey the huge number of films and television plays based on Dickens's work,[2] the present chapter will focus on some of the central issues in adaptation which are also relevant to my general argument, the discussion being restricted to relatively few examples. In making this attempt, and in formulating the book as a whole, I am clearly indebted to the work of some major twentieth-century thinkers. Walter Benjamin provides the essential theoretical under-pinning of the whole argument, with his concept of the epoch dreaming the period that is to follow, and he is also a constant recourse for aphorisms, insights and examples. Less in evidence, but almost as important, are Sergei Eisenstein and, for this chapter, André Bazin. Eisenstein has still not been fully assimilated into mainstream thinking or academic scholarship in literary studies, despite the major edition of his writings currently being published by the British Film Institute.[3] Within literary and specifically Dickens studies Eisenstein is mentioned, when at all, in relation to issues of filmic adaptation, but there is little recognition of the fact that his analysis of *Oliver Twist* in the seminal essay 'Dickens, Griffith and the Film Today'[4] is one of the most brilliant pieces of purely literary criticism written on that novel, although constantly inflected by his sense of the proto-filmic aspects of *Oliver Twist*, and of Dickens's work in general.

Turning to Bazin, there is a sense in which, as with Eisenstein, the sheer originality of his thought seems to have inhibited its full recognition; indeed, there was some danger of its being over-looked in recent years, even in film studies, and so a debt is owed to James Naremore for bringing it back into active circulation.[5] Bazin has the potential to be a powerfully liberating force with regard to adaptation, a field of study which is hardly one of the more bracing areas of criticism or scholarship, as the epigraph to this chapter indicates. As Naremore points out,[6] the proliferation of work in this field may have as much to do with the frequency with which film is studied in university literature departments as with the intrinsic intellectual richness of the topic itself. One of the more persuasive recent accounts is provided by Brian MacFarlane who makes a distinction between 'those elements of the original novel which are transferable because not tied to one or other semiotic system – that is, essentially, *narrative*' and those 'which involve intricate processes of adaptation because their effects are closely tied to the semiotic system in which they are manifested – that is, *enunciation*'. He goes on to explain that by 'enunciation, I mean the whole expressive apparatus that governs the pre-sentation – and reception – of the narrative'.[7] These are subtle distinctions, but they still leave us struggling with the old problem of two kinds of novelistic material that present adapters with radically different choices. The necessity of such distinctions is challenged by what might be called Bazin's inspired common sense in dissolving the differences between artistic forms. Writing as early as 1948, he claims that we are 'moving towards a reign of adaptation in which the notion of the unity of the work of art, if not the very notion of the author himself, will be destroyed. If the film that was made of Steinbeck's *Of Mice and Men* (1940; directed by Lewis Milestone) had been successful ... the (literary?) critic of the year 2050 would find not a novel out of which a play and a film had been "made," but rather a single work reflected through three art forms, an artistic pyramid with three sides, all equal in the eyes of the critic'.[8] Bazin is not merely anticipating one of the great coups of literary theory here, the death of the author, he is also proposing a way through all the endless difficulties that adaptation theory seems determined to make for itself. In doing so, he adds weight to one of my own governing ideas, that the appearance of cinema makes possible a proto-filmic reading of Dickens's novels. In Bazin's view we 'are witnessing the making of films that dare to take their inspiration from a novel-like style one might describe as ultracinematographic'.[9] Ultracinematographic is another way of expressing my point, that the advent of cinema enables us to see what is filmic in the language and structure of, say, *Our Mutual Friend*. Writing of Robert Bresson's *Diary of a Country Priest* on its appearance in 1950, Bazin suggests that the novel on which a film is based may be 'affirmed by the film and not dissolved into it. It is hardly enough to say of this work ... that it is in essence faithful to the original because ... it *is* the novel ... The aesthetic pleasure we derive from Bresson's film ... includes all that the novel has to offer plus ... its refraction in the cinema'.[10]

We cannot, unfortunately, test Bazin's statement against the existence of a film of *Our Mutual Friend* made by an artist of the stature of Bresson but, as I have argued earlier, the novel waits, shimmering with the full range of cinematic possibilities, needing only the creative engagement of a different kind of artist to make it spring into *another* form of life. I stress another because it already does exist in its fullest possible completion *as a novel*. If we cannot discover an example in Dickens, however, verification might be found in an example which appears fairly unlikely, Ian Softley's version of Henry James's *The Wings of the Dove* of 1997.[11] The novel belongs to James's late phase, one of a group of works characterised by their moral, psychological and social complexity, qualities embodied in a prose style that is remarkably complicated, filled with qualifications and ambiguities that tease the reader towards a resolution that is the reverse of a closed ending. Nothing, it seems, could be more *written*, but Softley and his adapter, Hossein Amini, continually find ways of rendering the original in filmic terms which mirror the novel's seemingly infinite gradations of sympathy, revulsion, commitment and withdrawal. Camera movement, lighting, colour and, above all, performance and setting fuse to create a *Wings of the Dove* in which the novel is not lost but is, rather, enhanced by existing in another universe than the one for which it was originally formed. In other words, for those who have read the book and seen the film, the world is a more interesting and beautiful place, one in which our minds can play over a new *Wings of the Dove* as it were, a fusion of novel and film, instead of indulging in the tiresome questions associated with adaptation: is the film true to the 'spirit' of the novel, is the novel 'better' than the film? And so on. Bazin suggests that we can put these meaningless distinctions to one side in recognising that out of the relationship of both forms a new kind of beauty is born.

Such a dissolution of the boundaries between artistic forms is for Bazin a widespread social and cultural phenomenon, one which reinforces the major concept of Benjamin's famous essay, 'The Work of Art in an Age of Mechanical Reproduction'.[12] Bazin uses photography and engraving as examples of the fact that 'the adaptation and summary of original works of art have become so customary and so frequent that it would be next to impossible to question their existence today'.[13] What Bazin's thinking provides for those who venture into the field of adaptation is freedom from the cul-de-sac of fidelity to the original, although this by no means involves the disappearance of value judgements. If film-makers have enough 'visual imagination' then 'faithfulness to a form, literary or otherwise, is illusory: what matters is the *equivalence in meaning of the forms*'.[14] With equivalence in meaning as a criterion of judgement, discriminations become possible freed from the tyranny of a fidelity which is at once mechanically reductive and frustratingly intangible. 'But is it Shakespeare?' is a cry that has rolled down the years and 'But is it Dickens?' is equally unhelpful. What, for a start, is Shakespeare, and of course Dickens, questions impossible to answer and which should not be posed in the first place. 'Is there equivalence in meaning of the forms?' is a much better question because it actually admits of some answers, as a brief examination of David Lean's celebrated film of *Great Expectations* (1946) makes clear.

In attempting to deal with this question, ideas developed in other chapters start to bear fruit, the concept of structural imagery from 'Theatre and Spectacle', for example, and the development of Eisenstein's theory of montage or parallel action presented later in the 'Panorama' section of 'Language and Form' (Chapter 9). Of course, any challenge to Lean's *Expectations* elicits surprise since it is a film that has been accorded almost unanimous praise. For the editors of *Screening the Novel*, for example, it is the only adaptation that 'is universally admitted to be a great film'.[15] And there is a great deal of evidence to support this view, from critics of all periods. For Zambrano, for example, '*Great Expectations* fulfils Edward Fischer's basic requirement for a great motion picture – the novel is presented so visually that it would remain a powerful, coherent work without the narrative, but the narrative could not successfully survive without the dramatic visual technique Dickens masters'.[16] Much more recently, Brian MacFarlane states that the film possesses 'a visual stylistic verve that may be compared to the novel's peculiar rhetorical powers'.[17] However, neither of these responses really engages with Bazin's equivalence of forms, relying rather on a somewhat generalised sense of the visual in both novel and film. It is undoubtedly this near unanimity that permits *Screening the Novel*'s editors to claim that 'wherever you look you will find this film acclaimed'.[18] Unfortunately they didn't look as far as Graham Petrie's mordantly brilliant piece, 'Dickens, Godard and the Film Today', published in 1975.[19] Petrie's essay is essential reading in this field, especially his central point that Lean separates out the realistic and poetic elements of the text, frequently dispensing with the poetic, whereas in the novel they co-exist, often simultaneously; from a Benjaminian standpoint that was touched on earlier, the novel is porous. For example, in his guise as commuter and do-it-yourself-er Wemmick is a highly realistic figure who relates directly to Dickens's understanding of important social changes in Victorian society, but his actual embodiment in the novel is full of heightened comic exaggeration, as in his Castle's state of near collapse every time the Stinger, its nightly gun, is set off. This dimension of comic fantasy is, of course, just as pregnant with meaning as the more realistic moments, showing us how precarious Wemmick's attempted retreat from the world really is. Equivalence of forms demands that both aspects of the character and his presentation be honoured, but the film falls back on caricature in an evasion of this complexity. What this amounts to is the charge that Lean and his collaborators simply do not understand the book they are attempting to adapt deeply enough, and the same point can be made in relation to my criteria of structural imagery and parallel action. By stripping the novel to the bare bones of its linear narrative the film loses almost all possibility of density of effect and thematic complexity. The removal of Dolge Orlick, to take only one omission, destroys the darker side of Pip's character which is reinforced by Orlick in his role as double. Similarly, Pip's journey to London dilutes the text's sombre resonances through its concentration on the quaintly picturesque. The obtrusive use of a post-horn just as the coach is commencing its journey strikes a reassuring note of Merrie England, which is reinforced by images of London at a complete remove from the crime-stained metropolis of Dickens's imagination. The film contains many local successes, some of which enhance one's understanding of the book, the comic contrast between the vulgarity of Pip's new clothes and the gentlemanly restraint of Herbert's attire, for example. And its opening, Pip's first encounter with Magwitch, is justly praised as one of the best in the history of cinema. On the other hand, a major thematic centre of the novel is Pip's ownership by Magwitch, not merely at the personal level but as part of Dickens's understanding of class relationships in Victorian Britain. This is a profound insight and any adaptation that fails to grasp it, or is unable to enact it filmically, is doomed to ultimate failure, however lively it may be visually.

The objection to Lean's omission of material from the novel is not an objection in principle, of course, a fact demonstrated by the more or less complete success of his *Oliver Twist* (1948), my personal candidate for the most successful film adaptation of a Dickens novel so far attempted. Its excision of the Rose Maylie aspect of the text involves no loss of equivalence of meaning between the forms. It might, indeed, be regarded as an enhancement of our total imaginative experience of the film and novel coexisting in our mental world since for many Rose represents an indulgence in escapist sentimentality on the part of a still inexperienced writer. Without it, the film achieves something of the fierce irony and savage comedy which characterise the novel's brilliant opening before it is somewhat dissipated by the uninteresting subplot involving Rose, her aunt, and her lover.

My discussion of Christine Edzard's attempt on *Little Dorrit* will point to her apparent unawareness of Eisenstein's essay, and the damaging effects of this on her film. Conversely, the dark-hued tone and stylistic brilliance of Lean's *Oliver* suggest a striking similarity between essay and film, although the date of its first appearance in English makes its impossible that Lean should have read it. Despite this, and in the spirit of Bazin's mixture of forms, it becomes possible to create a complex relationship between Dickens's novel, Eisenstein's proto-cinematic version of it, the films of D. W. Griffith, and Lean's film of *Oliver Twist!* This exercise in cross-fertilisation might begin with Eisenstein's commandeering of Chapter 21 of Dickens's text, the episode beginning 'It was a cheerless morning when they got into the street; blowing and raining hard; and the clouds looking dull and stormy' and which focuses, from a narrative point of view, on Sikes taking an unwilling Oliver on an 'expedition' to rob the Maylie country house, although much more than a plot point is achieved in the process. Eisenstein reproduces the chapter's first two pages, explaining that for 'demonstration purposes I have broken this beginning of the chapter into smaller pieces than did its author; the numbering is, of course, also mine'.[20] In the process he creates a new text, the effect of which can be indicated by a small example:

4. It was market morning.
The ground was covered, nearly ankle-deep, with filth and mire; and a thick steam, perpetually rising from the reeking bodies of the cattle, and mingling with fog,
which seemed to rest upon the chimney tops, hung heavily above ...
Countrymen,
butchers,
drovers,
hawkers,
boys,
thieves,
idlers,
and vagabonds of every low grade,
were mingled together in a dense mass.[21]

What follows is Eisenstein's evocation of the effect of the whole passage: 'This austere accumulation and quickening tempo, this gradual play of light ... this calculated transition from purely visual elements to an interweaving of them with aural elements ... these magnificently typical details, the reeking bodies of the cattle, from which the steam rises and mingles with the over-all cloud of morning fog'. Eisenstein's observations read like Chesterton (of whom he was a great admirer) at his best, a superbly impressionistic account of the passage leading to the unassailable assertion that the whole thing 'gives the fullest cinematic sensation of the panorama of a market'. The reader will need no reminding at this point that the panorama plays a special role in my argument as perhaps the major example of Victorian spectacular entertainments, one with which Dickens was deeply familiar and which feeds into his work at many levels, above all as a crucial influence in forming the vast structures of his later novels.

Eisenstein goes on to make the crucial connection between the panorama and the city in claiming that Dickens 'was the first to bring factories, machines and railways into literature'[22] and then follows up the observation with the link central to all literary criticism worthy of the name: 'But indication of this "urbanism" in Dickens may be found not only in his thematic material, but also in that head-spinning tempo of changing impressions with which Dickens sketches the city in the form of a dynamic (montage) picture'.[23] This is first-rate criticism, illuminating Dickens's prose and his wider purposes with fresh insights but, as the last words show, it is a criticism suffused with awareness of where Dickens stands in relation to film. His quotation from the novel finishes with 'the unwashed, unshaven, squalid, and dirty figures constantly running to and fro, and bursting in and out of the throng rendered it a stunning and bewildering scene, which quite confused the senses' and the question immediately following it is: 'How often have we encountered just such a structure in the work of Griffith?' A lively passage from *Nicholas Nickleby* provokes: 'Isn't this an anticipation of a "symphony of a big city"?' (A reference to *Berlin: Symphony of a Big City*, directed by Ruttmann and Freund in 1927.) A brief quotation from *Hard Times* leads to another surprising juxtaposition: 'Is this Dickens's Coketown of 1853, or King Vidor's *The Crowd* of 1928?'

Eisenstein then moves on to the analysis of an extended passage from *Oliver Twist*, the section where Oliver is entrusted with money by Mr Brownlow and falls back into the clutches of Fagin and the gang. The layout of the chapter as an example of montage, of moving between two lines of parallel action, is too long to be reproduced here, but the cinematic conclusions drawn from it must not be overlooked, as in this splendidly acute observation: 'These scenes are unrolled absolutely à la Griffith: both in their inner emotional line, as well as in the unusual sculptural relief and delineation of the characters; in the uncommon full-bloodedness of the dramatic as well as the humorous traits in them; finally, also in the typical Griffith-esque montage of parallel interlocking of all the links of the separate episodes'.[24] The well-known story of Griffith's indebtedness to Dickens is sufficiently germane to the argument of the book as a whole to demand inclusion at this point. In making the connection, Eisenstein proposes a series of steps in cultural history whose detail was teased out only later by film and theatre historians. In brief, he sees Dickens as drawing from, and contributing to, stage melodrama which, as we have seen in the previous chapter, crossed the Atlantic and 'attained on American soil by the end of the nineteenth century its most complete and exuberant ripeness'.[25] Griffith was nurtured in this artistic milieu before turning to cinema and so Dickens can be seen as a crucial factor in the moral atmosphere of his work. But at the aesthetic level the connection is even more direct, Griffith acknowledging Dickens not merely as a favourite author, but as the originator of one of his most striking cinematic techniques, parallel montage. This is the narrative device, made famous by *Intolerance*, whereby various lines of action are carried forward together, with easy transitions from one to the other despite their wide disparity in historical place and time and which Eisenstein sees as having its origins in Dickens, in the story of Oliver's recapture by Nancy, for example, which alternates with scenes in which Mr Brownlow and his friend, Grimwig, await the boy's return from his expedition to the bookseller, equipped with his new clothes, valuable books and a five pound note. The technique is clearly revealed at the end of Chapter 15 which moves from Oliver being 'dragged into a labyrinth of dark narrow courts' into 'The gas-lamps were lighted; Mrs Bedwin was waiting anxiously at the open door; the servant had run up the street twenty times to see if there were any traces of Oliver; and still the two old gentlemen sat, perseveringly, in the dark parlour, with the watch between them'.

One final example of Eisenstein's insight demands attention, his analysis of the curious little digression at the beginning of Chapter 17 of *Oliver Twist*, which states that 'in all good murderous melodramas' it is customary to 'present the tragic and the comic scenes, in as regular alternation, as the layers of red and white in a side of streaky bacon'. This custom leads to one of the best-known features of melodrama, its abrupt transitions from one emotional register to another. As the passage acknowledges, 'such changes appear absurd; but they are not so unnatural as they would seem at first sight'. The fact is that they occur just as frequently in reality itself, but in those cases we are actors in the drama of life rather than simply spectators in the theatre. In real life we 'are blind to violent transitions and abrupt impulses of passion and feeling, which, presented before the eyes of mere spectators, are at once condemned as outrageous and preposterous'. This thought-provoking observation has been understood in a number of different ways, as evidence of Dickens's theoretical understanding of melodrama and what he himself was up to in using it, for example. But what we are concerned with is Eisenstein's conclusion that: 'It is Dickens's own "treatise" on the principles of this montage construction of the story which he carries out so fascinatingly, and which passed into the style of

Griffith'.[26] And so rather in the manner of Abel Gance, in Chapter 1, forecasting that Shakespeare would make films, Dickens appears here as theorist as well as practitioner, the uncanny creator of filmic shadows waiting to be released into their celluloid form by Griffith and those who came after him.

It is time to bring Lean's *Oliver* into the equation and with it the realisation that there is not merely a more or less complete equivalence in meaning between his film and the novel, but that we seem to be looking at a film which displays an intelligent grasp of the principles set out in Eisenstein's essay. As I have already pointed out, dates of publication as well as other factors make this unlikely, although the similarities may have something to do with Lean's almost certainly having seen, and to some extent, absorbed, Eistenstein's own creative work. Be that as it may, Oliver's first entrance into London in Chapter 7 is a perfect embodiment of the 'panorama of a market' that Eisenstein sees in the novel, a masterful sequence that makes the strongest possible contrast to the bland images of the city presented in the film version of *Great Expectations*. Interestingly, Lean and his collaborators use poetic licence to take the evocation of this moment in *Oliver* from the description of dawn in the streets in Chapter 21, when Oliver is being taken by Sikes on the expedition to rob the Maylies. We see Oliver, strained and exhausted, in continual movement and part of an isolating crowd that constantly jostles him, the whole effect gaining its intensity from focusing on him in a medium–close shot so that he appears alone even though he is surrounded by the truncated figures of a mass of people. Here, as throughout the film, the use of sound is exemplary as is the invariably apt musical score. We cut to Oliver in the city on a blast of almost overwhelming noise, including the raucous uproar of a street band, the bleating of sheep heading for market, and the patter of an auctioneer spouting what sounds like gibberish. Everything contributes to Oliver's evidently growing exhaustion, the perfect preparation for the appearance of the Dodger, faultlessly got-up, at his most malign in the close-up of his appraising stare at Oliver, with the looming presence of St Paul's in the background.

The riches on display in the film are almost limitless. Comedy is never far away but is either suitably grotesque, as in the scenes between Mr Bumble and Mrs Corney, or with a hint of the sinister, even in the superbly choreographed scene of the boys playing at thieves, with Fagin as the innocent bourgeois gentleman. The latter is a moment when we see Oliver's first outburst of happy laughter, and the visual irony at work in the scene is a completely successful transposition of the book's verbal irony.

Every aspect of cinematic technique – lighting, especially the use of chiaroscuro, editing and camera movement – operates with maximum effectiveness to create a film which stands as a work of art on a par with its inspiration. Again, unlike Lean's *Great Expectations*, his *Oliver* displays a complete grasp of the city as labyrinth, reproducing its sense of mythic horror and Freudian overtones as well as the more mundane aspects of filth, drunkenness and poverty. Two sequences, both tours de force, illustrate this to perfection. After their first meeting, the Dodger hurries Oliver off to the den with breathtaking speed, around corners, through alleys and up seemingly endless flights of stairs to a dizzying conclusion, their crossing of a precarious looking bridge from the 'normal' world to that of Fagin with, as so often, St Paul's looming over their tiny figures. The spirits of Piranesi and Gustave Doré inhabit the whole sequence, with the city as a moral as well as a physical maze in which the innocent child is hustled not merely into the presence of Fagin but also into that of his own deepest fears. Just as powerful is the bravura sequence when Oliver is taken on his first criminal outing and is mistaken for the perpetrator when the efforts of the Dodger and his accomplice go awry. To cries of 'Stop thief', Oliver hares off, again into a maze of alleys, courts, flights of stairs, the whole breathless movement orchestrated through a combination of editing, tracking shots and deep focus, ending with a fade to black representing the punch he has just run into at breakneck speed. This is 'equivalence of meaning of the forms' with a vengeance because such moments do not merely effect a transposition into another medium of what the novel is about; their stylistic richness mimics one of Dickens's most striking characteristics as a novelist, his love of displaying his total command over all aspects of fictional technique.

It is tempting to run through every scene of this well-nigh perfect film, characterised as it is by compassion as well as technical virtuosity. The scene in which the baby Oliver is carried through the workhouse combines both, the infant in his swaddling clothes forming a poignant contrast to the horrors of his future 'home' which is rendered in a complex set whose visual power can only be fully appreciated in the cinema. Everything that is best in Lean's version might be summed up by the scenes leading to Oliver asking for more. 'You're to be presented to the Board' says a huge Mr Bumble to the tiny scrap and we cut to that body discussing their charges. 'This workhouse has become a regular place of entertainment for the poorer classes' is followed by a jarringly savage cut to a deafeningly loud laundry room where scrawny wretches toil desperately at backbreaking tasks, Oliver and Mr Bumble crossing it in a complex tracking shot. We cut back to the Board's discussion, followed by their information to Oliver that he is to be 'educated', by picking oakum. An imprisoning overhead shot, through the curved spikes of the workhouse gate, captures a line of children crossing the snow-covered yard on their way to virtually prison-like hard labour to the accompaniment of a sinister march tune. Again we cut, with no transition, to the surface of a cauldron of watery gruel, bowls of which the children grasp with pathetic eagerness. There follows one of the film's most striking moments, a scene that could have come out of Eisenstein's *Strike*, but which also belongs perfectly to its own time and so forms a justification for Bazin's co-existence of artistic forms. A group of workhouse children, the boys with shaven heads, all wan with hunger, gaze down through bars at their elders and betters making pigs of themselves over a grotesquely abundant meal. It goes without saying that this is a perfect embodiment of the near-starvation prevalent in Victorian workhouses, but it is also an image that echoes the concentration camps of the Second World War. Beyond all this, the moment has intimations of Goya as well as Eisenstein; in other words, it takes its place in a Western tradition of images of suffering inflicted by human cruelty. Again we cut without transition to the boys drawing lots, a moment that is only explicable in terms of what follows. Oliver is held briefly in pathetic isolation after having drawn the short straw and we cut immediately to a tracking shot down a table as the children eat their skimpy meal to the clang of cutlery on plates. Oliver is again isolated, surrounded by threatening gazes at his unwillingness to act; he embarks on his task in deep focus, a tiny figure approaching a swishing cane. Finally, he makes his request and uproar follows.

What Lean highlights for us here with such skill is the distinction between an adaptation and what might be called a version of one medium in terms of another, an additional way of making the point that the director and his collaborators understood what Dickens was up to in his novel. Their removal of the Rose Maylie episodes constitutes a triumphant justification of Bazin's sense of works of art co-existing in a world of equivalent forms in which pettifogging distinctions can be put to one side in favour of the recognition that '*Oliver Twist*' is now an amalgam of book and film in which both have contributed to our sense of the mixed final product, a conclusion that takes us on to Bazin's concept of a mixed cinema.

Bazin's thought is both challenging and helpful, never more so than in his defence of the essential impurity of art. He takes as his starting point the 'aesthetic history of influence in art in general' which 'would almost certainly reveal ... that at some stage in their evolution there has been a definite commerce between the technique of the various arts. Our prejudice about "pure art" is a critical development of relatively recent origins'.[27] One hopes that Bazin would have been gratified to discover that this is a prejudice that has weakened in recent years under what some would regard as the pressures generated by the moves into post-structuralism and the post-modern. Whatever the explanation, it is certainly not difficult to point to examples of, say, the break-down in generic classification brought about by such works as Alasdair Gray's novel *Lanark*.[28] Gray is, of course, a painter as well as a writer and his book is not so much illustrated as decorated with a constant stream of drawings, typographical games, curlicues of every possible kind. *Lanark* is clearly an art object in which the visual and the written carry more or less equal weight. Again, searching for Iain Sinclair's *Lights Out for the Territory*[29] on the shelves of a bookshop is no easy task since his text is a fantastic amalgam of travelogue, graffiti, tall tales, politics and mysticism, what he himself calls psycho-geography – not a category that one is likely to find listed in a bookshop. The sounds of everyday life taped into the music of Steve Reich, in his *Different Trains* for example, shows how widespread such developments are as does the creation of the film essay in Welles's *F for Fake* which, as early as 1973, anticipated the full panoply of post-modern effects in its self-reflexive playing with time, subjectivity and the creation of the medium itself.

Bazin stands, in fact, midway between the contemporary distrust of the purity of art forms and an earlier manifestation of particular relevance to Dickens. Despite the success of Jane Austen and Walter Scott there was still a debate in the 1830s as to the merits of the novel as a form and whether, indeed, it deserved the description of art, arguments not dissimilar to those that greeted the appearance of film, and which to some extent have still not been resolved, especially in a culture so dominated by the prestige of literature as Britain's. The problem was only exacerbated for the Victorians by Dickens's explosive success in a mode of publication, the monthly serial, which many soberly minded critics and readers regarded with suspicion. Its combination of text, illustrations and advertisements was often presented as essentially ephemeral, more of a magazine or miscellany than anything that could be described as art. Dickens succeeded in imposing himself as artist as well as entertainer on a vast public, but it is noteworthy that he never abandoned the serial as the form in which his work made its first appearance. As I have already pointed out in Chapter 1, Dickens's situation in the culture of his period was further complicated by his addiction to what he himself called working his copyright, so that at any given moment any given work might be appearing before the public in a myriad of manifestations, as a monthly or weekly serial as well as in a number of different formats, single-volume cheap editions alongside more elaborately presented de luxe ones. In addition, Dickens's work was constantly being pirated, with unauthorised texts appearing in the United States, for example. This has led to debate among scholars as to what constitutes the definitive text of any given novel, a situation not entirely dissimilar to that described by Usai in exploding the concept of an original print in cinema. Usai's working out of the complications ensuing from the distribution of two copies of a film, one for America and one for Europe, made in 1914 is too detailed to be reproduced here and so his conclusions will have to suffice: 'Take any Chaplin short, and you will soon realise that the "big bang" of the original camera negative has created a constellation of copies we will never be able to quantify'.[30]

Martin Meisel takes the argument a stage further in relation to Victorian theatre when he notes that 'drama itself was so much a serial pictorial form', one whose pictures were 'chiefly composed of a novel's illustrations "realized"', a phenomenon which reflects the 'imaginative appeal of those particular pictures ... and (more remotely) on how the whole genre of serial illustrated fiction was originally experienced'.[31] If we add to this our knowledge of some of Dickens's favourite amusements, such as Astley's, where plays were performed on horseback and famous battles were celebrated with huge casts of people and animals, we may not be quite so surprised by the extravaganzas put on by Alfred John West whose film shows were known as *Our Navy and Our Army* and 'contained a mixture of film, magic lantern slides, sound effects, musical accompaniment, narration and jingoistic songs sung with great patriotic fervour', shows which 'required up to fifty people to stage'.[32] The point to be made here is that Dickens emerged from, and contributed to, a world in which entertainments were composed of any material that came to hand and seemed relevant, exactly the world out of which film itself made its appearance. And if the visual was a dominating presence in this world, existing across a range of forms, this is equally true of narrative which, for the nineteenth century, was a part of all media, painting as much as theatre and the novel.

There is no reason to feel that Bazin would have been appalled by these populist manifestations; indeed, far from carping at the impure merging of forms, Bazin celebrates it, as we can see in his response to the filming of paintings, an activity almost guaranteed to raise purist hackles: 'Instead of complaining that the cinema cannot give us paintings as they really are, should we not rather marvel that we have at last found an open sesame for the masses to the treasures of the world of art?[33] He continues with his favourite image of a new form created out of existing ones: 'The film of a painting is an aesthetic symbiosis of screen and painting, as is the lichen of the algae and mushroom. To be annoyed by this is as ridiculous as to condemn the opera on behalf of theatre and music'.[34] Such open-mindedness to art and all its possibilities is a far cry from the attitude adopted by the writers of *Screening the Novel*, in their assertion that 'Dickens was a writer of genius and naturally his stock in trade is words. This is the first, and totally unbridgeable, gap we face when discussing Dickens and films, or Dickens and television. It helps us to account for the fact that what we get on the screen is not Dickens. It may look like Dickens and occasionally it may sound like Dickens, but it isn't really Dickens at all'.[35] This is hardly a helpful comment. If the gap between media is 'totally unbridgeable' there seems absolutely no way forward, but since adaptations, or versions, of Dickens exist and continue to be made there must be some way of talking about them sensibly. Yet again, Bazin comes to the rescue with his metaphor of adaptation as a form of translation: 'The best translation is that which demonstrates a close intimacy with the genius of both languages and, likewise, a mastery of both'.[36] As I suggested earlier, David Lean has a mastery of *Oliver Twist* which enables him to translate the language of text into the language of film with brilliant success, although he is on less sure ground with *Great Expectations.*

With characteristic daring, Bazin is not afraid to push the argument into the area of film and theatre, another field where clichés and stereotyped responses abound. Once again, his views are rooted in facts and practicalities, that filmed theatre does actually exist, whether or not it is good, bad or indifferent, as we can see in his reference to 'the practice (certain) ... the theory (possible) of successful filmed theatre'.[37] Bazin takes this further with his characteristic use of paradox; that is, paradox in the service of meaning rather than pyrotechnical display for its own sake: 'The theatre needed the cinema before it could freely express what it had to say ... The function of the cinema is to reveal, to bring to light certain details that the stage would have left untreated'[38] or, one might suggest, is incapable of showing clearly enough. An example from Baz Luhrmann's *William Shakespeare's Romeo and Juliet* (1996) comes to mind, the moment when Juliet stirs from her drug-induced simulacrum of death at the very second when Romeo, unaware of her return to life, reaches for the knife to kill himself. The film enables us to see this in agonising close-up in a way that is technically impossible in the theatre, and so provides justification for the paradox of a play needing cinema before it can freely express what it has to say.

The expressiveness of artistic forms provides a final instance of the mixed nature of literature and film, a good starting point being provided by Dickens's contemporary, George Henry Lewes, in remarking that 'Dickens once declared to me that every word said by his characters was distinctly *heard* by him'.[39] I, as well as almost every other writer on Dickens, have stressed the visual element in his work, his power of seeing and of making us see. But as Eisenstein points out in his analysis of the panorama of the market depicted in *Oliver Twist*, Dickens hears and creates in his readers the illusion of hearing just as much as he gives the illusion of sight. If, then, Dickens's novels speak as well as show, the paradoxical nature of art is furthered by cinema, the essentially visual medium, in Eisenstein's claim that 'an understanding of montage as not merely a means of producing effects, but above all ... a means of *speaking*, a means of *communicating* ideas, of communicating them by way of film language, by way of a special form of film *speech*'.[40] In other words, both forms talk to us across the range of sensuous possibilities. In the cinema we do, of course, literally see and hear; on the other hand, we cannot smell although there are time-honoured devices for making us aware of both perfumes and evil stenches. In literature, seeing and hearing, and other sense impressions, are at a remove, illusions fostered by our imaginative surrender to powerful language. In Eisenstein's terms both forms speak to us, communicating abstractions as well as concrete particularities, and the explanation is a simple one – once it is pointed out to us by Bazin, in a passage that demands repetition: 'the vast majority of the images on the screen conform to the psychology of the theatre or to the novel of classical analysis. They proceed from the common-sense supposition that a necessary and unambiguous causal relationship exists between feelings and their outward manifestations. They postulate that all is in the consciousness and that this consciousness can be known'.[41] Despite all their obvious differences, then, film and literature share an awareness of consciousness as their essential subject matter, and the technical means for conveying an illusion of consciousness to viewers and readers. It is this which makes adaptation not merely possible but desirable.

Notes

1 Naremore, James (ed.), *Film Adaptation*, London: Athlone Press, 2000, p. 1.
2 I provide a brief survey of the field in my entries on 'films and film-makers of Dickens' and 'television adaptations of Dickens' in Schlicke, Paul (ed.), *Oxford Reader's Guide to Charles Dickens*, Oxford: Oxford University Press, 1999, pp. 233–6, 548–54.
3 The major editor and translator for this collection of Eisenstein's writings is Richard Taylor; important contributions have also been made by Ian Christie. To be published by British Film Institute.
4 Eisenstein, Sergei, *Film Form: essays in film theory*, ed. and trans. Jay Leyda, London: Dennis Dobson Ltd, 1977.
5 Naremore, *Adaptation*, p. 1.
6 Naremore, *Adaptation*, p. 1.
7 MacFarlane, Brian, *Novel into Film: an introduction to the theory of adaptation*, Oxford: Clarendon Press, 1996, p. 20.
8 Bazin, André, 'Adaptation, or the Cinema as Digest', in Naremore, *Adaptation*, p. 26.
9 Bazin, André, *What is Cinema? Essays selected and translated by Hugh Gray*, Vol. 1, Berkeley, Los Angeles: University of California Press, 1967, p. 64.
10 Bazin, *What is Cinema?*, p. 143.
11 Another interesting test case is the modern-day version of *Hard Times* (*Tempos Difíceis, Este Tempo*) made by the Portuguese director, Joao Botelho in 1988, but the film is difficult to obtain and is probably unfamiliar, except by name, to many readers.
12 See Benjamin,Walter, *Illuminations*, trans. Harry Zohn and ed. Hannah Arendt, Glasgow: Fontana, 1973.
13 Naremore, *Adaptation*, p. 19.
14 Naremore, *Adaptation*, p. 20.
15 Giddings, R., Selby, K. and Wensley, C. (eds.), *Screening the Novel: the theory and practice of literary dramatization*, Basingstoke: Macmillan, 1990, p. 16.
16 Zambrano, A. L., '*Great Expectations*: Dickens and David Lean', *Literature/Film Quarterly*, Vol. II, Spring, No. 2, 1974, p. 137.
17 MacFarlane, *Novel into Film*, p. 105.
18 Giddings, *Screening the Novel*, p. 16.
19 Petrie, Graham, 'Dickens, Godard, and the Film Today', *The Yale Review*, Vol. LXIV, No. 2, 1975.
20 Eisenstein, *Film Form*, p. 214, n.
21 Eisenstein, *Film Form*, p. 215.
22 The above quotations are all taken from Eisenstein, *Film Form*, p. 216.
23 Eisenstein, *Film Form*, pp. 216–17.
24 The above quotations are all taken from Eisenstein, *Film Form*, p. 216–18.
25 Eisenstein, *Film Form*, p. 226.
26 Eisenstein, *Film Form*, p. 223.
27 Bazin, *What is Cinema?*, p. 116.
28 Alasdair Gray's novel, *Lanark: a life in four books*, is a post-modern masterpiece and was first published in Edinburgh by Canongate Publishing Ltd, 1981.
29 Sinclair Iain, *Lights Out for the Territory: 9 excursions in the secret history of London*, London: Granta Books, 1997.

30 Usai, Paolo Cherchi, *Silent Cinema: an introduction*, London: British Film Institute, 2000, p. 47.
31 Meisel, Martin, *Realizations: narrative, pictorial, and theatrical arts in nineteenth-century England*, Princeton, NJ: Princeton University Press, 1983, p. 250.
32 Herbert, Stephen, and McKernan, Luke (eds.), *Who's Who of Victorian Cinema: a worldwide survey*, London: British Film Institute, 1996, p. 150.
33 Bazin, *What is Cinema?*, p. 167.
34 Bazin, *What is Cinema?*, p. 168.
35 Giddings, *Screening the Novel*, p. 15.
36 Bazin, *What is Cinema?*, p. 117.
37 Bazin, *What is Cinema?*, p. 114.
38 Bazin, *What is Cinema?*, p. 91.
39 Lewes, George Henry, 'Dickens in Relation to Criticism', in *The Fortnightly Review*, 1 February 1872, p. 149.
40 Eisenstein, *Film Form*, p. 245.
41 Bazin, *What is Cinema?*, p. 62.

Novel into film: the case of *Little Dorrit*

8

Something Wrong Somewhere.[1]

A major cinematic adaptation of one of Dickens's greatest novels is an important enough event to demand a chapter to itself. Literary and film theory, the sociology of artistic production, and the current role of the media in Britain are all brought together in the appearance of Christine Edzard's six-hour version of *Little Dorrit*, filmed in 1987 and divided into two parts: 'Nobody's Fault' and 'Little Dorrit's Story'. We have already seen that the adaptation of Dickens's work into any medium should have long ceased to be a matter of surprise; from almost its first appearance his work was taken over into myriad forms. The immense popular success of *Pickwick* led to instant commercial exploitation in the form of Boz cabs, Weller corduroys, and Pickwick cigars, and the novels were endlessly pirated for the stage, frequently as they were appearing in their serial parts, an impertinence for which their perpetrators were punished by having to work out for themselves how, say, *Nicholas Nickleby* was going to end. As we have seen, such invasions of his creative privacy did occasionally drive Dickens to frenzies of irritation,[2] but his general attitude might best be described as benign indifference. If nothing else, they testified to the breadth of his popular appeal and might well lead customers ignorant of the original to want to read, and therefore perhaps purchase, Dickens's books for themselves.

This stress on the economic makes a satisfying link from Dickens to the commercial and industrial base of feature film-making, an emphasis which the sociology of literary production has helped to make more acceptable than to earlier generations of readers and perhaps even viewers. The origins of cinema as a mass popular entertainment led to its rejection, especially in British culture, on grounds more rooted in the ideology of class than in an objective assessment of the limitations inseparable from the creation of a new medium of communication.[3] This response was then complicated, for those who succumbed to filmic pleasure, into a rejection of the commercial vulgarities of Hollywood in favour of the supposedly untainted purity of European art cinema. But such dichotomies are somewhat unreal, both in their unawareness of the possibility of art being produced from within the studio system (John Ford comes to mind)[4] and their ignorance of the commercial underpinning of all feature film production. *Little Dorrit*, for example, cost some five million pounds to make, a small amount by the standards of commercial blockbusters and yet on a totally different scale from the costs involved in the production of any other art form apart from architecture. But the provision of even this relatively modest sum was full of commercial ironies of a kind that Dickens would have understood. It was only with great difficulty that backing was obtained from the Screen Entertainment division of Thorn EMI, a gesture made to convince the nervous parent company that the division was busily engaged in the kinds of activity which it was supposed to be pursuing.[5]

Commercial considerations of this kind were, of course, commonplace for Dickens as a glance at his relations with his publishers makes clear.[6] One example concerns the genesis of *Hard Times*, a novel explicitly undertaken for financial reasons, to bolster the falling sales of *Household Words*.[7] That the result was a Dickensian masterpiece of a rather special kind reveals both Dickens's response to the technical challenge of weekly serialisation and the degree to which his imagination could be fired at this stage in his career, even when the initiating stimulus was the external one of promptings from publishers and his own keen awareness of the economic worth of his periodical. This unforced acceptance of his role in the marketplace makes Dickens particularly useful in unravelling yet further the complex knot of responses to film in British culture, especially in its relation to literature.[8] To only a slightly lesser degree than Shakespeare, Dickens exists as a 'great' writer, a national (and even international) icon, and a popular genius, a combination of qualities that make him peculiarly difficult to pigeonhole. Dickens is now safely established as a canonical writer, taught in university courses via texts which contain the full paraphanelia of introductions, notes and so on. But we have seen that in his own day Dickens's method of publication caused him to be looked at askance by some as a parvenu, just as Forster, and others, attempted to dissuade him from the public readings undertaken for money on the grounds that they were an ungentlemanly activity.

Of course, Dickens's popularity triumphed in the end and, aided by the novels' appearance in a conventional format, he came to be regarded as a 'classic'. In this role, his works served a double function in relation to film. As part of the corpus of 'great' literature they could be used as a stick with which to beat the upstart inferior, cinema. But at the same time, and from a very early stage in the silent period, they could be manipulated to confer a status on film which it could not then claim for itself, one which allowed the audience 'to enjoy basking in a certain pre-established presence and to call up new or especially powerful aspects of a cherished work'.[9] The issue at stake here is obviously adaptation, a topic which was dealt with in the previous chapter, from which it is clear that like James Naremore[10] I find the socio-logical implications of the subject more interesting than its theoretical aspects. As a practical necessity, feature film-making has been from its earliest days dependent on adaptation: the novel, drama, poetry, biography and autobiography, and journalism have all provided raw material for the cinema. But this provision for an apparently insatiable maw has consistently been accom-panied by that supposed enhancement to which I have just referred. Viewers of a certain generation will be familiar with the Hollywood convention of a film's opening on a shot of a Folio Society-like volume whose pages are turned, reverently, while its perfectly visible words are frequently intoned by a voice-over. The whole process was clearly calculated to create what the producers of the day might have called 'a touch of class', a 'product' which, in a time-honoured maxim, 'looks like art and smells like money'. The Hollywood of the 'movie brats'[11] and independent production has become too self-conscious for such quaint devices, but the baton has been passed to what can fairly be regarded as one of the major television genres, the classic serial. The meaning for Britain's national life of the seemingly inexhaustible popularity of such adaptations, from Jane Austen's Miss Bates to Agatha Christie's Miss Marple, is a fascinating field of speculation, although too far from my topic to be examined in detail.

Orson Welles is, of course, an adaptor of genius, a translator from one medium to another, a maker of versions, and his views on adaptation are, like those of Bazin, a kind of sublime common sense. Despite his life-long veneration for Shakespeare – or perhaps because of it – Welles sees the plays as existing in the public domain. And with a characteristic touch of false modesty, he remarks that if Verdi can make operas out of Shakespeare he sees no reason why he shouldn't make films out of them. The key to this approach is its conviction that the end-product is a reading of the original rather than an adaptation in the strict sense. This contrast between versions and adaptations is the distinction on which much New Wave critical writing turned in the period of journalistic turmoil that led up to the invasion of French cinema by Truffaut, Godard, Rohmer, and the rest. In 'Une certaine tendance du cinéma francais' Truffaut enunciated what he saw as a crucial conflict between the '*Tradition de la Qualité*' and a '*cinéma d'auteurs*'.[12] Truffaut rejects the films of directors such as Delannoy, Allegret, and Autant-Lara and, above all, the adaptations of distinguished novels by the screen-writing team of Aurenche and Bost. What he objects to is the domination of their work by psychological realism and the fact that their screenplays are finished products which require only to be visualised by a *metteur en scène*. The *metteur* is ideally suited to this task as he has 'no truly personal style'[13] while the cinematic *auteur* cannot refrain from injecting elements of his own personality into a work, frequently at the actual moment of shooting in the studio or on location. Exactly the same points are made by Grigori Kosintsev, working within an entirely different cinematic tradition, in his notable book *The Space of Tragedy: the diary of a film director*, a sustained meditation on his transference of *King Lear* to the screen:

The best part of Orson Welles's films seemed to me those which had no mention in the play: Iago in the iron cage hoisted up in the air ... the coffin of enormous proportions which is dragged along the ramparts [in *Chimes at Midnight*] ... If the poetic structure of the words in a particular place remains intangible and this place has to be 'set up for the cinema' ... I feel that it is awkward and unnecessary to turn the play into a film script. But when you discover, in the very poetry, seedlings of what can be developed into dynamic visual reality, the whole business begins to have a point and one's work succeeds.[14]

A powerful example of this process in Kosintsev's *Lear* occurs when the play's animal imagery is transmuted into the 'dynamic visual reality' of Lear striding imperiously towards the camera, as it tracks backwards, pointing out the animals, excited horses and fearsome dogs, that he is selecting for his entourage after his first dismissal by Goneril. Kurosawa also makes brilliant use of horses in his rendering of *Macbeth, Throne of Blood*, especially in the extraordinary sequence in which Macbeth and Banquo are lost in a mist on horseback where the visceral energy of their charging horses acts as a perfect metaphor for their mental states.

To refer to the work of Kosintsev, Kurosawa and Welles as versions, rather than adaptations, is more than verbal juggling because, as Dudley Andrew has shown, the concepts of connotation and semiotics can form a theoretical bridge between the novel and film. Drawing on the thinking of Keith Cohen and Christian Metz, Andrew suggests that 'despite their very different material character, despite even the different ways we process them at the primary level, verbal and cinematic signs share a common fate: that of being condemned to connotation. This is especially true in their fictional use where every signifier identifies a signified but also elicits a chain reaction of other relations which permits the elaboration of the fictional world'. And so, for example, 'imagery functions equivalently in films and novels',[15] as in the examples I have just given. This is particularly relevant in the area of narrative which is itself a semiotic system available to both literature and cinema. The semiotic systems specific to novel and film, rooted in the verbal and visual, may be radically dissimilar, but this is no bar to the achievement of Bazin's equivalence in the meaning of forms between them. And Cohen suggests a stage beyond narrative in arguing that 'both words and images are sets of signs that belong to systems and that, at a certain level of abstraction, these systems bear resemblances to one another',[16] a proposition that I shall try to validate later in analysis of the stylistic features of Edzard's film of *Little Dorrit*.

To write interestingly about both literature and film is not the easiest of tasks but Graham Petrie's essay 'Dickens, Godard and the Film Today', to which I have already referred,[17] inspires confidence because of his inwardness with both forms. The distinction he draws between Dickens and George Eliot, for example, is clearly that of a literary critic of real discrimination: 'While ... George Eliot can enable us to respond to the everyday world more comprehensively, generously, and intelligently, a novelist like Dickens transforms our perception of the normal world, makes us see and understand it from a radically different angle'.[18] And he commands total assent in a convincing account of the strengths of Godard's *Weekend* in relation to Antonioni's *Zabriskie Point*. Both end in apocalyptic destruction, but Petrie demonstrates the lack of any organic relationship between the conclusion of Antonioni's film and what has gone before, whereas *Weekend* is rooted in an everyday world which has a mythic dimension so that its final upheavals achieve a force similar to the collapse of the Clennam house in *Little Dorrit*. I have already pointed to Petrie's convincing rejection of David Lean's *Great Expectations*, a critique rooted in Lean's failure to grasp the crucial element of simultaneity in Dickens's writing: '[It] results from the way in which his characters come to us surrounded by the associations of imagery, the rhythm and pattern of words, and the wild flights of language that have been built up around them, so that they seem to belong to the worlds of social and psychological reality, dream, myth, and fairy tale, all together. Their actions assimilate them to the world of objects and yet prove their essential humanity'.[19] This observation contrasts interestingly with Lean's assertion that *Great Expectations* is solely a fairy tale, a reduction of the novel's complexity which seems to foredoom his adaptation to some degree of failure.[20]

It is not, of course, sensible to expect film-makers to be literary critics in the professional sense but Neil Sinyard, another perceptive commentator on these matters, is surely right in asserting that the adaptation of a novel into film is essentially 'an activity of literary criticism'.[21] The same point is made by Dudley Andrew, perhaps a shade more acceptably, in arguing for adaptation as a form of the hermeneutic circle in which 'a leap and a process' can only be accomplished 'in response to a general understanding' of the work to be adapted.[22] And so, however much one is willing to trust the film rather than the film-maker, there is no denying the dismay aroused by Edzard's description of her intentions: 'What we wanted to do was to make Dickens come across as real, as a journalist's piece ... Incoherence is unreal. What makes a thing real is making it believable and making it coherent'.[23] That there is a journalistic element in Dickens's work is incontestable – as in the Victorian critic Bagehot's description of him as a 'special correspondent for posterity'[24] – but this is separating out and discarding, in the Lean manner, with a vengeance since one of Dickens's major strengths as a writer is a kind of controlled incoherence, a refusal to render the fictional world into neat and tidy patterns, creating instead a structure that admits mystery, confusion, uncertainty.

Despite the co-operative nature of film, one must assume that as writer–director Edzard had a fair amount of authorial control over her project, a freedom reinforced by the fact that the production company, Sands Films, is her own and the producer her husband. A year was spent in casting the film and great attention was given to the costumes which were handsewn by studio staff. Such attention to detail suggests that the larger creative choices were carefully considered and these might best be organised under the headings of style and narrative. By style I mean the totality of devices used to bring to the screen what we see and hear in the cinema. The question of narrative clearly involves practical issues as well as more purely artistic choices. With a novel as long as *Little Dorrit* something has to be omitted, although ideally such omissions should be governed by some general principles rather than simply the exigencies of length. Edzard may well have been influenced by the two-part, six-hour structure of Bertolucci's *Novecento* (1976); in any event, the novel itself is divided into two books, 'Poverty', and 'Riches'. Edzard ignores this obvious thematic opposition in favour of 'Nobody's Fault' and 'Little Dorrit's Story', and it is here that the first of many problems presents itself. Part Two is not without its successes and it does represent a contemporary response to aspects of the novel that are perhaps buried or, even, invisible to Dickens himself in attempting something of a feminist reading of the text. It foregrounds Little Dorrit's love (desire is perhaps not too strong) for Clennam, especially in a striking moment when we see her seated, partially undressed, before a candle-lit mirror, clearly intent on maximising her attractiveness before her final appeal to Clennam in the Marshalsea. Again, the film legitimately fills in something of the human value of the father–daughter relationship by breaking in on them laughing together over an amusing incident of daily life which remains unexplained. But the pivotal device of repeating moments from Part One as they are seen from Little Dorrit's perspective, interesting in itself, becomes wearisome through repetition and is a crucial factor in preventing the film from covering more of the novel's territory. This is simply too high a price to pay for an emphasis on Little Dorrit which is not daring enough to be truly revisionist. An otherwise physically miscast Derek Jacobi, as Clennam, does have the advantage of looking faintly like the film's Mr Dorrit. But this aspect of Little Dorrit's feeling for him remains unexplored despite being hinted at in the final scene in the Marshalsea where she bustles round an enfeebled Clennam sitting in her father's old chair. A truly feminist confrontation with the text would have demanded the inclusion of the probably lesbian Miss Wade, her relationship with Tattycoram, and the critique of femininity suggested by their contrast to Pet Meagles and Little Dorrit.

If Part Two has its strengths, Part One is, however, a severe disappointment, totally lacking in narrative complexity, and concentrating in a linear fashion on Clennam's pursuit of the mystery of his father's dying injunction, his own attack on the Circumlocution Office, and the revelation of the Dorrit inheritance. Most puzzling of all is the omission of Merdle – especially given the fact that Part One is 'Nobody's Fault' – although his name is mentioned from time to time and he is glimpsed briefly in the street. The implications of this missed opportunity are manifold. Some play is made with Casby, and the assault on him by Pancks comes towards the end of Part One; but the absence of Merdle nullifies the Patriarch's representative force and leaves Mr Dorrit's dependence on hand-outs as an isolated, personal phenomenon. Indeed, the whole tract-for-the-times aspect of the venture, the attack on yuppies and stock-exchange manipulation, goes for nothing without Merdle. And although he appears to some extent in Part Two, this is too late for a presence whose activities circulate through the 'blood of the book'[25] as much as those of any other character.

What is perhaps most disturbing in all this is an apparently wilful disregard of the insights contained in Eisenstein's 'Dickens, Griffiths and the Film Today', discussed in detail in the previous chapter. It is hard to believe that anyone venturing on a project such as Edzard's would not have read this seminal piece, above all its analysis of parallel montage which Eisenstein says he undertook 'for the use of future film-exponents',[26] but her film shows no evidence of it and suffers disastrously as a consequence. It goes without saying that both formally and in its content *Little Dorrit* lends itself to multiple montage, but the film's essentially linear progression misses almost all of the opportunities the text presents to the creative film-maker. The problems of adapting Dickens in this way would have been acute, no doubt, but when we grasp what an immense amount of time six hours is in cinematic terms, the possibilities of a rich alternation from the Marshalsea Prison to the Circumlocution Office, from Bleeding Heart Yard to the Merdle mansion, from Meagles to Casby, and so on, become evident and perfectly realisable in film terms.

I commented in the previous chapter on Eisenstein's analysis of the market as a panorama in *Oliver Twist* and a sense of panorama is what Edzard's film singularly lacks, whether in its presentation of the life of the streets or in the social, political, and economic diversity that are of the essence of Dickens's fiction. An external constraint here may have been financial limitations on production values, although I have already pointed out that five million pounds in 1987 was not a minuscule sum. It seems clear that choices were made to expend resources on the cast and on costumes, but this cannot excuse the threadbare nature of much of the rest of the film's *mise en scène*. A central weakness here is the embarrassing attempt to imply the labyrinthine complexity of the city, central to Dickens's vision, through the use of back-cloths, matching shots, and process work. The objection is not to the use of such devices in themselves. For many, cinema is at its most successful as a 'ribbon of dreams', a 'magic world'[27] in which a whole range of technical devices can transform and enhance reality. But the context in which they are used is all-important. In the baroque world of *Citizen Kane*, for example, process work of outrageous artificiality is not in the least jarring, and the transition from mundane reality to the heightened world of Fagin in Lean's *Oliver* is effected by a bridge hovering over a seemingly bottomless space against a backdrop of an obviously artificial St Paul's. It is, however, much harder to accommodate this level of artifice given the flatly realistic surface of Edzard's film. The visual extravagance of Welles and Lean is a way of conveying meaning – that Kane is a megalomaniac, for example, and Fagin a monster – but it is impossible to integrate such artifice successfully within the journalistic realism that is Edzard's guiding principle.

Even more important, such devices must be achieved with a modicum of technical expertise; their use here is nothing less than a catalogue of disasters. The film contains no location shooting, the Dickens world having been created entirely within the studio, a situation which might have led to greater success in matching studio sets and process work. In fact, in the film's street scenes joins are clearly discernible, a weakness exacerbated in the night scenes by hopelessly ill-controlled lighting. When Clennam follows Little Dorrit and Maggie into a supposedly darkened London in Part One, for example, the levels of lighting are so uneven as to destroy any credible illusion of that sinister mystery of midnight streets so central to Dickens's vision. A similar failure is evident in the studio-confected 'countryside' which stands in for the Meagles garden, the rural approaches to their house, and the country inn where Little Dorrit as a child enjoys a treat with Bob the turnkey. Perhaps the clearest example of this lack of mastery of the medium is the repeated shot, always from the same angle, of Little Dorrit's refuge, the iron bridge. The bridge itself is so evidently a tiny structure that it is impossible to move the camera for fear of revealing its edges, and the painted backcloth of the London skyline beyond is more on the level of a puppet show than a medium which has subtle resources of technical illusion at its command. (Those who have seen Bill Forsyth's *Housekeeping* of 1987 might be interested to know that the railway bridge so crucial to that film's success was a small, purpose-built replica handled in such a way as to give it an awe-inspiring sense of size and perspective.)[28] This failure relates to a pervasive stylistic weakness which is illuminated by Graham Petrie's comment: 'In Dickens what matters is less the substance of the material than the vision that permeates it. To isolate a series of spectacular events and vivid characterisations without, in film terms, finding some equivalent to the way in which Dickens's use of language makes words and gestures and notions reverberate and take on multiple associations in our minds is to impoverish the books utterly'.[29] This focuses attention on some of the most crucial creative choices involved in film-making, the essential mode in which the visual world is transmitted to us. The aural world counts for little, unfortunately, apart from the intelligent choice of Verdi for the musical soundtrack, although even here the appropriately melodramatic musical overtones are contradicted by the flatly realistic visual surface. And the non-vocal, non-musical soundtrack is an assortment of often undifferentiated noises which contribute little to the film's atmosphere. One feature of the work's visual quality is its total lack of depth which can be accounted for in a number of ways, lighting being a key example. The cinematographer and, perhaps, the director opt for lighting which is flat and even which brings nothing into predominance within individual scenes. The resulting flatness of surface relates directly to Petrie's 'vision that permeates' the Dickens novel, for which chiaroscuro would seem to be essential. The novel's dualism operates at every level: the division into 'Poverty' and 'Riches', the opposition between Little Dorrit and Blandois (omitted from the film), even the detail on the novel's first page of the 'foul water within the harbour' and 'the beautiful sea without' which never mix. The play of light and shadow in subtle lighting could embody these contrasts moment by moment while also reinforcing the opposition of good and evil at the core of the novel's moral scheme.

Depth is also denied by the use of a totally static camera and a lens which permits only the recording of an endlessly two-dimensional surface. Edzard's use of the camera is, in fact, one of the most puzzling features of the whole film. It remains in a fixed position throughout, framing the action in a persistent medium shot that becomes almost unbearably monotonous, varied only by modest panning and tilting movements through its axis and a very occasional close-up. The constraints of space in a small studio, partly financial, may have inhibited the use of a crane, but it seems inconceivable that the camera is never allowed to track. When Clennam carries the fainting Little Dorrit from the Marshalsea in Part Two, the use of a hand-held camera and rapid cutting creates a dizzying sense of the moment's disturbance, but this is almost the only vividly cinematic episode in six hours. Apart from this, the editing is in the classic Hollywood style whose invisibility does nothing to embody the richness of the medium which is conveying this particular message. There is, of course, no justification for the camera moving restlessly for its own sake as the, in its own way, equally monotonous prowling of Olivier's *Hamlet* (1948) makes clear, and there is a classic precedent for a fixed camera position in the films of Ozu (*Tokyo Story*, 1953, for example). Indeed, it seems at first that Edzard's static framing might be justified as an embodiment of the imprisoning world of *Little Dorrit*. But the effect is deadening at such length, and leaves out all those aspects of the novel's vision that could have been encompasssed in a camera tracking inquisitively forward, or distancingly backwards, in swooping over a dark labyrinth of city streets and descending to a quick confrontation with one of the myriad characters or settings that make the book so vividly alive. Again, the choice of lens is a crucial factor in the mediating process between the object photographed and its impinging on the human eye as a moving image. Modern film-makers are in the happy position of being able to draw on a wide choice, each with its own expressive possibilities. Within mainstream cinema, Nicholas Roeg (a former cinematographer) is a striking example of a director who exploits the full range of possibilities within a single film. Alternatively, in Peter Weir's *Witness* (1985) the zoom lens is employed consistently, although not excessively, to create a sense of inexorable power, of fate moving to a chilling conclusion. What Dickens's novel seem to demand at this level of cinematic realisation is the wide-angle lens, both of whose properties are peculiarly suited to the rendering of his vision in another medium. As is well known, this lens creates a sense of deep space in which all objects are in focus and permits therefore a complex choreographing of figures within a richly detailed physical setting, a striking contrast to the flatly realised surface of Edzard's film. It also introduces an element of distortion into its recording of figures and objects, and the wider the angle the more extreme this distortion becomes. The wide-angle lens thus becomes the perfect instrument for the poetic or symbolic heightening of reality, for caricature, for the 'excesses' of satirical indignation. And so Edzard's negative choices reinforce, at the level of practice, the theoretical validity of the claim that cinematographic versions of great works of literature do not have to involve gross distortions of the original. In the case of Dickens, the elements of *mise en scène*, camera movement and framing, editing, choice of lens, and so on, could all be deployed to create a visual realisation of works across time and the media.

If Edzard has failed so signally this is not because the task is fit only for genius. Neil Jordan's *Mona Lisa* (1986), for example, was strikingly successful in creating a hellish image of modern London, a surreal world of degradation and cruelty. And within the limits of its technical and financial resources BBC television's 1985 adaptation of *Bleak House* embodied a vision of the city which was modestly faithful to the novel's labyrinthine gloom. As I pointed out earlier, Edzard's film is not without its successes, especially in some of its splendid performances. Derek Jacobi is acutely sensitive within the limits of physical miscasting, a weakness which detracts from Joan Greenwood's Mrs Clennam. Greenwood is a highly connotative actor, especially vocally, and the unavoidable resonance of seductive beauty in her physical presence, even as an old woman, is totally at odds with the character's repressed denial of sensuality. Max Wall's fusion of caricature and menace is perfectly judged and Alex Guinness is particularly successful in Part Two in conveying Mr Dorrit's complex degeneration, one of the triumphs of Dickens's art in implying inner turmoil by way of external detail. And it is hard to see how Eleonor Bron's languid eye to the main chance as Mrs Merdle could have been bettered. However, there is one performance that must be seen as outstanding in its complete inwardness with the novel, that of Miriam Margolyes as Flora Finching. Her moment of triumph occurs in Part Two, the whirlwind account to Little Dorrit – between bites of a sandwich, pouring cups of tea, and manic sweeps around the room – of her early life in Book the First, Chapter 24: "'... ere we had yet fully detected the housemaid in selling the feathers out of the spare bed Gout flying upwards soared with Mr F. to another sphere'". For a moment the film itself soars into life as a perfect embodiment of the novel's spirit and vision, the actor's uncontrollable body language an exact reinforcement of her ability to free Dickens's language into surreal flight. Significantly, it is by far the funniest moment in the entire six hours.

Edzard's attempt can be put in perspective by comparison to a masterpiece of British cinema, Bill Douglas's *Comrades* (1986), an evocation of the Tolpuddle Martyrs' story with evident contemporary overtones. At a stroke, Douglas cuts through the debilitating dangers of the British obsession with the past embodied in a highly coloured realism and 'great' performances. The audience is denied the dubious satisfaction of picking out a knight or a dame by a magnificent cast of largely unknown faces. Clothes look shabbily lived in and the actors are actually unwashed (close-ups reveal the dirt under their fingernails). Faces are pinched, famished, common, but can be lit into a sometimes transcendent beauty, a transcendence quite missing in Edzard's film from the spiritually motivated Little Dorrit. In addition, *Comrades'* vein of realism is fused with a magical reliance on all the resources of cinema so that, for example, moments of unusual joy in the daily round are cinematically heightened. And the transportation of the martyrs to Australia is handled through a defiantly non-realistic, and highly amusing, use of drawings purporting to be maps. Above all, the medium itself is brought into question, and thus its supposed truthfulness, by a constant reference to early forms of visual entertainment (peep-shows, the travelling lanternist, and so on) and Brechtian reminders that this vision of the Tolpuddle martyrs is mediated by the very form in which it is communicated to us.

In contrast, Edzard opts for the invisibility of classic Hollywood cinema, most fictional television and certain forms of 'serious' film-making, especially in the field of richly costumed historical reconstruction. As in *Out of Africa* (1985) and *A Room With a View* (1985) the screen is a window on a supposedly real world which can be thought of as either invisible or swung open to reveal, say, Florence in the early 1900s. Given the resources of modern cinema the experience is, of course, fascinating. We are taken out of ourselves and identify with the Streeps and Redfords. But the negative arguments are too familiar to need pursuing in detail. Despite their high entertainment value, the ultimate result of such films is consolation and complacency, a view of the world conveyed by a 'classic' work of literature whose power to disturb is nullified by the smoothing out of all contradictions. This is particularly distressing in the case of Dickens because, despite his responsible concern to entertain a huge public, his work is continuously dangerous in its social and personal implications, and in its form. Aesthetically, Dickens's work is the reverse of the art that modestly conceals itself. There can hardly be a more virtuoso display of writing than the opening of *Little Dorrit* itself, and Dickens dares to leave readers to work out the relevance of the opening chapters to what follows. The novel begins in Marseilles, in a literal prison, and then moves to a group of travellers in the metaphorical prison of quarantine. We as readers are given an interpretative role in seeing how this opening relates to what comes after, just as we are not *told* about the fore-shadowing of Little Dorrit's goodness in the prison turnkey's little daughter who appears so briefly in the first chapter. Formally, Dickens's novels are opaque, drawing self-reflexive attention to themselves as created works of fiction. A filmic embodiment which ignores this is false to Dickens's vision and spirit in a fundamentally disqualifying way.

A great opportunity, and responsibility, has then been missed. The stage version of *Nicholas Nickleby* made Dickens live again in a form entirely appropriate to the novel. Television itself has done great work in making Dickens a vital part of contemporary culture. But the scale and resources of modern cinema seem made for a creatively sympathetic assault on Dickens's greatest novels. Christine Edzard's attempt will have to remain as a monument to How Not To Do It.[30]

Notes

1 This is the title of Chapter 5, Book the Second, of Dickens's *Little Dorrit.*
2 See Ch. 1.
3 In recommending D. H. Lawrence as a contributor to *Close Up 1927– 1933: cinema and modernism* (Donald, J., Friedberg, A. and Marcus, L. (eds.), London: Cassell, 1998), Dorothy Richardson remarked 'You know Lawrence loathes films? *Foams* about them. I'm sure he'd foam for you', (p. 150). The response of British literary intellectuals to film is a fascinating topic in its own right, one that continues to weaken the possibilities of an active film culture in the United Kingdom.
4 A 'Dickensian' example of artistic greatness and popular appeal in Ford's work is his Western, 'The Searchers' (1956).
5 Useful information on the film's production can be found in Phelps, Guy, 'Victorian Values', *Sight & Sound,* 57, London: British Film Institute, Spring, 1988.
6 See Patten, Robert L., *Charles Dickens and his Publishers,* Oxford: Oxford University Press, 1978.
7 See the Introduction to Dickens, Charles, *Hard Times,* ed. Grahame Smith, London: Everyman, 1994.
8 See Mulhern, Francis, *The Moment of 'Scrutiny',* London: New Left Books, 1979, pp. 51–2.
9 Andrew, Dudley, *Concepts in Film Theory,* Oxford: Oxford University Press, 1984, p. 98.
10 Naremore, James (ed.), Introduction, *Film Adaptation,* London: Athlone Press, 2000.
11 The phrase has been used to describe film-makers such as Steven Spielberg and Martin Scorsese who grew up with cinema as part of their formative experience.
12 Extracts from Caughie, John (ed.), *Theories of Authorship: a reader,* London: Routledge & Kegan Paul in association with British Film Institute, 1981, p. 39.
13 The phrase is Bazin's in Caughie, *Theories,* p. 23.
14 Kosintsev, Grigori, *The Space of Tragedy: the diary of a film director,* London: Heinemann, 1977, pp. 53–4.
15 Andrew, *Concepts in Film Theory,* p. 103.
16 Andrew, *Concepts in Film Theory,* p. 102.
17 See Ch. 7.
18 Petrie, Graham, 'Dickens, Godard and the Film Today', *The Yale Review,* Vol. LXIV, No. 2, 1975, p. 197.
19 Petrie, 'Dickens, Godard and the Film Today', pp. 198–9.
20 Zambrano, A. L., 'Dickens's Style in Terms of Film', *Hartford Studies in Literature,* Vol. IV, No. 2, 1972, pp. 103–4.
21 Sinyard, Neil, *Filming Literature: the art of screen adaptation,* London: Croom Helm, 1986, p. 117.

22 Andrew, *Concepts in Film Theory*, p. 97.

23 Phelps, 'Victorian Values', p. 110.

24 Collins, Philip (ed.), *Dickens: the critical heritage*, London: Routledge, 1971, p. 394.

25 Dickens used the phrase regarding Miss Wade to John Forster. See House, M., Storey, G. and Tillotson, K., *et al.* (eds.), *The British Academy Pilgrim Edition of The Letters of Charles Dickens*, Vols. 1–12, Oxford: Clarendon Press, 1965–2002; ? 9 February 1857, Vol. 8, p. 280.

26 Eisenstein, Sergei, *Film Form: essays in film theory*, ed. and trans. Jay Leyda, London: Dennis Dobson Ltd, 1977, p. 213.

27 According to Welles, 'A film is a ribbon of dreams', in Cowie, Peter, *The Cinema of Orson Welles*, London, The Tantivy Press, 1973, title page. One of the best studies of a director to have appeared so far is Naremore, James, *The Magic World of Orson Welles*, New York: Oxford University Press, 1978.

28 Information conveyed by Bill Forsyth, the director of *Housekeeping* (1987), after a presentation of his film at the MacRobert Arts Centre, University of Stirling.

29 Petrie, 'Dickens, Godard and the Film Today', p. 198.

30 This summarises the incompetence of the Circumlocution Office, the heart of Dickens's satire of Victorian bureaucracy in Chapter 10 of *Little Dorrit*, 'Containing the whole Science of Government'.

9

Language and form

Great literature is simply language charged with meaning to the utmost possible degree.[1]

This book has pursued the dreamlike connections between Dickens and film in a whole number of ways, through discussions of the city and technology, stage spectacle, the impurity of art, and consciousness. The final, most difficult, and yet most necessary, link has to be at the level of language and fictional form. Passages have been examined, from Chapter 1 onwards, in the attempt to locate the dream landscape in the reality of the textual, but this is the moment to attempt something larger and more all-embracing by taking further a point made earlier about the double nature of *Our Mutual Friend* as both a completely self-contained, and great, work of fiction and a shadowy double of its other, film. Such a recognition is, of course, entirely dependent on a surrender to the possibilities this book has tried to open up and make plausible. The reward for those willing to enter the dream may be an enhanced understanding of the general cultural field within which novel and film co-exist as well of the penumbra that might be said to flicker around *Our Mutual Friend* if my argument is accepted.

'Writing in movement'[2]

We sometimes seem to take for granted an incomparable descriptive power in Dickens, possibly because of the difficulty of giving any adequate explanation of marvels such as the following, from *Bleak House*:

Mr Chadband is a large yellow man, with a fat smile, and a general appearance of having a good deal of train oil in his system ... Mr Chadband moves softly and cumbrously, not unlike a bear who has been taught to walk upright. He is very much embarrassed about the arms, as if they were inconvenient to him, and he wanted to grovel; is very much in a perspiration about the head; and never speaks without first putting up his great hand, as delivering a token to his hearers that he is going to edify them. (Ch. 19)

If we look closely at passages like these we are bound to register that, linguistically, they are poetic in their nature. The unpunctuated smoothness of 'a large yellow man' and its unctuous relation to a 'fat smile' and the horror of train oil in the system fuse into a perfect comic unity. His greasy plumpness is reinforced by the fact that he 'moves softly' and this is brilliantly embodied in the sound of 'cumbrously', which avoids the relative harshness of the more usual 'encumbered'. Mr Chadband as an embarrassed bear conjures the image of his arms waving fatuously about his head, a perfect represenation of the fact that his gestures are as meaningless as his words. The raising of his hand is a 'token' of edification, but Mr Chadband's entire life is a matter of tokens or signs rather than reality; one feels the force of the colloquial 'token gesture' behind this. Dickens's ability to create a totally convincing fictional reality out of the accretion of a series of finely judged details in the swift introductory sketching of a minor character is just as evident in more extended passages; for example, Nemo's room just after his death:

The air of the room is almost bad enough to have extinguished it [Mr Tulkinghorn's candle], if he had not. It is a small room, nearly black with soot, and grease, and dirt. In the rusty skeleton of a grate, pinched at the middle as if Poverty had gripped it, a red coke fire burns low. In the corner by the chimney, stand a deal table and a broken desk: a wilderness marked with a rain of ink. In another corner, a ragged old portmanteau on one of the two chairs, serves for cabinet or wardrobe; no larger one is needed, for it collapses like the cheeks of a starved man. The floor is bare; except that one old mat, trodden to shreds of rope-yarn, lies perishing upon the hearth. No curtain veils the darkness of the night, but the discoloured shutters are drawn together; and through the two gaunt holes pierced in them, famine might be staring in – the Banshee of the man upon the bed. (Ch. 10)

Dickens's art is imbued with intensity here, both as a preparation for what is to be found on the bed and as a context within which to place the life that is now over. The unpleasant mention of bad air and dirt leads to the 'skeleton' which foreshadows Nemo's eventual dissolution and the fire which has burnt low as his life has dwindled. It is part of the core of mystery in *Bleak House* that we should know almost nothing of Nemo (whose name means 'no one'). We piece together a little from what is said of him by Jo and George Rouncewell (his former lover, Lady Dedlock, says nothing) and the third-person narrator permits us only the most oblique of views. Our truest sense of Nemo's life is, in fact, conveyed by this passage. In the 'wilderness marked with a rain of ink' we see the only remains of the endless hours spent copying those documents which are so much the life-blood, or death-blood, of the Court of Chancery. The dreadful privation of his existence is objectified in the collapsed portmanteau 'like the cheeks of a starved man' and the gaunt eyeholes of the shutters through which famine might be 'staring' in, the spirit of death that has come to announce Nemo's solitary end.

It is hardly necessary to stress the extent to which this writing is dramatic as well as visual, dramatic in the sense of actualising characters and situations through a constant reference to objects and gestures, a striking anticipation of Pudovkin's claim that 'the playing of an actor which is connected with an object and is built around it ... is always one of the strongest methods of cinematic construction'.[3] This is also one of the strongest methods of characterisation in Dickens. His characters are embedded in their contexts of clothing, food, physical gestures, objects, and seem almost to exist more through their direct imprint on the physical world than through speech. A notable example is provided by Phil Squod, the passionately devoted employee of George Rouncewell in *Bleak House* whose whole life is committed to the Shooting Gallery through which George ekes out a meagre living. Phil's dialogue is touching as well as lively, especially when he recounts how some of his physical disabilities resulted from the 'larking' of his mates in a steelworks. But it is his 'mark' that really distinguishes him as a little fragment of individualised human life:

As Phil moves about to execute this order, it appears that he is lame, though able to move very quickly. On the speckled side of his face he has no eyebrow, and on the other side he has a bushy black one, which want of uniformity gives him a very singular and rather sinister appearance. Everything seems to have happened to his hands that could possibly take place, consistently with the retention of all the fingers; for they are notched, and seamed, and crumpled all over. He appears to be very strong, and lifts heavy benches about as if he had no idea what weight was. He has a curious way of limping round the gallery with his shoulder against the wall, and tacking off at objects he wants to lay hold of, instead of going straight to them, which has left a smear all round the four walls, conventionally called 'Phil's Mark'. (Ch. 21)

Dickens takes continual delight in manipulating commonplace expressions for his own purposes and the suggestion of making one's mark lurks behind this passage. Phil's mark is no metaphor, however, but an actual 'smear' which forms the ultimate affirmation of his place in the world. This is about as limited a mode of being as could be imagined and yet it is redeemed by the love that he and George so obviously feel for one another.

It seems clear from his letters that Dickens possessed a hallucinatory power of observation in his response to the world around him, but this quality is equally at work in the actualisation of what he had presumably seen in his mind's eye. This grasp of two realities, the inner and outer, and the ability to objectify them in language and form connects with yet another aspect of cinema, what Benjamin refers to as 'unconscious optics': 'The act of reaching for a lighter or a spoon is familiar routine, yet we hardly know what really goes on between hand and metal ... The camera introduces us to unconscious optics as does psychoanalysis to unconscious impulses'.[4] But Dickens seems to anticipate such a filling in of the gaps in normal observation in even tiny details. His novels are full of whistles, winks, nods, gestures with the hands, odd walks, all the paraphernalia of living at the most minute level, and it is not uncommon for these minutiae to carry the weight of insights akin to those of psychoanalysis for, as Ned Lukacher states, 'In the culture of psychoanalysis, Dickens has always been the figure of both its prehistory and its future'.[5] Those who doubt such claims might wish to consider the talking cure effected in the conversation in *A Tale of Two Cities* between Mr Lorry and Dr Manette concerning the latter's regression to the shoe-making he practised in the Bastille, occasioned by his daughter's marriage to a member of the family responsible for his incarceration.[6] More directly relevant to the argument I am pursuing at this point is the weight of significance that coheres around the detailed description of how Mr Lorry and Miss Pross destroy the tools of the doctor's prison trade after he has left home to join his daughter and Charles Darnay on their honeymoon:

On the night of the day on which he left the house, Mr Lorry went into his room with a chopper, saw, chisel, and hammer, attended by Miss Pross carrying a light. There, with closed doors, and in a mysterious and guilty manner, Mr Lorry hacked the shoemaker's bench to pieces, while Miss Pross held the candle as if she were assisting in a murder – for which, indeed, in her grimness, she was no unsuitable figure. The burning of the body (previously reduced to pieces convenient for the purpose) was commenced without delay in the kitchen fire; and the tools, shoes, and leather, were buried in the garden. (Book the Second, Ch. 19)

This episode, described entirely in terms of physical detail – hacking, burning, burying – is nonetheless imbued with the presence of Dr Manette's inner world, the realm into which he slips unconsciously whenever the pressures of his mundane existence become intolerable. Indeed, as the passage so suggestively indicates, Lorry and Miss Pross *are* engaged in a benign kind of murder in which the doubled other of Dr Manette's existence, his retreat into shoe-making during his incarceration in the Bastille and his later return to this form of activity under stress, is taken to pieces and buried. Cinematic foreshadowing is again evident in the hypnotic visual power of the writing combined with its seemingly effortless access to a life below the surface made possible by the imaginative precision of the objects and actions that make up that surface.

Bleak House, specifically in its opening lines, reveals another aspect of the dual effect in Dickens's writing, this time his tendency towards what might be called the urban sublime: 'Smoke lowering down from chimney-pots, making a soft black drizzle with flakes of soot in it as big as full-grown snowflakes – gone into mourning, one might imagine, for the death of the sun' (Ch. 1). The sense of cosmic disaster in the 'death of the sun' initiates the sombre mood characteristic of many aspects of the novel, with 'flakes of soot ... as big as full-grown snowflakes' suggesting an inversion of the natural order which anticipates the unnaturalness of much of its world. The darkness and unnaturalness of this opening, albeit expressed by a typical energy of image and style, provide an opportunity to move to a wider perspective on how language works in the book. Again, a kind of shadowing comes into play at this point because if Dickens (fore)shadows cinema, *Bleak House* is doubled in another, more commonsensical manner, in being saturated in references to Shakespeare, specifically *Macbeth*. In this way, the novel might be seen as an example of Benjamin's monad, in holding past, present and future together in a complex balancing act.[7] References to *Macbeth* abound in *Bleak House*. They include direct quotation, 'For myself, my children', said Mr Turveydrop, 'I am falling into the sear and yellow leaf' (Ch. 23), and 'equitably waltzing ourselves off to dusty death' (Ch. 8). But there are also echoes of the play in 'Or unless she fancies it 's blood ... She'd as soon walk through that as anything else' (Ch. 18), and 'very red blood of the superior quality, like inferior blood unlawfully shed, *will* cry aloud, and *will* be heard' (Ch. 28). Finally, there is sometimes nothing more than a general tonal resemblance: 'it is the subtle poison of such abuses to breed such diseases. His blood is infected, and objects lose their natural aspects in his sight' (Ch. 33). Dickens's use of Shakespeare in this way clearly illustrates the kind of relationship that can exist between major artists. The creative vitality of Dickens's imagination in *Bleak House* expresses itself in a fertility that draws sustenance from a wide range of sources and it seems only appropriate that one of the most important should be a play of Shakespeare's which even within his canon displays an outstanding degree of linguistic virtuosity. The quality in *Macbeth* that I think must have struck Dickens's imagination can be seen in the speech beginning, 'If it were done when 'tis done, then 'twere well/It were done quickly'[8] whose enigmatic complexity is embodied in the puns and word-play of its opening. The similarity to *Bleak House* is surely evident in a line such as 'running their goat-hair and horse-hair warded heads against walls of words' (Ch. 1).

What conclusions can we draw from this? I would argue that Shakespeare's play provided both a sanction and an inspiration to Dickens to give full rein to his verbal exuberance, a linguistic complexity which expresses itself insistently in visual terms. For example, the passage just quoted is an abstract condemnation of the law, but one that reduces its practitioners to the level of animals fatuously butting at something they cannot even dent.

It would be foolish, however, to ignore resemblances between these two works on a level other than the purely verbal. There is an important similarity of mood and atmosphere between them, the most obvious being their pervasive quality of darkness. Both works are saturated in a sense of night and the unnatural deeds that may occur then. One thinks of Lady Dedlock's visit, conducted by Jo, to the rat-infested grave of Nemo, but perhaps the best extended example is the vigil of Guppy and Tony Weevle in Nemo's room as they wait for their midnight assignation with Krook. This whole chapter, 32, is a fine example of Dickens's very special combination of comedy and horror. It begins with the kind of *Macbeth*-like appropriateness we have come to expect:

It is night in Lincoln's Inn – perplexed and troublous valley of the shadow of the law, where suitors generally find but little day ... The bell that rings at nine o'clock, has ceased its doleful clangour about nothing ... and the night-porter, a solemn warder with a mighty power of sleep, keeps guard in his lodge ... Mrs Piper and Mrs Perkins ... have something to say ... of the Harmonic Meeting at the Sol's Arms; where ... Little Swills, after keeping the lovers of harmony in a roar like a very Yorick, may now be heard taking the gruff line in a concerted piece.

There is of course a great deal to notice here at the linguistic level: the reference to the valley of the shadow of death, an echo of 'the death of the sun' (Ch. 1), in the suitors generally finding little day; the clear link with *Macbeth* through the bell and the night-porter; and yet another reference to Shakespeare in Yorick, our only acquaintance with whom is through his skull in the grave-diggers' scene in *Hamlet*. It is interesting to observe that the unnatural horrors of *Bleak House*, expressed often in cosmic terms, have a strongly social dimension: 'It is a close night, though the damp cold is searching too; and there is a laggard mist a little way up in the air. It is a fine steaming night to turn the slaughter houses, the unwholesome trades, the sewerage, bad water, and burial grounds to account, and give the Registrar of Deaths some extra business'. The chapter's almost overwhelming sense of nightmare begins with a question from the inoffensive Mr Snagsby: '"Don't you observe ... Mr Weevle, that you're – not to put too fine a point upon it – that you're rather greasy here, sir?"' And this is confirmed by the unusual behaviour of the candle in Nemo's room, which is a 'heavily burning taper ... with a great cabbage head and a long winding-sheet'. The mood is skilfully lightened by some passages between Guppy and Weevle on the subject of love: '"You, Tony, possess in yourself all that is calculated to charm the eye, and allure the taste, It is not – happily for you, perhaps, and I may wish that I could say the same – it is not your character to hover around one flower. The ole garden is open to you, and your airy pinions carry you through it"'. But this is only a prelude to the final disintegration of Krook whose spontaneous combustion announces itself by spreading throughout the house, in the same way as the diseases engendered by poverty spread throughout the entire novel:

'What in the Devil's name ... is this! Look at my fingers!'
A thick, yellow liquor defiles them, which is offensive to the touch and sight, and more offensive to the smell. A stagnant, sickening oil, with some natural repulsion in it that makes them both shudder ... look here – and look here! When he brings the candle, here, from the corner of the window-sill, it slowly drips, and creeps away down the bricks; here, lies in a little thick nauseous pool.

I have already pointed out the dramatic quality at work in this chapter, which we can now notice operates in the popular as well as the technical sense of the word. The creation of atmosphere through richly suggestive language, the development of tension made possible by the careful use of comedy, the connections from the vividness of the scene itself to the work's wider concerns, all of this is very close to Shakespeare's characteristic way of working.

But the link to Shakespeare is also relevant to Dickens's position as both a popular novelist and a great creative genius. Without any condescension or writing down, which he consistently deplored, Dickens can appeal to different levels in his audience by the inclusion of material that can enhance the understanding for those who notice, but will do nothing to destroy the pleasure for those who do not. Passages such as those I have quoted surely suggest the unique richness of Dickens's writing and will, perhaps, convince or remind the reader that there is nothing in the work of his contemporaries at all akin to Dickens's mixture of social realism and the uncanny; the comic and the horrific; his rendering of character in terms of objects, gesture and body language; his ability to animate the world of things so that they move, breathe, take on a life almost more intense than the beings who inhabit it; dialogue which is suffused with verbal tics, redolent of the streets, as far from the everyday in its moments of exaltation as in its cries of despair. In other words, if Dickens holds a mirror up to nature, it is a highly distorted one; his is a realism heightened by poetic and symbolic exaggeration. To find anything like this in the European novel, we shall have to wait for Dostoevsky, an admitted disciple, and even later, Joyce.

This is an ideal moment to remember that earlier chapters of my book have suggested that the sources of Dickens's uniquely rendered verbal universe lie in the city. The pulse that beats through his language is the roar of crowded thoroughfares, of street lights shimmering on wet pavements, of fogs that render the external world invisible, obscene contrasts of unparalled luxury and degradation, raucous delight in theatre and circus, the isolation of lonely individuals slipping unobserved through the press of an indifferent humanity. It is part of Dickens's greatness that he is capable of other effects, moments of charm and delicacy, for example, but the surge of verbal energy I am trying to indentify here is a dominant one. It is this that makes *Bleak House* – indeed, Dickens's writing as a whole – Janus-faced. In relation to the past, the novel encompasses *Macbeth* and assimilates it for its own purposes, while at the same time gazing into an unknowable future with a prescience that is uncanny if we are willing to read with a sense of what comes after.

What I am seeking to isolate as a key mode of communication between novel and reader is the continued *process* of Dickens's language, a moment at which the problem of quotation presents itself in an acute form. The point at issue can only be made, however, by way of a lengthy passage, and I have chosen some paragraphs which constitute a *tour de force* of Dickens's Janus-like stylistic complexity, the conclusion of Chapter 11 of *Bleak House*, focusing on the death of Nemo. The reader is, of course, invited to contemplate this passage in cinematic terms:

Thus, gradually the Sol's Arms melts into the shadowy night, and then flares out of it strong in gas. The Harmonic Meeting hour arriving, the gentleman of professional celebrity takes the chair; is faced (redfaced) by Little Swills; their friends rally round them, and support first-rate talent. In the zenith of the evening, Little Swills says, Gentlemen, if you'll permit me, I'll attempt a short description of a scene of real life that came off here to-day. Is much applauded and encouraged; goes out of the room as Swills; comes in as the Coroner (not the least in the world like him); describes the Inquest, with recreative intervals of piano-forte accompaniment to the refrain – With his (the Coroner's) tippy tol lo doll, tippy tol li doll, Dee!

The jingling piano at last is silent, and the Harmonic friends rally round their pillows. Then there is rest around the lonely figure, now laid in its last earthly habitation; and it is watched by the gaunt eyes in the shutters through some quiet hours of night. If this forlorn man could have been prophetically seen lying here, by the mother at whose breast he nestled, a little child, with eyes upraised to her loving face, and soft hand scarcely knowing how to close upon the neck to which it crept, what an impossibility the vision would have seemed! O, if, in brighter days, the now extinguished fire within him ever burned for one woman who held him in her heart, where is she, while these ashes are above the ground!

It is anything but a night of rest at Mr Snagsby's, in Cook's Court; where Guster murders sleep, by going, as Mr Snagsby himself allows – not to put too fine a point upon it – out of one fit into twenty. The occasion of this seizure is, that Guster has a tender heart, and a susceptible something that possibly might have been imagination, but for Tooting and her patron saint. Be it what it may, now, it was so direfully impressed at tea-time by Mr Snagsby's account of the inquiry at which he had assisted, that at supper-time she projected herself into the kitchen, preceded by a flying Dutch-cheese, and fell into a fit of unusual duration: which she only came out of to go into another; and another, and so on through a chain of fits, with short intervals between, of which she has pathetically availed herself by consuming them in entreaties to Mrs Snagsby not to give her warning 'when she quite comes to;' and also in appeals to the whole establishment to lay her down on the stones, and go to bed. Hence, Mr Snagsby, at last hearing the cock at the little dairy in Cursitor Street go into that disinterested ecstasy of his on the subject of daylight, says, drawing a long breath, though the most patient of men, 'I thought you was dead, I am sure!'

What question this enthusiastic fowl supposes he settles when he strains himself to such an extent, or why he should thus crow (so men crow on various triumphant public occasions, however) about what cannot be of any moment to him, is his affair. It is enough that daylight comes, morning comes, noon comes.

Then the active and intelligent, who has got into the morning papers as such, comes with his pauper company to Mr Krook's, and bears off the body of our dear brother here departed, to a hemmed-in churchyard, pestiferous and obscene, whence malignant diseases are communicated to the bodies of our dear brothers and sisters who have not departed; while our dear brothers and sisters who hang about official backstairs – would to Heaven they *had* departed! – are very complacent and agreeable. Into a beastly scrap of ground which a Turk would reject as a savage abomination, and a Caffre would shudder at, they bring our dear brother here departed, to receive Christian burial.

With houses looking on, on every side, save where a reeking little tunnel of a court gives access to the iron gate – with every villainy of life in action close on death, and every poisonous element of death in action close on life – here, they lower our dear brother down a foot or two: here, sow him in corruption, to be raised in corruption: an avenging ghost at many a sick-bedside: a shameful testimony to future ages, how civilization and barbarism walked this boastful island together.

Come night, come darkness, for you cannot come too soon or stay too long, by such a place as this! Come, straggling lights into the windows of the ugly houses; and you who do iniquity therein, do it at least with this dread scene shut out! Come, flame of gas, burning so sullenly above the iron gate, on which the poisoned air deposits its witch-ointment slimy to the touch! It is well that you should call to every passer-by, 'Look here!'

With the night, comes a slouching figure through the tunnel-court, to the outside of the iron gate. It holds the gate with its hands, and looks in between the bars; stands looking in, for a little while.

It then, with an old broom it carries, softly sweeps the step, and makes the archway clean. It does so, very busily and trimly; looks in again, a little while; and so departs.

Jo, is it thou? Well, well! Though a rejected witness, who 'can't exactly say' what will be done to him in greater hands than men's, thou art not quite in outer darkness. There is something like a distant ray of light in thy muttered reason for this:

'He wos wery good to me, he wos!'

'Shadowy night' is once more the setting of an important moment in the novel and we notice the poetic exactness with which the Sol 'melts' into it and then 'flares' out with a sense of garish and unnatural vigour, a movement emphasised by the placing of 'strong' rather than the conventional 'flares out strongly'. Typically, the normality of day passes into illumination by gas-light and not the normality of moon and stars. The highly compressed quality of the novel's language which I have pointed out as being similar to *Macbeth* ('walls of words' and 'If it were done, when 'tis done') recurs at 'is faced (red-faced) by Little Swills' and there is an amusing integration into the narrative of the Sol's publicity for its nightly entertainment which, like so much else in the novel, is far from the truth. The friends may at least rally round, but there is precious little evidence of 'first-rate talent' as these scenes amply make clear. Just as the characters of *Bleak House* are so often different from how they appear or wish to appear – Mr Chadband for example – so Little Swills's attempt to become like someone else is a complete failure: 'not the least in the world like him'. The gibberish of his song's refrain is only an extreme form of the meaninglessness of so much of the language uttered in the novel, the jargon of lawyers, for example. The limitations of this little segment of human life are placed, without contempt or patronage, by the modulation into another tone in the next paragraph; enjoyment there may be at the Sol, but its music is 'jingling' and not the harmony we would naturally associate with meetings held under the auspices of the sun (the joviality of this Sol is invariably associated with night, and by day it shines with a distinctly bleary eye). The transition into serious- ness is achieved by one of those effects in Dickens that seem to defy analysis and are the cause of extraordinary delight: 'the Harmonic friends rally round their pillows'. One's response has something to do, I think, with the humorous compassion of this, the pathetic pleasures and vanities of the evening recalled by the repetition of the phrase 'rally round' for the activity of sleep. The next few lines require a delicate adjustment of our critical responses. It would be easy to dismiss them as sentimental, but the commonplace is a great and universal one as all parents know. The thought of what the tiny speck of life may become, the thought that the complex and corrupt adult *was* once a tiny speck of life, is a source of endless fascination. This is also the moment at which the novel's strong current of erotic feeling surfaces in one of its rare examples of explicitness. The passion is unmistak- able in 'if ... the now extinguished fire within him ever burned for one woman who held him in her heart' and in her arms as we, of course, are privileged to know.

The tone changes as Guster, like Macbeth, 'murders sleep', but there is an interval of farce as we are made to visualise Guster projecting herself into the kitchen 'preceded by a flying Dutch cheese'. The inversion of normality which Cook's Court shares with so much of *Bleak House* is lightly touched on through the wit of the cock's 'disinterested ecstasy' in crowing, disinterested because he spends his life in a cellar and never sees the sunrise, supposing it were visible in such an unlikely locality. A link is suggested between the 'enthusiastic fowl' and the world of public affairs and this flicker of satire suddenly modulates into a solemnity that conveys the inevitable movement forward of human life: 'It is enough that daylight comes, morning comes, noon comes'. The horrors of the grave-yard are embodied with a sensuous precision of language and exactness of detail – 'pestiferous and obscene ... a reeking little tunnel of a court ... they lower our dear brother down a foot or two ... sow him in corruption, to be raised in corruption' – that takes them above the level of a local abuse to a universal example of what man is capable of doing to man: 'a shameful testimony to future ages, how civilization and barbarism walked this boastful island together'. For a moment we inhabit a nightmare almost as dark as that of *Macbeth* itself and so 'Come night, come darkness' reminds us of 'Come, seeling night'.[9] Gaslight reappears, this time 'sullenly', and the 'poisoned ... witch-ointment slimy to the touch' seems to foreshadow the nauseating stuff attendant on the dissolution of Krook. We see Jo for a moment as the world sees him, as 'it' rather than an individual human being, but this is corrected by an amazing mixture of elevation, 'thou art', and intimacy, 'Well, well!'. This conclusion's power to move stems partly from its willingness to allow Jo's humble words to bear the weight of moral statement: 'He wos wery good to me, he wos!'

Such passages as these, *Bleak House* as a whole, and Dickens's work in general seem to cry out for actualisation in *mise en scène* not, as I have said before, to remedy any lack – there is none to be remedied in this way – but, rather, to render explicit the shadowy promise implied in their complex interweaving of sound, image, gesture, atmosphere, dialogue, movement. The novels of Dickens's English contemporaries – George Eliot, Thackeray, Trollope, the Brontës – have been adapted to sometimes notable effect for film and television, but this has been in response to commercial pressures of programme filling rather than the aesthetic demands of the essential, if shadowy, imperative at work in Dickens's fiction. In short, *Bleak House* demands *in its nature* to be visualised; *Vanity Fair*, say, does not. Moments in the passage quoted that seem already to exist in quasi-cinematic terms come instantly to mind: the pathos and comedy of the entertainment on offer at the 'Sol's Arms' followed by the image of the actors in the little scene asleep; Guster being precipitated through a door, preceded by a cheese; a cock crowing in a cellar completely excluded from light; the nightmare of Nemo's grave. More subtly cinematic, however, than these moments of evidently visual power is what I have referred to as the element of process in Dickens's writing, the continuously unfolding movement of his prose which can be analysed in the terms of literary criticism, but which is at least as convincingly understandable in the ways in which his language seems to track, dissolve, pan, cut – in short, to anticipate those qualities which are so characteristic of film's continuous movement through time. Noël Burch points to an interesting difference in how film pioneers named their apparatus: Edison and Dickson called their projector the Vitascope – that is, 'the vision of life' – while for Lumière it was the Cinématographe, 'writing in movement'.[10] Dickens's work encompasses both, although this section has concentrated on the second.

If, then, film can be seen to have a ghostly existence in the detail of Dickens's prose, the role of the next section will be to demonstrate how this operates at the level of form and structure on a larger scale.

The novel as panorama

If any character in literature lives a life of quiet desperation it is Mrs Plornish, the careworn companion of an impoverished working man, in Dickens's *Little Dorrit*. Against all the odds Mrs Plornish attempts to respond positively to life, giving weekly succour to her workhouse-bound father, Mr Nandy, and taking the best care she can of her children. She also enjoys the dubious advantage of having been 'established in the small grocery and general trade in a snug little shop' purchased for her when the Dorrit family came into their fortune. Being situated 'at the crack end of the Yard' (Bleeding Heart Yard, that is) makes, as she says herself, '"an excellent connection"'; in fact, the '"only thing that stands in its way ... is the Credit"'. Mrs Plornish's sliver of capitalist enterprise is, then, aligned with the monstrous activities of the great financier, Mr Merdle, because 'if the Bleeding Hearts had but paid, the undertaking would have been a complete success; whereas, by reason of their exclusively confining themselves to owing, the profits actually realised had not yet begun to appear in the books'. In the face of all these difficulties Mrs Plornish clearly needs some comfort, and solace is provided by her Happy Cottage:

Mrs Plornish's shop-parlour had been decorated under her own eye, and presented, on the side towards the shop, a little fiction in which Mrs Plornish unspeakably rejoiced. This poetical heightening of the parlour consisted in the wall being painted to represent the exterior of a thatched cottage; the artist having introduced (in as effective a manner as he found compatible with their highly disproportionate dimensions) the real door and window. The modest sunflower and hollyhock were depicted as flourishing with great luxuriance on this rustic dwelling, while a quantity of dense smoke issuing from the chimney indicated good cheer within, and also, perhaps, that it had not been lately swept. A faithful dog was represented as flying at the legs of the friendly visitor, from the threshold; and a circular pigeon-house, enveloped in a cloud of pigeons, arose from behind the garden-paling. On the door (when it was shut), appeared the semblance of a brass plate, presenting the inscription, Happy Cottage, T. and M. Plornish; the partnership expressing man and wife. No Poetry and no Art ever charmed the imagination more than the union of the two in this counterfeit cottage charmed Mrs Plornish. It was nothing to her that Plornish had a habit of leaning against it as he smoked his pipe after work, when his hat blotted out the pigeon-house and all the pigeons, when his back swallowed up the dwelling, when his hands in his pockets uprooted the blooming garden and laid waste the adjacent country. To Mrs Plornish, it was still a most beautiful cottage, a most wonderful deception; and it made no difference that Mr Plornish's eye was some inches above the level of the gable bedroom in the thatch. To come out into the shop after it was shut, and hear her father sing a song inside this cottage, was a perfect Pastoral to Mrs Plornish, the Golden Age revived. (Book the Second, Ch. 13)

Charm and profundity are so perfectly poised here that they tempt analysis to extend beyond the boundaries of what is strictly relevant to the matter in hand. A passage from Benjamin, referring to the reign of Louis Philippe, does however point in a direction germane to the discussion: 'For the private individual, the place of dwelling is for the first time opposed to the place of work. The former constitutes itself as the interior. Its complement is the office. The private individual, who in the office has to deal with reality, needs the domestic interior to sustain him in his illusions'.[11] Of course, for Mrs Plornish work and home are the same place, but the point holds. When her days of trying endlessly to convert the Bleeding Hearts' credit into cash are over, she finds refreshment and pleasure in her deceptive fiction in ways that may recall the delights of picture-going for the poor and dispossessed, a social reality embodied with delicate humour in Woody Allen's *The Purple Rose of Cairo* (1985).

Yet more to the point, Dickens's Happy Cottage may well have found its formal inspiration in panorama painting, stage sets or some other nineteenth-century visual entertainment. And Mrs Plornish's pleasure in its deceptiveness harks back to the *trompe-l'oeil* aspects of panoramas discussed in Chapter 2. It is clear that she enjoys, not the rendering of reality provided by art, but its imitation which, despite its defects of scale, is for her the thing itself, such is the power of her longing for something other than the sordid urban world in which she spends her days. Humdrum as it may seem, the effect of Happy Cottage on Mrs Plornish may be likened to the more elaborately magical experience described in another passage from Benjamin:

The innermost glowing cells of the city of light, the old dioramas, nested in the arcades, one of which today still bears the name Passage des Panoramas. It was, in the first moment, as though you had entered an aquarium. Along the wall of the great darkened hall, broken at intervals by narrow joints, it stretched like a ribbon of illuminated water behind glass. The play of colours among deep-sea fauna cannot be more fiery. But what came to light here were open-air, atmospheric wonders. Seraglios were mirrored on moonlit waters; bright nights in deserted parks loomed large. In the moonlight you could recognise the château of Saint-Leu, where the last Condé was found hanged in a window. A light was still burning in the window of the château... It was an ingenious experiment on the moonstruck magic night of Romanticism, and its noble substance emerged from the trial victorious.[12]

Bringing Mrs Plornish's homely pleasures into contact with Benjamin's ecstatic vision may seem like comparing a day out to Margate with a weekend in Marrakech; Benjamin's picture of the wonders of old Paris is suffused with hints of orientalism and the *ancien régime*. But if Benjamin entrances *us*, Mrs Plornish is equally enchanted, transported on the magic carpet of Dickens's, and her own, imagination. We can find in Happy Cottage, then, justification for Martin Meisel's claim that 'panorama and diorama modes affect the style, the form, and the scope of Dickens's fiction'. He goes on to say that no 'novel of Dickens can be said to be built on a literal imitation of dioramic or panoramic form'[13] which is, of course, true although it is hard to imagine what such a literal imitation in the form of a literary text might be.

I am in danger here of entering territory already explored, the one-to-one equation of the novel with the camera, for example. Nonetheless, panoramic elements are everywhere present in Dickens's work, an area where Benjamin is yet again indispensably useful in his discussion of the 'feuilleton', a journalistic form which, making its appearance in the Paris of the 1830s, consists of 'individual sketches, whose anecdotal form corresponds to the panorama's plastically arranged foreground, and whose informational base corresponds to their painted background. This literature is also socially panoramic'.[14] His somewhat cryptic utterance is is filled out by another scholar who describes the feuilleton as 'collections of descriptive sketches of contemporary Parisian life and habits'. She then goes on to reinforce a fairly widely accepted claim that panoramic literature 'is but one short-lived genre of the everyday produced during the July Monarchy';[15] that is, in the Paris of the 1830s. But the fact that the form is not restricted to a single historical period in the political life of France, above all Paris, is proved by the material collected by Dickens for his first major publication, *The Sketches by Boz*, the First Series of which appeared in 1836, followed rapidly by the Second Series in two volumes. The *Sketches* collected, in addition to some new work, essays and stories which had appeared in newspapers and magazines between 1833 and 1836. They were recognised, when they appeared in book form, as something new in English literature although their reputation, if not their success, was eclipsed by the triumphant arrival in 1836 of Dickens's first novel, *Pickwick Papers*, which swept all before it. Dickens scholars have tended to place this material in a tradition inaugurated by some of his favourite writers, the eighteenth-century essayists associated with the *Spectator* magazine and, above all, Charles Lamb whose work belongs to the period of Dickens's youth. These writers may have provided an initial inspiration to a hard-pressed young journalist seeking to make his mark in the world, but there is evidence that contemporaries were struck by the freshness of the sketches, the sense that they held a mirror up to a world which readers recognised although they had not had the wit or vision to formulate such impressions for themselves. The material which makes up *Sketches by Boz* can be classified in a number of ways, but the pieces usually arranged under the heading of 'Scenes' are instantly recognisable as a form of panoramic literature, as a selection of their titles reveals: 'The Streets – Morning', 'The Streets – Night', 'Hackney Coach Stands', 'The River', 'Gin Shops', 'A Visit to Newgate' and so on. In other words, the feuilleton was not confined solely to Paris and so its emergence in the work of an unknown young writer suggests that it was prompted by the pressure of a set of widespread social forces. The most significant of these forces was the transformation of the city into metropolis, a process in which London clearly took the lead in terms of size and economic importance, a reason perhaps why the form was not short-lived for Dickens but one to which he returned throughout his career. Indeed, the urban sketches collected as *The Uncommercial Traveller* in 1860, and subsequent editions, contain some of his greatest writing. Taken as a whole, *Sketches by Boz* might be regarded as a panoramic exploration of London life and its characters, focusing on the class territory which Dickens made peculiarly his own, that hard-to-define area between the upper-working and lower-middle classes. But individual sketches have their own panoramic quality, a point that can be demonstrated by a brief analysis of a representative example.

'The Streets – Morning' was first published in the *Evening*

Chronicle on 21 July 1835, appearing later in the Second Series of *Sketches by Boz.*[16] It opens with an evocation of 'the streets of London an hour before sunrise' with their 'air of cold, solitary desolation' in places which one would expect 'to see thronged at other times by a busy, eager crowd' (p. 49). As so often in these pieces and the early fiction, such as *Oliver Twist*, Dickens – or his narrator – takes on the role of explorer, presenting to his readers incidents and settings which most of them may have experienced only rarely for themselves, such as being up and about in London before dawn. In doing so, he identifies a key moment in the urban panorama, the brief interval between the disappearance of the 'drunken, the dissipated, and the wretched' and the appearance of 'the more sober and orderly part of the population', a moment when 'the stillness of death is over the streets' (p. 49). Almost nothing is to be seen except an 'occasional policeman' (p. 49), and 'a rakish-looking cat' running 'stealthily across the road' (p. 51). The imaginary cat is brought to life in a way that anticipates key features of the language analysed in this chapter from the much later *Bleak House*, the animal's movements being enacted in the movement of the prose itself: from running, the cat 'descends' into its own domain, after which it is 'seen' (the illusion is a powerful one) 'bounding', first onto a water butt, then onto a dust hole, after which it is observed 'alighting' on the 'flagstones', at all times 'as if he were conscious that his character depended on his gallantry of the preceding night escaping public observation'. It is easy enough to guess what he has been up to! The animal is imbued with a consciousness of himself and his own movements; even more surprisingly, the streets themselves are endowed with a life of their own as, 'by almost imperceptible degrees', they begin 'to resume their bustle and animation' (p. 51). Again, the emphasis is on movement: 'market carts roll slowly along'; people with 'heavy baskets of fruit' on their heads 'toil' down Piccadilly towards Covent Garden, 'following each other in rapid succession' (p. 51). In addition to movement, another distinguishing feature of the sketch is its stress on urban contrasts: 'a bricklayer's labourer ... walks briskly to his work'; truanting schoolboys 'rattle merrily' over the 'pavement'; in doing so, they contrast 'forcibly' with the 'demeanour of the little sweep', tired before his day even begins by having 'knocked and rung till his arm aches' (p. 51) in trying to gain admission to carry out his grim employment. As the day gets into full swing, we are again presented with Eisenstein's 'panorama of a market'; in this case, Covent Garden: 'men are shouting, cars backing, horses neighing, boys fighting, basket-women talking, piemen expatiating on the excellence of their pastry, and donkeys braying' (pp. 51–2). These, and 'a hundred other noises' form 'a compound' (p. 52) which distils the discordant uproar of the city awake and about its business. The passing scene is then individualised by its concentration on the flirtatious goings-on of two servant-girls who use the routine of taking in the day's milk as an opportunity to rouse the interest of 'Mr Todd's young man over the way' (p. 52). The focus moves to the onlookers gathered for the departure of a coach, some attempting to sell odds and ends to the passengers, which prompts a query: 'Heaven knows why' but it seems 'quite impossible any man can mount a coach without requiring at least sixpennyworth of oranges, a penknife, a pocket book, a last year's annual, a pencil case, a piece of sponge, and a small series of caricatures' (p. 53). Cab drivers are then brought into service to register some of the changes that are transforming the urban scene by way of the question of how 'people can prefer "them wild beast cariwans of homnibuses, to a riglar cab with a fast trotter"' (p. 53). By now the shops are 'completely opened' and 'the bakers' shops in town are filled with servants and children waiting for the drawing of the first batch of rolls – an operation which was performed a full hour ago in the suburbs' (p. 53). The suburbs themselves are a relatively new feature of city life in 1835 – a phenomenon destined to grow hugely with the growth of railway travel – and their mention allows Dickens to introduce one of his favourite urban types, the clerk, and to display his knowledge of their varieties:

Middle-aged men, whose salaries have by no means increased in the same proportion as their families, plod steadily along, apparently with no object in view but the counting house; knowing by sight almost everybody they meet or overtake, for they have seen them every morning (Sundays excepted) during the last twenty years, but speaking to no one. If they do happen to overtake a personal acquaintance, they just exchange a hurried salutation, and keep walking on, either by his side or in front of him, as his rate of walking may chance to be. As to stopping to shake hands, or to take the friend's arm, they seem to think that as it is not included in their salary, they have no right to do it. Small office lads in large hats, who are made men before they are boys, hurry along in pairs, with their first coat carefully brushed, and the white trousers of last Sunday plentifully besmeared with dust and ink. It evidently requires a considerable mental struggle to avoid investing part of the day's dinner money in the purchase of the stale tarts so temptingly exposed in dusty tins at the pastry cooks' doors; but a consciousness of their own importance and the receipt of seven shillings a week, with the prospect of an early rise to eight, comes to their aid, and they accordingly put their hats a little more on one side, and look under the bonnets of all the milliners' and staymakers' apprentices they meet – poor girls! – the hardest worked, the worst paid, and too often, the worst used class of humanity. (pp. 53–4)

By eleven o'clock 'a new set of people fills the streets' and they are 'thronged with a vast concourse of people, gay and shabby, rich and poor, idle and industrious; and we come to the heat, bustle, and activity of NOON', (p. 54) which brings the sketch to its conclusion.

The eye/I of a 'kaleidoscope gifted with consciousness' is working at full strength here. Like the separate dots of pigment in an Impressionist painting which cohere into a whole, the varied details of the urban scene coalesce into a panoramic image of the bustle, noise, variety and contrasts of the, for Dickens, modern city in which the brush strokes are finely adjusted as well as broad. The alienated lives of those middle-aged clerks are conveyed with insight as well as in vivid detail, their aversion to shaking hands anticipating a scene in one of Dickens's later works, the puzzlement expressed in *Great Expectations* by the quintessentially urban Wemmick at Pip's readiness to shake hands with him. And the knowledgeable man of the world is on show in the unstated understanding between the narrator and the adult reader as to why milliners and staymakers were 'too often the worst used class of humanity', because they were frequently driven or seduced into prostitution. Finally, the movement of Dickens's language, the sketch's distinguishing feature, is insistently cinematic, in its reliance on what can only be called tracking shots, close-ups, dissolves, editing and montage, crane shots, and so on. One further example will clarify the point: 'A partially opened bedroom window here and there, bespeaks the heat of the weather, and the uneasy slumbers of its occupant; and the dim scanty flicker of the rushlight, through the window blind, denotes the chamber of watching or sickness' (p. 51). The overwhelmingly visual quality of this little sequence surely renders further analysis of its filmic aspects redundant.

Another way in which Dickens's work can be seen to be panoramic is in the juxtaposition of images of the metropolis with mirrors, reflections, shop windows and street illumination, life as a dream, the whole coalescing into a panoramic spectacle of human experience. Benjamin's meditations on mirrors could form a starting point for this particular line of approach, beginning with his sense of the socially conditioned egotism of Parisian life: 'that is what one becomes in Paris [an egotist], where you can hardly take a step without catching sight of your dearly beloved self. Mirror after mirror! In cafés and restaurants, in shops and stores, in haircutting salons and literary salons, in baths and everywhere'.[17] As the passage makes clear, the explanation is simple, but nonetheless fascinating:

Paris is the city of mirrors. The asphalt of its roadways smooth as glass, and at the entrance to all bistros glass partitions. A profusion of windowpanes and mirrors in cafés, so as to make the inside brighter and to give all the tiny nooks and crannies, into which Parisian taverns separate, a pleasing amplitude. Women here look at themselves more than elsewhere, and from this comes the distinctive beauty of the Parisienne. Before any man catches sight of her, she already sees herself ten times reflected. But the man, too, sees his own physiognomy flash by. He gains his image more quickly here than elsewhere and also sees himself more quickly merged with this, his image. Even the eyes of passers by are veiled mirrors, and over that wide bed of the Seine, over Paris, the sky is spread out like the crystal mirror hanging over the drab beds in brothels ... Paris has a passion for mirror-like perspectives. The Arc de Triomphe, the Sacré Coeur, and even the Panthéon appear, from a distance, like images hovering above the ground and opening, architecturally, a fata morgana.[18]

The vision is rounded off with a final, dreamlike touch in his evocation of bars and cafés: 'Through mirrors extending along walls, and reflecting rows of merchandise right and left, these establishments all obtain an artificial expansion, a fantastical magnitude, by lamplight'.[19] But, again, this dream-world is not restricted to nineteenth-century Paris. In Dickens's London the urban dream may often appear in its guise as nightmare, but this is not invariably the case as a passage from only his third novel, *Nicholas Nickleby*, indicates: 'They rattled on through the noisy, bustling crowded streets of London, now displaying long double rows of brightly-burning lamps, dotted here and there with the chemists' glaring lights, and illuminated besides with the brilliant flood that streamed from the windows of the shops, where sparkling jewellery, silks and velvets of the richest colours, the most inviting delicacies, and most sumptious articles of luxurious ornament, succeeded each other in rich and glittering profusion' (Ch. 32). Passages such as these seem almost like an anticipation of Zola's near-delirious celebration of that amazing nineteenth-century invention, the huge department-store in *The Ladies' Paradise* of 1883:

In this lingering daylight, electric lamps were lighting up one by one, and their opaque white globes studded the distant depths of the departments with bright moons. They shed a white brightness of blinding fixity, like the reflection of some colourless star, which was killing the dusk. Then, when all the lamps were lit, there was a rapturous murmur from the crowd; the great display of white took on fairy-like splendour beneath this new lighting. It seemed as if the colossal orgy of white was burning too, was itself becoming changed into light. The song of white was taking wing in the blazing whiteness of a dawn.[20]

There is a glorious extravagance in this writing, a palpable sense of excitement generated by the wonders of the city in a moment of almost orgasmic capitalist activity. A similar response is generated at some key moments in Dickens's last completed novel, *Our Mutual Friend*, especially in its gradual transition from a world permeated by a dust composed of every possible form of garbage into a golden dust which is the harbinger of a previously inconceivable positive outcome for the book's major players. A key moment in this transformation is a distinctively urban scene, the hotel dinner to celebrate the wedding of Bella Wilfer, attended only by Bella, her husband and her father:

What a dinner! Specimens of all the fishes that swim in the sea, surely had swum their way to it, and if samples of the fishes of divers colours that made a speech in the Arabian Nights ... and then jumped out of the frying-pan, were not to be recognized, it was only because thay had all become of one hue by being cooked in batter among the whitebait. And the dishes being seasoned with Bliss – an article which they are sometimes out of, at Greeenwich – were of perfect flavour, and the golden drinks had been bottled in the golden age and hoarding up their sparkle ever since. (Book the Fourth, Ch. 4)

This magical view of the urban world is also recorded in a final glimpse of the Boffins who, after having spent a lifetime in sordid toil, are now 'exquisitely happy, and daily cruising about, to look at shops' (Book the Fourth, Ch. 16).

It seem clear that we can trace an overlapping series of influences in Dickens's work at this point. The intensely visual quality of his writing, on the large as well as the small scale, can be related to his immersion in the full range of Victorian visual entertainments – the magic lantern, the panorama and diorama, the huge elaborations of stage machinery. At the same time, these aspects of his daily life as a man who loved to be amused, as well as to amuse, cannot be separated from his involvement in the city as a spectacle which he experienced continuously at first hand, above all in the urban walks for which he is so famous, and which formed the essential setting for his novels. But, as this study has been attempting to portray, Dickens is not simply the passive observer of these visual pageants. He contributes, for his contemporaries as much as for us, to the meanings that inhere in the city as metropolis through the imaginative power which creates images of the urban world at the same moment as it critiques them. His London is an act of creation as well as reflection. Dickens is, however, as much literary producer as he is lonely creator, and the contribution of his culture to his own idiosyncratic view of urban capitalism must be acknowledged. If it is, then Dickens's place on a cultural continuum of the visual is once again reinforced. To take a single example, the panorama feeds into Dickens's work at a range of levels; he seizes on it for his own purposes, making it work for him in a whole number of ways; his novels then pass on into the cultural stream that flows towards the end of the nineteenth century and the appearance of film. Given the force of the arguments, and the range of material, presented throughout this book, is this not the moment to exclaim, with Eisenstein, 'How many such "cinematic" surprises must be hiding in Dickens's pages!',[21] especially if we remember that the panoramic aspects of his work relate to one major strand of film-making, the cinema of spectacle and technical display? The vastness of scope of such works as *Bleak House*, *Little Dorrit* and *Our Mutual Friend*; the glittering visual brilliance of their writing; the sheer range of characters and situations they embody; the Byzantine complexity of their plots, which are the vehicles of meaning as much as of melodramatic mystery-making – all of these point to a cinema which will find its Dickensian equivalences in the epics of Griffith, in Vidor's *The Crowd*, in Gance's *Napoleon* and, later, the work of Orson Welles whose version of *The Trial*, for example, is as Dickensian as it is Kafkaesque. Again, as this study has sought to show, this is not a matter of direct influence, except in the case of Griffith but, rather, a sigificant contribution to a range of forces which made film possible without determining its existence.

Finally, Dickens's work can be seen as cinematic in ways other than the purely visual, in his anticipation of the parallel montage which Griffith acknowledged as a major influence on his own work, an example in which a crucial difference must be drawn between Dickens and his filmic disciple. Despite his admiration for Griffith, Eisenstein criticises what he sees as a defect in his handling of the multiple stories that make up, say, *Intolerance*. He contrasts what he calls 'the dual *parallel rows*' of Griffith with Soviet montage as a 'means of achieving *a unity of a higher order* – a means *through the montage image of achieving an organic embodiment of a single idea conception, embracing all elements, parts, details of the film-work*'.[22] In other words, Soviet montage is a means towards the fusion of artistic unity and intellectual understanding which is the hallmark of the greatest art and which Griffith, in the last analysis, lacks. Conversely, it is evidently a feature of the potentially unwieldy range of material which makes up *Bleak House*, that Dickens is able to organise it in ways that have meaning and aesthetic validity. The concept of organic unity has become dangerous ground in literary studies, but it is nonetheless clear that in the hands of a lesser writer the sheer amount of *stuff* contained in *Bleak House* could easily disintegrate into a disconnected maelstrom of characters, events and settings. That it does not is a feat of the imagination, a combination of artistic control and thought, that can be perceived in the novel's handling of the case of Jarndyce versus Jarndyce. This law-suit, spiralling off into what looks like infinity, is organised around an insight central to a range of the novel's concerns, that it is a system of oppression whose evils are crystalised in its adherence to the 'one great principle of the English law' which is 'to make business for itself. There is no other principle distinctly, certainly, and consistently maintained through all its narrow turnings. Viewed by this light it becomes a coherent scheme, and not the monstrous maze the laity are apt to think it' (Ch. 39).

It is at this point that my argument on the nature of words, images and the merging of forms in relation to Dickens comes to a focus. I have suggested that structural imagery is crucial to the novels' success, but this large-scale and spectacular deployment of effects is also crucially dependent on parallel action in bringing together the juxtapositions that lie at the heart of the thematic and formal success of texts such as *Bleak House* and *Little Dorrit*. In *Bleak House*, we see the links between the worlds of Chancery and Fashion, the hopeless degradation of Tom-all-Alone's and the empty splendour of the Dedlock place in Lincolnshire; in *Little Dorrit*, we move from the literal gaol in Marseilles to the metaphorical prison of London, from the Poverty of the novel's first section to the Riches of its second. If adaptations of Dickens are considered in relation to this central feature of his work, as well as Bazin's equivalence of meaning in forms, then we have solid grounds for singling out some versions for praise. For example, the achievements of what might be described as the more traditional forms of adaptation are well represented by the BBC's television version of *Bleak House* (1984), adapted by Arthur Hopcraft, who scripted a brilliant version of *Hard Times* for Granada Television in 1977. But in the end the very triumphs of television only accentuate the disappointment expressed elsewhere in this book, that despite the sheer number of adaptations of Dickens's novels into film there is nothing to match the artistic quality of the versions of Shakespeare achieved by artists of the stature of Welles, Kurosawa and Kosintsev. For many, David Lean is a great film-maker, although not surely in the same league as the names just mentioned. His version of *Oliver Twist* is a splendid achievement and one that can be admired without reservation. But *Oliver* is an early, short, and relatively uncomplicated work. It seems significant that Lean falters, in my judgement at least, when he tackles one of the novels of Dickens's maturity, *Great Expectations.* There is panoramic richness in these late works, opportunities for cinematic visualisation on the grandest of scales, but they also possess intellectual complexity, and it is doubtful that their transformation into film has ever been attempted by an artist with even remotely the vision and imagination of Dickens himself. The dream of such a possibility is the subject of the next, and last, section of this book.

Notes

1 Pound, Ezra, *How to Read*, London: Desmond Harmsworth, 1931, Part 2.
2 Burch, Noël, *Life to those Shadows*, trans. Ben Brewster, London: British Film Institute, 1990, p. 29.
3 In Benjamin, Walter, *Illuminations*, trans. Harry Zohn, and ed. Hannah Arendt, Glasgow: Fontana, 1973. p. 259.
4 Benjamin, *Illuminations*, p. 239.
5 Lukacher, Ned, *Primal Scenes: literature, philosophy, psychoanalysis*, Ithaca/London: Cornell University Press, 1986, p. 336.
6 See Book the Second, *The Golden Thread*, Chapter 19.
7 The monad is a recurrent theme of Graeme Gilloch's *Myth and Metropolis: Walter Benjamin and the city*, Cambridge: Polity Press, 1997.
8 Shakespeare, *Macbeth*, I. vii. 1–2.
9 Shakespeare, *Macbeth*, III. ii. 46.
10 Burch, *Life to those Shadows*, p. 29.
11 Benjamin, Walter, *The Arcades Project*, trans. Howard Eiland and Kevin McLaughlin, Cambridge, Mass.: Belknap Press, 1999, p. 8.
12 Benjamin, *Arcades Project*, p. 533.
13 Meisel, Martin, *Realizations: narrative, pictorial, and theatrical arts in nineteenth-century England*, Princeton, NJ: Princeton University Press, 1983, pp. 64, 63–4.
14 Benjamin, *Arcades Project*, p. 6.
15 Charney, Leo and Schwarz, Vanessa R. (eds.), *Cinema and the Invention of Modern Life*, Berkeley, Los Angeles: Universisty of California Press, 1995, pp. 228, 230.
16 Page references are taken from Slater, Michael (ed.), *Dickens' Journalism: Sketches by Boz and other early papers 1833–39*, London: Phoenix, 1996.
17 Benjamin, *Arcades Project*, p. 539.
18 Benjamin, *Arcades Project*, pp. 537–8.
19 Benjamin, *Arcades Project*, p. 537.
20 Zola, Emile, *The Ladies' Paradise*, ed. and trans. Brian Nelson, Oxford: World's Classics, 1998, p. 426.
21 Eisenstein, Sergei, *Film Form: essays in film theory*, ed. and trans. Jay Leyda, London: Dennis Dobson Ltd, 1977, p. 214.
22 Eisenstein, *Film Form*, pp. 253–4.

A dream epilogue:
Charles Dickens and Orson Welles

The embarrassment of riches[1]

My epigraph starts, designedly, a good many hares, one of which is to play with two different senses of the word embarrassment. Poverty can certainly be embarrassing enough, but why riches? Is it possible to have too much of a good thing? And are riches other than material ones possible sources of embarrassment? Does this relate to a confusion which may be generated in readers and audiences by the sheer wealth of artistic talent that is a function of genius? Turning to the more popular sense of the word, Dickens certainly seems to have embarrassed his friends on occasion while simultaneously providing ammunition for his enemies. The hair that was slightly too long, those marginally over-decorated waistcoats, the insistence on the 'low vulgar form' of serial publication and, much later, the determination to make money from public readings of his own work – all gave rise to wincing remonstrance. As for Orson Welles, readers of a certain generation may still flinch at the memory of those dire sherry advertisements, the great voice booming softly, the huge frame decked out in its Spanish get-up. And what is a great, and supposedly serious film-maker, up to in sawing Marlene Dietrich in half, even as an entertainment for troops in the Second World War? [2]

The parallels between two figures distant from each other in time and, apparently, achievement may be pushed a stage further. When Dickens began working out the detailed future of *Household Words*, the first of the two popular weeklies that were to take up so much of his time and energy between 1850 and his death in 1870 (the second was *All the Year Round*), he contemplated creating an authorial persona for the magazine: 'I want to suppose a certain SHADOW, which may go into any place, by sunlight, moonlight, starlight, firelight, candlelight, and be in all homes, and all nooks and corners, and be supposed to be cognisant of everything, and go everywhere, without the least difficulty ... a kind of semi-omniscient, omnipresent, intangible creature ... I want him to loom as a fanciful thing all over London'.[3] The idea seemed a good one to Dickens himself and his friend and biographer, John Forster, but it proved impossible to work out successfully and was dropped. But an uncannily similar version appeared in the late 1930s and those who have heard a recording of it may experience a *frisson* of embarrassed pleasure at the memory of an unmistakable voice asking, 'who knows what evil lurks in the hearts of man? The Shadow knows ... the weed of crime bears bitter fruit. Crime does not pay! The Shadow knows!'[4] By the late 1930s Welles was an enormous success not merely on the New York stage but also in the relatively new form of radio.[5] And so in 1937 he was invited to take over the role – embarrassment surfaces again – of Lamont Cranston, the hero of an already successful radio series, *The Shadow*, in which he doubles as a '"wealthy young man about-town"' who wages war on crime 'aided only by his side-kick, the lovely Margot Lane'.[6]

These fortuitous similarities, fascinating to the enthusiast, need to be put on a firmer footing and this is provided by Robert Carringer's report of his conversation with Welles in 1979: 'Then there was a long, wistful meditation on his career – how he had started out wanting to be an American Charles Dickens'.[7] What *can* Welles have meant by this? Not, evidently, the desire to be a novelist or, indeed, a writer of any kind. The most fully formed of his early talents was music, but this disappeared at the age of nine with the death of his mother, and was followed, in rapid succession, by painting, acting, the stage in general, and the apotheosis of his magical encounter with film.[8] But although Welles was never primarily a writer, he and Dickens do have a great deal in common. (Apart from their love of dogs!) If Welles was not a professional writer, Dickens was not a professional actor, although contemporary reports provide ample testimony to his skill and intensity in the productions he masterminded in such detail, and he did unquestionably achieve professional status in his public readings, not merely in being paid for them, but in the total command of his performances, the fruit of immensely hard and detailed preparation.[9] In addition, both were highly skilled in magic tricks from an early age; both flung themselves into the joys of toy theatres for childhood productions in which each took all the major roles, of impresario and stage manager as well as actor; both had a passionate and life-long commitment to Shakespeare. There's a question, of course, as to how much of this would have been known to Welles and so one is forced to speculate as to the sources of his revelation to Carringer. My guess is that it was the desire for the kind of mythic status achieved by Dickens which I analysed in Chapter 3, a status marked by the combination of the highest standards in art with immense popular appeal.

Welles himself clearly embodies a number of complex and even contradictory myths. Just as 'Dickensian' stands for the opposing worlds of Christmas jollity and squalid poverty, Welles's mythic status can be traced in a number of ways. Peter Bogdanovich says of his role as The Shadow, 'it's become part of American mythology'[10] and he achieved something like world stature through his ten-minute role as Harry Lime in Carol Reed's *The Third Man* in 1949, a part with which he was ever after identified and which crops up in his later career in a whole number of ways (in a BBC radio series, for example). In relation to film, Welles inhabits two contrasting mythic territories. On the one hand, he stands as a classic expression of artistic hubris, the descent into failure from a pinnacle of success achieved too early (the biographer Charles Higham is a major exponent of this position). Alternatively, he has been seen as the epitome of the lonely artist challenging a monolithic financial system, the directors' director who triumphs in the end through a combination of dedication and genius. Death often provides the occasion for the final conferment of mythic status, especially if it is marked by coincidences that might be seen as uncanny. Dickens's occurred on the fifth anniversary of his involvement in the frightful railway crash at Stapleford, and was marked in countless ways, one of the more striking being the reported comments of words overheard in a London tobacconist's shop: 'Whilst there a working man came in for a screw of tobacco, and, as he threw his twopence on the counter, he said: "Charles Dickens is dead. We have lost our best friend".'[11] On the day of Welles's death, at the same age as his most famous character Charles Foster Kane, the present writer overheard a 'working man' asking his family if they had heard that Orson Welles had gone with the sense that he was reporting a major event. This is undeniably a kind of fame and it is equally undeniable that Welles experienced it in a number of different guises throughout his career. If we discount media tittle-tattle concerning the boy genius – the notorious newspaper headline 'Cartoonist, Actor, Poet and Only Ten'[12] is a favourite example – a series of evidently extraordinary theatrical productions he staged in New York in the late

1930s under the aegis of the Mercury Company he had formed with John Houseman brought him adulation of a fairly conventional kind. The list is well enough known, but sufficiently amazing to bear repetition: the all-black *Macbeth*, set in Haiti; the farce *Horse Eats Hat*; Marlowe's *Dr Faustus*; the opera *The Cradle Will Rock*; a version of Shakespeare's *Julius Caesar* up-dated to Hitler's Germany; Thomas Dekker's *The Shoemaker's Holiday*; Shaw's *Heartbreak House*. These were productions distinguished by innovative settings, imaginative reconstructions and, significantly for Welles's later career, new departures in stage lighting, a body of work sufficient to give him a permanent place in the history of modern theatre. Welles had achieved all this by the age of twenty-three but, as Joan Plowright testifies, these gifts did not desert him in later life. She describes appearing in his London production of *Moby Dick* in 1955 as 'the most brilliantly imaginative, exciting and unpredictable theatrical experience of my career' and goes on to provide a hint of what the show was actually like: 'Aided only by astonishing lighting effects, choreographed mime and movement, with the actors playing several parts each, the story of Melville's classic unfolded on a bare stage'.[13]

At the same time, and equally important in view of his film career, Welles was innovating in the new world of radio. In both fields he had the benefit of able collaborators, but there now seems little doubt that it was his genius that made the significant difference in setting new standards of artistic daring in these different media. It was radio, of course, that brought Welles notoriety on the American and, even, the world stage with the infamous 1938 broadcast of *The War of the Worlds*, presented in such a way as to suggest that the other Wells's (H. G.) science fantasy was actually occurring in reality. The programme was heard by roughly six million people of whom, it has been estimated, approaching two million were sufficiently disturbed to take some kind of evasive action.[14] The uproar generated by this episode and Welles's incarnation as Harry Lime probably represent the apex of his fame in the popular sense, although throughout his life he remained, as did Dickens, a media personality, liable to be recognised in the street and always good for a 'guest spot' on television shows from *I Love Lucy*[15] to *The Muppet Show*.

The position I am seeking to clarify here is well summed up by Michael Anderegg, at least partly on the basis of youthful memories:

In short, Welles, who had virtually dominated the cultural landscape of the late thirties and early forties, continued, albeit in a subterranean way, to be a presence in 1950s culture. Though no longer a seemingly omnipotent figure, he was, at least, omnipresent, difficult to avoid. At the same time, he was an enigma: what, exactly, did Welles represent in the culture to which he contributed? What was the connection between *King Lear* and Harry Lime, Shakespeare and Steve Allen?[16]

My own version of such memories focuses on being entranced by a BBC series of the mid-1950s produced by Huw Weldon, *Orson Welles' Sketch Book*, a fifteen-minute close-up of Welles talking on a wide range of topics which he illustrated by drawings made while he spoke. The first of these, a hilarious account of his boyhood debut on the stage of the Gate Theatre in Dublin, lives on in a golden glow of glamour and laughter, but I had real difficulty in persuading friends that the purveyor of these entertainments had created some of the greatest works of art in the history of cinema. In other words, Welles's way of life was about as far as it's possible to be from the perceived behaviour of such icons of Modernism as Flaubert, Conrad, Woolf, and so on, a comparison made relevant by the fact that Welles is in his essence a Modernist film-maker. And we can relate this dismay about Welles's 'life-style' to the unease generated by some of Dickens's activities in his own lifetime. By all means write novels, and great ones that aspire to classic status, but do they always have to be published in serial form, did Dickens have to spend twenty years of his life running two popular weekly magazines, did he have to appear so fervently in amateur theatricals, did he have to spend precious years reading his novels in public for money instead of writing them? These are some of the questions posed by friends and foes alike as the pattern of his career unfolded, a pattern which unmistakably revealed Dickens as, in his own eyes, an entertainer, a role embraced just as fervently by Welles. And it is this, I think, that helps to account for the unease generated by Dickens in the years after his death, an uncertainty of status powerfully reinforced by Oscar Wilde's famous jibe concerning Little Nell,[17] the critical responses of such members of the Bloomsbury Group as Lytton Strachey and, in the world of academic criticism, the infamous strictures, later modified, of Dr Leavis. In referring to some Modernist icons a moment ago, I used the phrase 'perceived behaviour' advisedly since a closer look at lives of supposed artistic purity and dedication reveals how frequently the high priests of Modernism dabbled in the popular. Henry James sought in vain to create a larger public for himself through his five-year involvement with the theatre; Joyce made a stab at cinema ownership in Dublin as a way of repairing his fortunes; and Lawrence thought nothing of working in popular journalism or seeking, in *The Lost Girl*, to write an avowed potboiler. But both Dickens and Welles pushed this unavoidable contact with the realities of economic survival to extreme lengths, into forms of behaviour which seem, to the purist, to compromise their artistic integrity. And, what is worst of all, they evidently *enjoyed* the dubious activities that brought them into contact with a wider public.

Perhaps there is a serious loss involved in the four-year gap between *Great Expectations* and *Our Mutual Friend* and the five years between that book and Dickens's last, uncompleted, novel *The Mystery of Edwin Drood*, although it is not at all clear that Dickens would have filled these years with novel writing if he had not been involved in the public readings. Similarly, self-righteous indignation is sometimes generated by the supposed paucity of Welles's output (although this still amounts to twelve remarkable feature films made over some thirty years) even allowing for the sheer expense of film-making, and his difficulties in generating finance. But, like Dickens, he too has often seemed to admirers and detractors alike to have wasted his time in ventures far beneath him, one of the more bizarre being *The Green Goddess* episode of 1939, the ripe horror of which is conveyed by the following:

Welles was told by all his friends that he should not go into vaudeville. When they heard that he definitely was, they all told him they hoped for the sake of his career he would do something dignified. So instead of doing his magic act he decided to cut *The Green Goddess* [in its day a famous comedy-melodrama] down to twenty minutes ... He opened in Chicago and all went fairly well until the time came for a quick change before the last scene. As the Maharajah of Rook, Welles wore a turban, a long robe and black patent-leather boots. Under this were the rolled-up trousers of the dress suit he wore in the next scene – simply by dropping them. When he made the quick change, his dresser carefully removed the robe and then just as carefully put it back on him. This happened twice in the dark. So did several other things. Finally, after the music cue had been played for the third time by the anxious orchestra and extras were getting lost out on the stage, Welles made his entrance as the presumably nonchalant and immaculate Rajah, with his snap-on tie and collar reversed, pants still rolled up and an unlit and broken cigar in his hand. Welles couldn't understand the wonderful laughter he got with his opening speech.[18]

It is doubtful if Dickens was ever entangled in anything quite so ignominious, although he did come close to disaster once or twice in his theatricals and in the public readings. But it is here, I believe, that we may discern what Welles had in mind in his claim that he had started out wanting to be an American Charles Dickens. What he desired more than anything was a public, a public of the kind seemingly effortlessly commanded by Dickens in his lifetime, and beyond. The phrase 'the public' does indeed echo throughout interviews, biographies, reminiscences, and so on, and it is perhaps the core of Welles's tragedy as an artist that he won over a public for so many of his activities, but never in sufficient numbers to enable him to pursue, even relatively untroubled, the destiny as film-maker that he seems, with hindsight, so clearly marked out for. Welles's situation was by no means unique, of course, but it is undeniably dismaying that the series of masterpieces his output represents should have been poured out to such, on the whole, public neglect. The audiences who succumbed to the charm of the star actor, the magician, the television performer were, on the whole, resistant to the films for a whole variety of reasons. The essential point is made well by Michael Anderegg in his comparison of the public responses to *Touch of Evil* and *The Trial*: '... neither film had crossover potential: the elite audience could not get past the pulp fiction elements of the former and the general audience had little patience for the sound-image dislocations of the latter. Welles was uncompromising at both ends of the spectrum, either unwilling or unable to gauge the nature of his potential viewers'.[19] The heart of this problem lies, I think, in a fundamental contradiction in Welles's life and work. The public persona he acquired, or constructed, over so many years had the ability to reach out to a great many audiences for whom he was genius in its genial aspect, a charming and amusing oddity who made a pleasant companion for, say, a half-hour's television viewing. But the work, by which I mean his films, is distinguished by an ineradicable commitment to truth-telling which makes it deeply uningratiating, both thematically and at the level of surface *mise en scène*. Those who love the films, who agree with Bazin in finding them marked by 'formal brilliance' and 'overwhelming originality',[20] are puzzled by their lack of wide public appeal; but it has to be admitted that, far from seeking identification from the viewer, they seem almost to repel it in their determination to create artistic worlds which embody, with total complexity, the truths they are examining. These worlds are sometimes suffused in charm and delicacy, one thinks of the almost ecstatic nostalgia embodied in the opening scenes of *The Magnificent Ambersons* and the delightful self-presentation of Welles as creator in *F for Fake*. There is evidence to suggest that, better handled by its publicists, Welles's films might have reached wider audiences on their first appearance. For example, *Citizen Kane*'s production studio, RKO, lacked the nerve to capitalise on the furore created by the hostility to the film shown by the immensely wealthy newspaper owner, William Randolph Hearst, and so put it before the public in a half-hearted manner. *F for Fake* highlights a different problem. As so often, Welles himself was convinced that the film would be a success, at least partly because he rightly believed that with it he had invented a new genre, the film essay. But once again, as with the dark comedy of *Touch of Evil*, Welles needed to create an audience for work which was challengingly original. Factors such as these undoubtedly played a role in dooming his output to a large measure of incomprehension or indifference on its first appearance.

But there may be another reason for this lack of public acclaim, one that returns me, although from a different angle, to my theme of embarrassment. I can only appeal to experience at this point in suggesting that Welles's films can produce a kind of nervous laughter in audiences, a response not dissimilar to what may be occasionally evoked, if we are honest, in reading Dickens. In other words, my claim here is that their work can itself be embarrassing and that this may, in the end, be a kind of strength. This is a sensitive issue, especially perhaps in relation to Dickens, whose reputation is as high in the twenty-first century as it has ever been. He is now widely accepted in intellectual and academic circles as a very great artist indeed; in fact, it is possible to read academic articles, books even, that contain not the slightest hint that he is a comic writer. But I want to go further than trying to reinstate the comedy which is a central part of his appeal. My point is that there are elements in Dickens's work that may sometimes prompt us to laugh *at* and not *with* him. Another characteristic passage from H.D., her evocation of the early film experience, helps to clarify my point here:

I suppose we might begin rhetorically by asking, what is the cinema, what are the classics? For I don't in my heart believe one out of ten of us highbrow intellectuals, Golders Greenites, Chautauqua lecturers [speakers on an American lecture circuit], knows the least little bit about either. Classics. Cinema. The word cinema (or movies) would bring to nine out of ten of us a memory of crowds and crowds and saccharine music and long drawn out embraces and the artificially enhanced thud-offs of galloping bronchoes. What would be our word-reaction to Classics? What to Cinema? Take Cinema to begin with (cinema = movies), boredom, tedium, suffocation, pink lemonade, saw-dust even: old reactions connected with cheap circuses, crowds and crowds and crowds and illiteracy and more crowds and breathless suffocation and (if 'we' the editorial 'us' is an American) peanut shells and grit and perhaps a sudden collapse of jerry-built scaffoldings. Danger somewhere anyhow. Danger to the physical safety, danger to the moral safety, a shivering away as when 'politics' or 'graft' is mentioned, a great thing that must be accepted (like the pre-cinema days circus) with abashed guilt, sneaked to at least intellectually. The cinema or the movies is to the vast horde of the fair-to-middling intellectuals a Juggernaut crushing out mind and perception in one vast orgy of the senses.[21]

A major aim of this chapter is to show that the world evoked by H. D., a world of crowds and dust and circuses, of noise and danger, is precisely a world with which Dickens and Welles would not merely be familiar but one they would have gloried in. This is the world of Astley's Circus, loved byDickens, where Shakespeare was performed on horseback, and of the Riviera Hotel in Las Vegas where, in 1956, Welles performed a '25-minute act featuring magic and recitations from *Julius Caesar*, *King Lear*, and *The Merchant of Venice*'. (It is gratifying to learn that his 'four-week engagement' was 'held over for an additional two weeks'.)[22] In short, these two great artists are vulgar, they are of the people, and this vulgarity is a felt presence in their work, for reasons suggested by Michael Anderegg in discussing Welles the actor: 'Although Welles was able to shape his acting persona into a key element of his creative personality, he has been perceived, almost from the beginning of his career, as representing excess, as someone whose acting lay outside the boundaries of what was acceptable or at least desirable in the twentieth century'.[23] Excess is, I would suggest, a key aspect of Welles the actor, Welles the film-maker and of Dickens the novelist. Both are capable of fashioning moments of delicacy and refinement; Bernstein's memory of the glimpse of a girl on a ferry from *Kane* comes to mind, as does the sleigh ride in *Ambersons*. And the opening chapters of *David Copperfield* set a standard in the charmingly humorous evocation of childhood. More characteristic, however, is the bravura technical command which both Welles and Dickens delight in displaying; the dazzling opening shot of *Touch of Evil* and the beginning of *Bleak House* serve as representative examples. But this element of excess, this insistence on the creation of a *tour de force*, spills over into the body of the work taken as a whole, into an over-egging of the pudding that may irk the sensibilities of the literal mind. The baroque extravagance of *Kane*'s opening scenes seems more than is strictly necessary to make the point. And is the London of *Bleak House* muddy enough to demand that 'Megalosauros, forty feet long or so, waddling like an elephantine lizard up Holborn Hill'? How, precisely, are we meant to respond to such moments, where artistic embodiment might be said to race ahead of thematic significance? Are we, perhaps, just a shade puzzled and does our discomfiture find release in the faintest of blushes, in a temptation to giggle? I have deliberately avoided obvious examples in trying to make this point. Moments of sentimental and melodramatic exaggeration in Dickens are obviously risible and everyone laughs, in my experience, at the final spoken credit of *The Magnificent Ambersons*, 'My name is Orson Welles' or, even, at Tanya's last words in *Touch of Evil*: 'He was some kind of a man. What does it matter what you say about people?' It goes without saying that this kind of laughter should be distinguished from the contemptuous rejection of *Ambersons* by some of the audience at its notorious sneak preview in Pomona, California in 1942, after the showing of a Dorothy Lamour musical, *The Fleet's In*. It is also worth noting that, of the 125 comment cards collected, 53 were positive, including remarks such as 'the best the cinema has yet offered', 'the picture was a masterpiece', 'photography rivalled that of superb *Citizen Kane*', 'I think it was the best picture I have ever seen'.[24] But the negative cards and, above all, the derisive laughter of some sections of the audience sank the film in the eyes of its producers and so led inexorably to the partial destruction of one of the twentieth century's great works of art. Derision apart, my general point involves the two different senses of embarrassment that I began with and two different explanations as to why we may respond as we do. The element of vulgarity in both Dickens and Welles may bring a blush to the sensitive cheek of the intellectual just as it clearly did to their contemporaries. But we can also be staggered by an extravagance of technique which embodies the determination of these artists to push novel and film to the limits of what was possible expressively in their own time.

These links between Dickens and Welles do, however, run even deeper, to the sense of their own identity as artists. In 1866 Dickens wrote a letter to the editor of the *Atheneum* which began 'Sir As the Author of the Pickwick Papers (and of one or two other books)'.[25] This somewhat oddly worded introduction, the prelude to a complex issue of authorship, was occasioned by a challenge to Dickens's role as sole creator of his first novel, the immensely successful and popular *Pickwick Papers*. Given that this challenge appeared relatively late in his career, when his position as England's premier novelist might have seemed impregnable, it is interesting to note how deeply the matter irritated him. The story of the novel's origins is a complex one. As a bright young man Dickens seemed an obvious choice to provide the written text for a series of comic illustrations, a format popular in the early Victorian period, by the well-known artist, Robert Seymour. The story of what followed is well known, but it remains one of the rattling good yarns of literary history. Seymour committed suicide at an early stage, Dickens took command, the illustrations became secondary, and possibly the most famous first novel in the history of English literature was born. In 1854 Seymour's widow had circulated a privately printed account of the book's origins which claimed that the initial concept had been her husband's and that he was solely responsible for the physical appearance of Mr Pickwick, one of the best known characters in world literature. Dickens was clearly riled that this brouhaha had surfaced again more than ten years later, this time in a letter to the *Atheneum* from Seymour's son in which he repeated that 'the original plan was to give the adventures of a club of cockney sportsmen, and the idea and title of the work was my father's'.[26] Dickens's response is, first, to claim originality for himself: 'Mr Seymour the Artist never originated, suggested, or in any way had to do with, save as illustrator of what I devised, an incident, a character ... a name, a phrase, or a word, to be found in the Pickwick Papers'.[27] But he then goes on to acknowledge that there was a mildly co-operative aspect to the venture, including Seymour's contribution to the look of a character, Mr Pickwick, who has assumed mythic proportions in the literary landscape: 'My views being deferred to, I thought of Mr Pickwick, and wrote the first number; from the proof sheets of which Mr Seymour made his drawing of the Club, and that happy portrait of its founder, by which he is always recognised, and which may be said to have made him a reality'.[28]

Dickens's desire to set the record straight, given his power and fame, is perhaps surprising but closer examination suggests a number of reasons why it may have seemed important to him. He was without rivals in the early years of his career, but from the late 1840s a number of major writers appeared – Thackeray, George Eliot, the Brontës – whose work challenged his pre-eminence, especially given their commitment to a realism which some readers found superior to Dickens's fondness for melodrama. Again, although he was not to know it, Dickens had published his last completed novel, *Our Mutual Friend*, and was not to write another for five years, the uncompleted *Edwin Drood*. He may well have felt that his days as a novelist were over and so any attack on the originality of his first great success was not to be taken lightly. In addition, the mid- to late-1860s were a troubling time for Dickens. On a personal level, he had abandoned his wife of many years for a relationship, whatever its precise nature, with a woman young enough to be his daughter. And although he was proud and pleased by his success as a professional reader, this activity took a severe toll on his health. Finally, Dickens remained as savagely at odds as ever with what he regarded as the administrative shambles of so much of British public life, as a letter to a friend living abroad, bringing him up-to-date with current events, reveals: 'Lastly, a muddle of railways in all directions possible and impossible, with no general public scheme, no general public supervision, enormous waste of money, no fixable responsibility, no accountability'.[29] Clearly, Dickens was in no mood to have his originality as a novelist challenged.

Welles's letter, for he wrote one too, was to the London *Times* of 17 November 1971: 'The initial ideas for this film [*Citizen Kane*] and its basic structure were the result of direct collaboration between us [Welles and Herman J. Mankiewicz]; after this we separated and there were two screenplays: one written by Mr Mankiewicz, in Victorville, and the other, in Beverly Hills, by myself ... The final version of the screenplay ... was drawn from both sources'. Welles was moved to write, of course, in response to the infamous attack on *Citizen Kane* mounted by Pauline Kael in the same year as his letter.[30] There is something peculiarly painful in this assault by America's leading film critic on America's greatest film-maker. Apart from *F for Fake*, Welles's career as a creator of feature films was over, and there is reason to believe that Kael's influential attack did nothing to ease his situation as a director constantly in search of finance for his next project, to say nothing of the pain caused to an artist who had spent most of his time not practising the art for which he was supremely gifted.

The issue at hand is, again, that of originality, this time in relation to a work that looms even larger in Welles's career than *Pickwick Papers* did for Dickens. Both have mythic status, but *Kane* carries the additional burdens of being, in the journalistic cliché, 'the greatest film ever made' and of embodying a pitch of youthful genius that its originator was supposedly never to reach again. For those who have read it, and studied the whole matter, Kael's essay is clearly a tissue of contradictions and ignorant speculation. She understands, rightly, that *Citizen Kane* is 'a "popular" masterpiece – not in terms of actual popularity but in terms of its conceptions and the way it gets its laughs and makes its points', but this leads her to the élitist view that the film 'isn't a work of special depth or a work of subtle beauty. It is a shallow work, a *shallow* masterpiece'.[31] In other words, she fails to grasp what Dickens amply demonstrates, that great and complex works of art can be popular. The essence of Kael's position, however, is that the sole responsibility for the script of *Kane* should lie with its credited co-writer, Herman J. Mankiewicz, and that he is, in some essential way, the work's creator.

There is no need, at this late stage, to mount a defence of Welles's originality in relation to *Citizen Kane*, to substantiate the claim that the film is his artistic property as much as *Pickwick Papers* is Dickens's. For one thing, the task has been accomplished with meticulous fairness by Peter Bogdanovich in his essay 'The *Kane* Mutiny' in *Esquire* (October 1972). The interesting question is why the attempt to dislodge Welles from his authorship should have been made in the first place. To treat it with more dignity than it deserves, Kael's essay might be seen as part of her attempt to rehabilitate Hollywood's script-dominated comedies of the 1930s, of which she was particularly fond and which she felt had been displaced by the rise of *auteur* theory with its emphasis on the dominant role of the director, often at the moment of shooting in the studio or on location. It is impossible to doubt, of course, that Welles is an *auteur* in the fullest sense. In addition to being a writer-director, his thematic and stylistic preoccupations remain remarkably consistent, despite the varied freshness of the individual films, and despite also radical changes in technical personnel throughout his career. The use of deep-focus cinematography in *Kane* and *Ambersons*, realised by different cameramen, is a particularly striking example.

It might seem odd to refer to a novelist as an *auteur*, but it is clear that Dickens placed special emphasis on his creative gifts. Both of his weekly publications, *Household Words* and *All the Year Round*, carried the heading 'Conducted by Charles Dickens' and this conducting involved not merely selecting their material and writing a good deal of it himself, but subjecting the anonymous contributions of others to exhaustive and exhausting rewriting in a manner similar to the scripts for Welles's radio broadcasts. As Jonathan Rosenbaum points out: 'Drafts on [*sic*] the early shows were often done by outside writers, but Houseman or Welles usually took care of the final draft, with Welles almost always doing a polish'.[32] With regard to his own novels, Dickens's letters and other comments constantly stress their originality, but it is entirely in the spirit of this book that some of his most interesting insights into the nature of creativity are conveyed in his responses to painting and the theatre. In 1855 he reports to his greatest confidant, John Forster, his thoughts on the English paintings, some of them by close friends, shown at a major Paris exhibition:

It is of no use disguising the fact that what we know to be wanting in the men is wanting in their works – character, fire, purpose, and the power of using the vehicle and the model as mere means to an end.

There is a horrible respectability about most of the best of them – a little, finite, systematic routine in them, strangely expressive to me of the state of England itself ... There are no end of bad pictures among the French, but, Lord! the goodness also! – the fearlessness of them; the bold drawing; the dashing conception; the passion and action in them! ... Don't think it a part of my despondency about public affairs, and my fear that our national glory is on the decline, when I say that mere form and conventionalities usurp, in English art, as in English government and social relations, the place of living force and truth.[33]

It is obvious that what Dickens admired in French art – fearlessness, boldness, the dashing conception, passion and action – are precisely the qualities to be found in his greatest work. And the link he makes between artistic conventionality and the conventionalities of English government and social relations has a direct bearing on his own aims as an artist both thematically and in terms of form. Equally relevant is the praise Dickens heaps on the French actor Charles Fechter, who enjoyed a distinguished career on the London stage: 'You ask me about Fechter and his Hamlet. It was a performance of extraordinary merit; by far the most coherent, consistent, and intelligible Hamlet I ever saw ... a remorseless destruction of all conventionalities'.[34] In keeping with his views on painting and the theatre, we know that Dickens encouraged his friend Forster to review his work in a weekly paper, *The Examiner*, in a way that stressed the unity and coherence that stems from the presence of a governing idea, a judgement that Dickens clearly felt was largely absent from the general run of reviews his later novels received.

Indeed, Dickens's concern that his artistry should be properly appreciated was the occasion for a celebrated contribution to *Household Words*, the seemingly oddly named 'Curious Misprint in the Edinburgh Review' which appeared on 1 August 1857. Dickens's piece, written at high speed, was his reply to an anonymous article in the *Edinburgh Review* of July 1857, 'The Licence of Modern Novelists', by Sir James Fitzjames Stephen. Stephen was a pillar of the British establishment, the brother of Leslie Stephen who was Virginia Woolf's father, and the details of his biography remain deadeningly familiar even today: Eton and Trinity College, Cambridge; barrister, judge and professor; member, no doubt a worthy one, of numerous public bodies; eventually a baronet. Stephen wrote for many of the high-powered journals of his day, and clearly thought himself fully qualified by birth, education, experience and ability to take Dickens to task for his ignorant and Philistine satire of British institutions. Significantly, a piece by one of Dickens's defenders refers to attacks on him by 'certain

University-bred reviewers'[35] which reinforces the class-based nature of these diatribes with their stress on Dickens as, at best, an entertainer, who should not be meddling in matters beyond his education and comprehension. But Stephen reveals his own ignorance and Philistinism in his inability to read such a complex structure as *Little Dorrit*. One of his objections to Dickens is that writing in serial form enables him to make use of affairs of the moment in a purely opportunistic way, his example being the collapse of the Clennam house at the end of the novel, 'a catastrophe' which *Little Dorrit* 'evidently borrowed from the recent fall of houses in Tottenham Court Road'. Sir James Fitzjames Stephen may have been able to do a great many things, but reading a novel as complex as this was not one of them: as Dickens points out, in remorseless detail, his objection reveals him as possessed of a cloth ear in completely failing to grasp that this climax of the book had been hinted at hundreds of pages before its occurrence and kept constantly before the reader's attention by means of a subtle web of imagery. In short, Stephen attempts to use the book for his own purposes, to ridicule what he sees as Dickens's intellectual limitations, while failing himself to grasp that its greatness lies in the power of its imagination, and that in a work as long and complex as *Little Dorrit* imagination is a shorthand term for intellectual as well as artistic qualities. Indeed, the opposition is itself a false one, since artistry at this level cannot exist without thought.

For a different, but related response to Welles, we can turn to one of the biggest disappointments of his career, the studio's rejection of *Touch of Evil*, a masterpiece which he hoped would secure his return to Hollywood and the resumption of his filmmaking career. As Welles explained to Peter Bogdanovich, he was 'so sure I was going to go on making a lot of pictures at Universal ... They went out of their way to compliment me every night for the rushes ... Every day they kept asking me to sign the contract. Then they saw the cut version and barred me from the set'. In response to Bogdanovich's questioning, Welles stresses the mystery of their rebuff: 'There's something missing there that I don't know about, that I'll never understand'. But he does, in fact, go on to provide a fully adequate account, one reminiscent of Stephen's cloth ear in relation to *Little Dorrit*: 'The picture rocked them in some funny way. They particularly loathed the black comedy – the kind people now like ...They just didn't know what I was up to ... They were deeply shocked – they felt insulted by the film in a funny way. And hurt and injured – I'd taken them for some kind of awful ride'.[36] In other words, as he did so frequently throughout his career, Welles had collided with conventional minds not necessarily, in this case, because of any ill will, although that was a frequent enough ingredient in the responses he had to face. Welles joked to Bogdanovich at one point that he was sure that he was going to be loved after his death[37] but the pressure towards innovation in his work meant that it was constantly liable to be misunderstood or unappreciated on its first appearance. The tension in Welles between thinking constantly of film projects and realising so few of them meant that whenever he got the opportunity to make a film he was liable to pour a huge amount of material into it, another aspect of the excess to which I referred at the beginning of this chapter. This occurs thematically as well as stylistically so that his work is constantly anticipating what is to come later. It is now widely acknowledged that the use of sound and light-weight cameras in *Touch of Evil* was revolutionary, but so also was its drug taking and implied sexual violence. Most striking of all, however, is the use of a bugging device to trap Quinlan, the first example of a phenomenon which would be used to striking effect more than fifteen years later by Coppola in *The Conversation*. This grasp of new developments at the moment of their appearance, similar to Dickens's grasp of changes in the urban scene, is reinforced by Welles's comments on his version of Kafka's *The Trial*: 'Modern horror creeping up on the Austro-Hungarian Empire ... with I.B.M. machines in the background'.[38] This insight is embodied in some of the film's most strikingly contrasted scenes, with K. stumbling past impossibly bulging, hand-written files only to be confronted by serried ranks of humming computers, possibly the first serious use of this contraption in the history of cinema.

As I pointed out earlier, Welles believed that he had 'discovered a new kind of movie'[39] in *F for Fake*. However, stylistic and thematic originality of this magnitude is bound to conflict with those who 'wouldn't want to make a Renoir picture even if it was a success', a paradox Welles touches on again in claiming that 'the last thing they [the producers of *Touch of Evil*] wanted was a success'.[40] This returns us to another earlier point, the uningratiating quality of Welles's vision for those unwilling to tune themselves into it, which helps to account, along with a measure of sheer bad luck, for the public indifference or hostility to his films on their first appearance. It might seem as though the reception accorded to Dickens belongs to a wholly different world, but this is not entirely the case, despite the ever-increasing sales of his novels throughout his career. In 1865 the Victorian critic, Eneas Sweetland Dallas, reviewed *Our Mutual Friend* in the following terms: 'One thing is very remarkable about it, – the immense amount of thought which it contains ... What labour Mr Dickens has given to it is a labour of love ... he, who of all our living novelists has the most extraordinary genius, is also ... the most careful and painstaking in his work'.[41] Dickens responded with a delighted letter of thanks but also, in a unique gesture, the gift of the manuscript to its admirer. It is possible to account for this rather extraordinary reaction, I think, in relation to a curious phenomenon in Dickens's later career, the disparity between the popular and critical response to his later work, what a standard reference work refers to as 'a growing chorus of critical dissent ... even as Dickens's popularity with the common reader consolidated his status as a classic ... An emerging concern with the aesthetics of the novel as a legitimate art form, coupled with a narrowly realist conception of that form, led critics to decry his art as crude and implausible'.[42] These were responses directed at such masterpieces as *Bleak House*, *Little Dorrit* and *Our Mutual Friend*! Indeed, the accolades accorded to *Great Expectations* may have been almost as maddening for Dickens, as critics stressed this work's return to the happier and sunnier mode of his earlier fiction, a fairly comprehensive misreading of the text. Sweetland's review was, then, a relatively rare appreciation not merely of Dickens's artistry but of his capacity for thought, and the general critical puzzlement in the face of his later fiction may be accounted for by another specialist viewpoint, one we have already encountered, that his 'dense thematic compositions, striking use of imagery, rhetoric and dramatic device advanced fiction technically to the threshold of modernism'.[43] Like Welles, then, Dickens was ahead of his time in creating works that belonged in some essential way to an as yet unknown future although, unlike Welles, he was able to carry a huge public with him in the venture.

Given this chapter's title, the sympathetic reader will have grasped by now where my comparison of these two great artists is tending. Although it is tormenting that no direct evidence exists of Welles having read Dickens, it is certain that he did so. Indeed, given the similarities between his upbringing and that of Henry James, as described in Chapter 3, we can be pretty certain that Dickens was read to him as a child – except that, given what we know of the boyish Orson, it may have been he who did the reading. And we can presume that a man whose ambition was to be 'the American Charles Dickens' must have actually read the works of the writer he sought to emulate, even if not in writing itself. Indirect evidence of this involvement can be found in two major areas, the radio broadcasts and his first visit to Hollywood. For radio, Welles had at the very least a hand in adapting a number of works in which he also acted: *Pickwick* (as Jingle and Sergeant Buzzfuzz), *A Christmas Carol* (as the narrator and Scrooge), and *A Tale of Two Cities* (as Sydney Carton). Turning to films, and this is a painful thought, one of his early, unrealised projects was a *Pickwick Papers* with W. C. Fields as Micawber. We can only speculate what a Wellesian *Pickwick* might have been, but I am pleased to find confirmation of my own hunches in Fred Guida's splendid study of adaptations of *A Christmas Carol* when he remarks that even 'a cursory viewing of *Citizen Kane* ... suggests that Welles was probably very much in touch with the heart and pulse of *The Pickwick Papers*'.[44] My own example of this would be the sequence where the youthful Kane and Leland dash into the offices of the *Inquirer* and sweep out its old guard. From the dance-like movement with which they swing off the pavement up the newspaper office's steps to their balletic unseating of the bumbling editor – himself a 'Dickensian' figure – the whole episode is imbued with the boyish gaiety associated with a figure such as Nicholas Nickleby. But a further example is provided by one of the last of Welles's major projects, his original script, in collaboration with Oja Kodar for a projected film, *The Big Brass Ring*. Welles received major funding for the project from a sympathetic producer whose only condition was that the film be carried financially by a major star. Welles set aside two million dollars of the budget plus ten per cent of the profits to lure such figures as Jack Nicholson, Warren Beatty, Paul Newman and Robert Redford; none would agree to make the film, and the project collapsed. On the evidence of the script, this might have been a major work, echoing *Kane* but with a distinctive inflection towards the modern world. This remains speculation, but Jonathan Rosenbaum is surely correct in the analysis he gives of the script's genesis in his persuasive Afterword:

At the same time, it should be noted that *The Big Brass Ring* seems equally grounded in Anglo-American fiction of the nineteenth century. Even without the mediating narration of Marlow, the guilt-ridden darkness of Pellarin and Menaker suggests the universe of Conrad, and it is worth recalling that Welles's script adaptations of *Heart of Darkness*, *Lord Jim* and *Victory* span three decades of his career. On another plane, the gallery of fools comprising Pellarin's political entourage owes something to the caricatural energy of Dickens – think of the aforementioned J. Sheldon Buckle, or Dinty Benart – reminding one that a *Pickwick Papers* with W.C. Fields was one of Welles's earliest Hollywood projects.[45]

But Guida provides a clue to taking the shadow relationship between Dickens and Welles a stage further when he remarks, not apropos of Welles: 'One imagines a motion picture camera tracking its way through the labyrinth that was London, occasionally panning across the horizon for a new reference point, or zooming in to capture some minute bit of business. Everything is recorded for posterity; deep focus, sharp detail'.[46] This is, of course, the cinematic quality that I found so singularly lacking in Christine Edzard's adaptation of *Little Dorrit*, a vision of Dickens on film that the novels themselves seem to prompt one towards and which Welles, I believe, could have fulfilled. Victor Perkins's sensitive study of *The Magnificent Ambersons*[47] ends with a lovely dream concerning the missing forty minutes of this great work of art:

Let us suppose then – it seems reasonable – that a film plant must employ many persons of a preserving bent, people spontaneously impelled to take care of threatened celluloid. Why should we rather despair than hope that such a person may have been in place to frustrate the order for the destruction of Welles's film? On top of a cupboard, at the back of an attic, inside a chest, somewhere with an atmosphere convenient to the survival of the film stock, seven reels are stacked, awaiting discovery, a humble studio hand's gift to posterity. That is a good happy ending. It is not a delusion, but it is better than reality.[48]

My own study began in dreams and has now come full circle in suggesting that Welles had the full range of abilities to bring Dickens successfully to the screen. Intellectually, there is every reason to believe that he would have understood Dickens's use of structural imagery, large-scale imagery pregnant with meaning, which has been a major focus of my argument, from the passage in *Dombey and Son* – analysed in Chapter 6, 'Dickens, theatre and spectacle' – and throughout Dickens's career. Indeed, such imagery might be said to be a major feature of Welles's own output. *Citizen Kane* creates a panorama of the intertwined worlds of press and politics in twentieth-century America which is not merely a spectacle but a profound analysis of the mystery of personal identity in a society dominated by image creation and public fame. *The Magnificent Ambersons* charts no less a subject than the rise to domination of the motor car and its consequent effects on the lives of individuals and the cities they inhabit. As with Dickens, thought and artistry are inseparably linked in the scale of such works as *The Trial* and *Chimes at Midnight* where versions of the Austro-Hungarian Empire and late mediaeval England are brought to life in amazing detail, testimony to an imagination fully in control of its materials and its vision of the world. In addition to structural imagery, it is also clear by now that Welles's major stylistic tool, his reliance on long takes made possible by deep focus, would have been the perfect filmic embodiment of Dickens's vision, taking in the panoramic and the detailed with equal force and, through the distortion involved in deep focus, providing an exact equivalence for the heightened exaggerations that are central to Dickens's symbolic rendering of the real. *Touch of Evil* is perhaps the most striking example, its gothic extravagance rendered in the grotesque depiction of its protagonist, Hank Quinlan, a stylistic and thematic exaggeration which still permits pity and understanding. The whole work is, in fact, Dickensian in its masterly handling of chiaroscuro; its deployment of liminal spaces, in the proximity of Mexico and the United States, linked by a bridge below which flows a river as filthy as the Thames of *Our Mutual Friend*; and its constantly roving camera, moving as restlessly but with as much meaning as the movement of Dickens's prose. The thought of such a fusion of talents is, in Perkins's words, 'a good happy ending. It is not a delusion, but it is better than reality'.

Notes

1 This is the English translation of the title of a French play of 1726, *L'embarras des riches*, by Abbé d'Allainval.
2 Information on this, and other related matters, is provided by Callow, Simon, *Orson Welles: the road to Xanadu*, London: Jonathan Cape, 1995 and Welles, Orson and Bogdanovich, Peter, *This is Orson Welles*, ed. Jonathan Rosenbaum, New York: HarperCollins, 1992.
3 Forster, John, *The Life of Charles Dickens*, London: J. M. Dent & Sons, 1927, Vol. 2, pp. 63–4.
4 Callow, *Orson Welles*, p. 321.
5 These aspects of Welles's career are recounted by Callow, *Orson Welles*, and France, Richard, *The Theatre of Orson Welles*, Lewisburg: Bucknell University Press, 1977.
6 Callow, *Orson Welles*, p. 321.
7 Carringer, Robert, *The Making of Citizen Kane*, London: John Murray, 1985, p. 133.
8 Welles's first film was the five-minute, silent *Hearts of Age*, made as a prank in 1934. In 1938 he filmed the much more substantial introduction to a stage play, *Too Much Johnson*.
9 See Collins, Philip, *Charles Dickens: the public readings*, Oxford: Clarendon Press, 1975.
10 Welles and Bogdanovich, *Welles*, p. 11.
11 Dickens, Sir Henry F., *Memories of My Father*, London: Victor Gollancz Ltd, 1928, p. 29.
12 Welles and Bogdanovich, *Welles*, p. 326.
13 Plowright, Joan, *And That's Not All*, London: Weidenfeld & Nicolson, 2001, pp. 27, 28.
14 Welles and Bogdanovich, *Welles*, p. 346.
15 A particularly interesting account of the role of such appearances in Welles's career is provided by Anderegg, Michael, *Orson Welles:*

Shakespeare and popular culture, New York: Columbia University Press, 1999, pp. 3–4.

16 Anderegg, *Welles*, p. 2.

17 Wilde remarked that 'One must have a heart of stone to read the death of Nell without laughing', in Schlicke, Paul (ed.), *Oxford Reader's Companion to Dickens*, Oxford: Oxford University Press, 1999, p. 426.

18 Welles and Bogdanovich, *Welles*, p. 26.

19 Anderegg, *Welles*, p. 13.

20 Bazin, André, *Orson Welles: a critical view*, trans. Jonathan Rosenbaum, Los Angeles: Acrobat Books, 1991.

21 Donald, J., Friedberg, A. and Marcus, L. (eds.), *Close Up 1927–1933: cinema and modernism*, London: Cassell, 1998, p. 105.

22 Welles and Bogdanovich, *Welles*, p. 420.

23 Anderegg, *Welles*, p. 142.

24 Welles and Bogdanovich, *Welles*, pp. 116–25.

25 House, M., Storey, G. and Tillotson, K., *et al.* (eds.), *The British Academy Pilgrim Edition of Letters of Charles Dickens*, Vols. 1–12, Oxford: Clarendon Press, 1965–2002; 28 March 1866, Vol. 11, p. 175.

26 *Letters of Dickens*, 28 March 1866, Vol. 11, p. 176, n. 2.

27 *Letters of Dickens*, 28 March 1866, Vol. 11, p. 176.

28 *Letters of Dickens*, 28 March 1866, Vol. 11, p. 177.

29 *Letters of Dickens*, 30 November 1865, Vol. 11, p. 116.

30 Pauline Kael's essay 'Raising Kane' appeared in *The New Yorker*, 20 and 27 February 1971, and subsequently as the introduction to Kael, Pauline, *The Citizen Kane Book*, Frogmore, St Albans: Paladin, 1974.

31 Kael, *Citizen Kane Book*, pp. 3, 2.

32 Welles and Bogdanovich, *Welles*, pp. 323–4.

33 *Letters of Dickens*, 11-12 November, 1855, Vol. 7, p. 743.

34 *Letters of Dickens*, 16 March 1862, Vol. 10, p. 53.

35 *Letters of Dickens*, 27 July 1857, Vol. 8, p. 389, n. 3.

36 Welles and Bogdanovich, *Welles*, p. 322.

37 *The Lost Films of Orson Welles*, BBC Tx Series, 1995, written by Oja Kodar,.

38 *The Orson Welles Story*, Arena, BBC-TV, 1980.

39 Arena interview.

40 Arena interview.

41 *Letters of Dickens*, 30 November 1865, Vol. 11, p. 118, n. 1.

42 Schlicke, *Oxford Companion to Dickens*, p. 130.

43 Sutherland, John, *The Longman Companion to Victorian Fiction*, Harlow, Essex: Longman, 1988, p. 186.

44 Guida, Fred, *A Christmas Carol and Its Adaptations: a critical examination of Dickens's story and its productions on screen and television*, Jefferson, North Carolina: McFarland and Company, Inc., 2000, pp. 152–3.

45 Welles, Orson and Kodar, Oja, *The Big Brass Ring: an original screenplay by Orson Welles with Oja Kodar*, London: Black Spring Press, 1991, p. 146.

46 Guida, *Christmas Carol*, p. 26.

47 Perkins, V. F., *The Magnificent Ambersons*, BFI Film Classics, London, British Film Institute, 1999.

48 Perkins, *Ambersons*, p. 73.

Select bibliography

Unless otherwise stated in the text, quotations from Dickens can be consulted in any easily available edition.

Abel, Richard, 'Peak Practice' in 'Urban Legends: ten cities that shook cinema', *Sight & Sound*, London: British Film Institute, May 2001.

Ackroyd, Peter, *Dickens*, London: Guild Publishing, 1990.

Allen, Michael, *Family Secrets: the films of D. W. Griffith*, London: British Film Institute Publishing, 2000.

Allen, Richard, *Projection and Illusion: film spectatorship and the impression of reality*, Cambridge: Cambridge University Press, 1997.

Altick, Richard, *The Shows of London*, Cambridge, Mass.: Belknap Press, 1978.

Andrew, Dudley, *Concepts in Film Theory*, Oxford: Oxford University Press, 1984.

Armstrong, Isabel, 'Transparency: towards a poetics of glass in the nineteenth century' in Spufford, Frances and Uglow, Jenny (eds.), *Cultural Babbage: technology, time and invention*, London: Faber and Faber, 1996.

Arvidson, Linda, *When the Movies Were Young*, New York: Dover, 1969.

Asendorf, Christopher, *Batteries of Life: on the history of things and their perception in modernity*, trans. Don Reneau, Berkeley, Los Angeles: University of California Press, 1993.

Auerbach, Nina, *Private Theatricals: the lives of the Victorians*, Cambridge, Mass.: Harvard University Press, 1990.

Bachelard, Gaston, *The Poetics of Space*, trans. Maria Jolas, Boston, Mass.: Beacon Press, 1994.

Bailey, Peter, *Popular Culture and Performance in the Victorian City*, Cambridge: Cambridge University Press, 1998.

Bann, Stephen, *The Clothing of Clio*, Cambridge: Cambridge University Press, 1984.

Barnes, John, *The Beginnings of the Cinema in Britain*, Newton Abbot: David and Charles, 1976.

Barnouw, Erik, *The Magician and the Cinema*, Oxford: Oxford University Press, 1981.

Barr, Charles, *English Hitchcock*, Moffat:Cameron & Hollis, 1999.

Baudelaire, Charles, *The Painter of Modern Life, and other essays*, ed. and trans. Jonathan Mayne, London: Phaidon Press, 1964.

Baudelaire, Charles, *The Parisian Prowler: le spleen de Paris petis poèmes en prose*, trans. Edward K. Kaplan, second edition, Athens and London: University of Georgia Press, 1997.

Bazin, André, *What is Cinema? Essays selected and translated by Hugh Gray*, Vol. 1, Berkeley, Los Angeles: University of California Press, 1967.

Bazin, André, *Orson Welles: a critical view*, trans. Jonathan Rosenbaum, Los Angeles: Acrobat Books, 1991.

Benjamin, Walter, *Illuminations*, trans. Harry Zohn and ed. Hannah Arendt, Glasgow: Fontana, 1973.

Benjamin, Walter, *The Arcades Project*, trans. Howard Eiland and Kevin McLaughlin, Cambridge, Mass.: Belknap Press, 1999.

Booth, Michael R., *Victorian Spectacular Theatre*, London: Routledge, 1981.

Booth, Michael R., *Theatre in the Victorian Age*, Cambridge: Cambridge University Press, 1991.

Bordwell, D., Staiger, D. and Thompson, K., *The Classical Hollywood Cinema: film style and mode of production to 1960*, New York: Columbia University Press, 1985.

Bowser, Eileen, *The Transformation of Cinema 1907–1915*, New York: Scribner, 1990.

Boyer, Christine M., *The City of Collective Memory: its historical imagery and architectural entertainments*, Cambridge, Mass.: MIT Press, 1994.

Bradby, D., James, L. and Sharratt, B. (eds.), *Performance and Politics in Popular Drama: Aspects of Popular Entertainment in Theatre, Film and Television*, Cambridge: Cambridge University Press, 1980.

Braun, Marta, *Picturing Time: the work of Etienne-Jules Marey*, Chicago: University of Chicago Press, 1993.

Brewster, Ben, and Jacobs, Lea, *Theatre to Cinema: stage pictorialism and the early feature film*, Oxford: Oxford University Press, 1997.

Brownlow, Kevin, *The Parade's Gone By*, Berkeley: University of California Press, 1968.

Bullen, J. B. (ed.), *Writing and Victorianism*, London: Longman, 1997.

Burch Noël, *Correction Please, or, How We Got into Pictures*, London: Arts Council of Great Britain, 1979.

Burch, Noël, *Life to those Shadows*, trans. Ben Brewster, London: British Film Institute, 1990.

Calvino, Italo, *Invisible Cities*, trans. William Weaver, London: Picador, 1979.

Caughie, John, *Theories of Authorship: a reader*, London: Routledge & Kegan Paul in association with British Film Institute, 1981.

Caws, Mary Ann (ed.), *City Images: perspectives from literature, philosophy, and film*, Langhorne: Gordon and Breach, 1993.

Ceram, C. W., *Archaeology of the Cinema*, New York: Harcourt Brace & World, 1965.

Charney, Leo and Schwarz, Vanessa R. (eds.), *Cinema and the Invention of Modern Life*, Berkeley: University of California Press, 1995.

Chesterton, G. K., *Charles Dickens*, London: Methuen & Co. Ltd, 1906.

Christ, Carol T. and Jordan, John O. (eds.), *Victorian Literature and the Victorian Visual Imagination*, Berkeley: University of California Press, 1995.

Christie, Ian, *The Last Machine: early cinema and the birth of the modern world*, London: BBC Educational Developments, 1994.

Clarke, David B. (ed.), *The Cinematic City*, London: Routledge, 1997.

Coe, Brian, *The History of Movie Photography*, Westfield, NJ: Eastview, 1981.

Cohen, Keith, *Film and Literature: the dynamics of exchange*, New Haven: Yale University Press, 1979.

Cohen, Margaret, 'Panoramic Literature and the Invention of Everyday Games' in Charney and Schwarz, 1995.

Cook, David, *A History of Narrative Film*, New York: W. W. Norton, 1996.

Corkin, Stanley, *Realism and the Birth of the Modern United States: cinema, literature and culture*, Athens: University of Georgia Press, 1996.

Crary, Jonathan, *Techniques of the Observer: on vision and modernity in the nineteenth century*, Cambridge, Mass.: MIT Press, 1992.

Deleuze, Gilles, *Cinema: the movement – image*, trans. Hugh Tomlinson, Minneapolis: University of Minnesota Press, 1986.

Donald, J., Friedberg, A. and Marcus, L. (eds.), *Close Up 1927–1933: cinema and modernism*, London: Cassell, 1998.

Doré, Gustave, and Jerrold, Blanchard, *London: a pilgrimage*, New York: Dover Publications, 1872; reprinted in 1970.

Durgnat, Raymond, *The Cinematic Text: montage in film and literature*, Brighton: Harvester Press, 1987.

Edel, Leon, 'Novel and Camera' in Halperin, John (ed.), *The Theory of the Novel: new essays*, New York: Oxford University Press, 1974.

Edel, Leon (ed.), *Henry James Letters*, Cambridge, Mass.: Harvard University Press, 1974–1984.

Eigner, Edwin, *The Dickens Pantomime*, Berkeley: University of California Press, 1989.

Eisenstein, Sergei, *Film Form: essays in film theory*, ed. and trans. Jay Leyda, London: Dennis Dobson Ltd, 1977.

Eisenstein, Sergei, *The Memoirs of Sergei Eisenstein*, ed. Richard Taylor and trans. William Powell, London: British Film Institute, 1996.

Elsaesser, Thomas and Barker, Adam (eds.), *Early Cinema: space, frame, narrative*, London: British Film Institute, 1990.

Everson, William K., *American Silent Film*, New York: Oxford University Press, 1978.

Fell, John L. (ed.), *Film Before Griffith*, Berkeley: University of California Press, 1983.

Flint, Kate, *The Victorians and the Visual Imagination*, Cambridge: Cambridge University Press, 2000.

Forsyth, Neil, 'No, but I Saw the Film: David Lean Remakes *Oliver Twist*' in Anny Sadrin, 1999.

France, Richard, *The Theatre of Orson Welles*, Lewisburg: Bucknell University Press, 1977.

Giddings, R., Selby, K. and Wensley, C. (eds.), *Screening the Novel: the theory and practice of literary dramatization*, Basingstoke: Macmillan, 1990.

Gifford, Dennis, *The British Film Institute Catalogue 1895–1970*, London: British Film Institute, 1973.

Gilloch, Graeme, *Myth and Metropolis: Walter Benjamin and the city*, Cambridge: Polity Press,1997.

Gish, Lilian, *The Movies, Mr Griffith and Me*, Englewood Cliffs: Prentice-Hall, 1969.

Guida, Fred, *A Christmas Carol and Its Adaptations: a critical examination of Dickens's story and its productions on screen and television*, Jefferson, North Carolina: McFarland and Company, Inc., 2000.

Gunning, Tom, *D. W. Griffith and the Origins of American Narrative Film: the early years at Biograph*, Urbana, Illinois: University of Illinois Press, 1991.

Gunning, Tom, 'Tracing the Individual Body: Photography, Detectives and Early Cinema' in Charney and Schwartz, 1995.

Hanberry, Carol McKay, *Dramatic Dickens*, London: Macmillan, 1989.

Hansen, Miriam, *Babel and Babylon: spectatorship in American silent film*, Cambridge, Mass.: Harvard University Press, 1991.

Hepworth, Cecil M., *Came the Dawn*, London: Phoenix House, 1951.

Herbert, Stephen and McKernan, Luke (eds.), *Who's Who of Victorian Cinema: a worldwide survey*, London: British Film Institute, 1996.

Hollander, Anne, *Moving Pictures*, New York: Alfred A. Knopf, 1989.

Hollington, Michael, 'Dickens, *Household Words* and the Paris Boulevards' in Anny Sadrin, 1999.

House, M., Storey, G. and Tillotson, K., *et al.* (eds.), *The British Academy Pilgrim Edition of The Letters of Charles Dickens*, Vols. 1–12, Oxford: Clarendon Press, 1965–2002.

Hyde, Ralph, *Panoramania! The art of the 'all-embracing' view*, London: Trefoil Publications in association with Barbican Art Gallery, 1988.

James, Henry, *Autobiography*, ed. Frederick W. Dupee, London: W. H. Allen, 1956.

Johnson, Edgar, *Charles Dickens: his tragedy and triumph*, revised and abridged. Harmondsworth: Penguin Books Ltd, 1952.

Kaplan, Fred, *Henry James: the imagination of genius*, London: Hodder & Stoughton, 1992.

Kirby, Lynne, *Parallel Tracks: the railroad and the silent cinema*, Exeter: University of Exeter Press, 1997.

Lovell, Terry, *Consuming Fiction*, London: Verso, 1987.

Low, Rachael, *The History of British Film*, 3 vols. London: Allen & Unwin, 1948.

McFarlane, Brian, *Novel into Film: an introduction to the theory of adaptation*, Oxford: Clarendon Press, 1996.

McMaster, Juliet, *Dickens the Designer*, London: Macmillan, 1987.

Mannoni, Laurent, *The Great Art of Light and Shadow: archaeology of the cinema*, Exeter: University of Exeter Press, 2000.

Marsh, Joss, 'Dickens and Film', in Jordan, John, O. (ed.), *The Cambridge Companion to Charles Dickens*, Cambridge: Cambridge University Press, 2001.

Meisel, Martin, *Realizations: narrative, pictorial, and theatrical arts in nineteenth-century England*, Princeton, NJ: Princeton University Press, 1983.

Melchior-Bonnet, Sabine, *The Mirror: a history*, London: Routledge, 2001.

Miller, J. Hillis, and Borowitz, D., *Charles Dickens and George Cruikshank*, Berkeley: University of California Press, 1971.

Musser, Charles, *The Emergence of Cinema: the American screen to 1907*, New York: Scribner, 1990.

Naremore, James (ed.), *Film Adaptation*, London: Athlone Press, 2000.

Newsom, Robert, *Charles Dickens Revisited*, New York: Twayne Publishers, 2000.

Nord, Deborah, *Walking the Victorian Streets: women, representation and the city*, Ithaca, NY: Cornell University Press, 1995.

Paroissien, David, 'Dickens and the Cinema', *Dickens Studies Annual*, Vol. 7, Carbondale, Illinois: Southern Illinois University Press, 1980.

Petrie, Graham, 'Dickens, Godard, and the Film Today', *The Yale Review*, Vol. LXIV, No. 2,1975.

Petrie, Graham, 'Silent Film Adaptations of Dickens: Part I – Beginnings to 1911', 'Part II – 1912–1919', 'Part III – 1920–1927', *The Dickensian*, Vol. 97, Part I, Part II, Part III, 2001.

Pointer, Michael, *Charles Dickens on the Screen: the film, television, and video adaptations*, Lanham, MD: The Scarecrow Press, Inc., 1996.

Richardson, Robert, *Literature and Film*, Bloomington, Indiana: Indiana University Press, 1969.

Rignall, John, *Realist Fiction and the Strolling Spectator*, London: Routledge, 1992.

Robinson, David, *Chaplin: his life and art*, New York: McGraw-Hill, 1989.

Roston, Murray, *Victorian Contexts: literature and the visual arts*, Basingstoke: Macmillan, 1996.

Sadrin, Anny (ed.), *Dickens, Europe and the New Worlds*, London: Macmillan, 1999.

Samuel, Raphael, 'Dockland Dickens' in *Theatres of Memory*, London: Verso, 1994.

Schivelbusch, Wolfgang, *The Railway Journey: the industrialization and perception of time and space in the 19th century*, Leamington Spa: Berg, 1986.

Schivelbusch, Wolfgang, *Disenchanted Night: the industrialization of light in the nineteenth century*, Berkeley: University of California Press, 1988.

Schlicke, Paul, *Dickens and Popular Entertainment*, London: Allen & Unwin, 1985.

Sillars, Stuart, *Visualisation in Popular Fiction 1860–1960*, London: Routledge, 1995.

Sinyard, Neil, 'Dickensian Visions in Modern British Film', *The Dickensian*, Vol. 85 Part II, No. 41, 1989.

Slater, Michael (ed.), *Dickens' Journalism: sketches by Boz and other early papers 1833–39*, London: Phoenix, 1996.

from Household Words 1851–59, London: J. M. Dent & Sons, 1999.

Smith, Albert, *Cricket on the Hearth; or, a fairy tale of home*, New York: Samuel French; first performed in 1859.

Smith, Lindsay, *Victorian Photography, Painting and Poetry*, Cambridge: Cambridge University Press, 1995.

Spiegel, Alan, *Fiction and the Camera Eye: visual consciousness in film and literature*, Charlottesville: University of Virginia Press, 1976.

Stokes, Melvyn and Maltby, Richard, *American Movie Audiences From the Turn of the Century to the Early Sound Era*, London: British Film Institute, 2001.

Thomson, David, *Rosebud: the story of Orson Welles*, London: Little, Brown and Company, 1996.

Usai, Paolo Cherchi, *The Griffith Project, Vol. 1: Films Produced in 1907–1908*; *Vol. 2: Films Produced in January–June 1909*, London: British Film Institute, 1999.

Usai, Paolo Cherchi, *Silent Cinema: an introduction*, London: British Film Institute, 2000.

Vardac, Nicholas A., *Stage to Screen: theatrical method from Garrick to Griffith*, New York: Benjamin Blom, 1968.

Virilio, Paul, *The Vision Machine*, trans. Julie Rose, London: British Film Institute, 1994.

Vlock, Deborah, *Dickens, Novel Reading and the Popular Theatre*, Cambridge: Cambridge University Press, 1998.

Warren, Patricia, *British Film Studies*, London: Batsford, 1996.

Wicke, Jennifer, *Advertising Fictions: literature, advertisement and social reading*, New York: Columbia University Press, 1988.

Williams, Christopher (ed.), *Cinema: the beginnings and the future*, London: University of Westminster Press, 1996.

Witte, Bern, *Walter Benjamin: an intellectual biography*, trans. James Rolleston, Detroit: Wayne State University Press, 1991.

Zambrano, A. L., 'Dickens's Style in Terms of Film', *Hartford Studies in Literature*, Vol. IV, No. 2, 1972.

Zambrano, A. L., '*Great Expectations*: Dickens and David Lean', *Literature/Film Quarterly*, Vol. II, Spring, No. 2, 1974.

Index